All Things
Necessary

All Things Necessary

A Practical Guide for Episcopal Church Musicians

MARTI RIDEOUT

Morehouse Publishing
NEW YORK · HARRISBURG · DENVER

Church Publishing, Incorporated
445 Fifth Avenue
New York, New York 10016

www.churchpublishing.org

Cover design by Laurie Klein Westhafer
Typeset by Beth Oberholtzer

Library of Congress Cataloging-in-Publication Data
A catalog record for this title is available from the Library of Congress.

Printed in the United States of America

*This book is dedicated with gratitude and honor
to the course writers
of the original curriculum of the
Leadership Program for Musicians Serving Small Congregations (LPM)
with whom I was honored to serve,
for which I will ever be grateful,
teachers of teachers, mentors beyond measure:
Carol Doran, Mimi Farra, Raymond Glover
Marilyn Keiser, Edward Kryder, William Bradley Roberts.*

Contents

CHAPTER 7

Music for the Holy Eucharist/ Music for the Sacraments

CHAPTER 8

Music and Liturgical Planning

CHAPTER 9

Coda

Acknowledgments

The holy weavings of people and places, past to present, play an enormous role in accumulating the experiences called life. While compiling this resource, my thoughts and prayers of thanksgiving for those people rose above my moments of writer's anxiety. I am grateful for the love of music imparted by my father who, without training, filled our home with exuberant hymn playing and jazzy song improvisations on both piano and organ. When I was compelled to take piano lessons at the age of six my mother set the kitchen timer for twenty minutes of practice time each day, knowing I would rather have been climbing trees, and I am ever grateful for her immense love and encouragement throughout my vocation. Exceptional teachers of piano and organ and choir directors imparted words of wisdom that echo today. I give thanks for mentors, friends, and colleagues who manage to see in me that which I cannot, encouraging me to do things I never dreamed possible. I give special thanks to the Rev. Cricket Park, who read through the history and terms and definitions portions and offered her wit and wisdom, and to my daughter Lissa Rideout Wade, whose proofreading skills gave confidence to my words. Nancy Bryan, editorial director of Books and Music at Church Publishing, was a thoroughly professional, knowledgeable, and patient guide to this neophyte writer, and I am most appreciative for her presence throughout the process. The clergy, choirs, and congregations with whom I have had the pleasure to serve, whether in long-term or interim positions, have given me stories and experiences of a lifetime. Choristers and students have inspired me to learn more, strive harder, and offer my best. The constant love and support of my husband Rob, children Lissa and Brian (USMC) and their spouses Andrew and Emily, and the enthusiasm and unparalleled joy of six grandchildren (Cameron, Adam, Elyse, Sophia, Henry, and Samuel) give to me far more than I could ever imagine, but I am humbly and forever grateful. I am aware of this single journey and honored to serve the One whose love demands my soul, my life, my all. Thanks be to God!

Prelude

A group of organists, all serving in Episcopal parishes, gathered one Saturday a month for ten months for a day of classes and worship, collegiality, and a growing awareness of vocation through the two-year Leadership Program for Musicians (LPM). The participants came from all over the diocese, prepared to engage in class, turn in completed coursework, and perform skills assignments. That year I taught the Leadership of Congregational Song—Organ Track, one of six LPM courses offered then, and observed quite a range of abilities among the students, all of whom were eager to learn and had many more questions about their own church situations than could be covered in class, lunch, or coffee breaks. So, I offered to drive to their churches and spend a morning or afternoon or day listening to them play the required course assignments of hymns and service music on the organs in their churches, to play their hymn registrations while they walked around the empty church and heard what they cannot hear on Sunday morning, talk about choir placement, choral library, challenges they were having, clergy and congregational support, budgets, liturgical questions, and whatever else they needed in our time together.

The church of one participant was almost two hours from the LPM meeting site. I thoroughly enjoyed the scenery while driving to her church, mentally leaving behind my own job for a span. I reminisced about my years in small congregations and looked forward to being with her. She was probably the oldest participant in that class, perhaps in her early seventies, retired from her day job and the organist in a small Episcopal church for about thirty years. She met me at the door with a legal pad, not a letter-size pad, with a question written on each line of two pages. As she handed the pad to me she said, "Marti, I haven't got much time left to be an organist. But in the time I've got left, I want to be the best organist I can be!"

Every teacher should be so blessed with such a student. Here was someone whose quest for knowledge in the field of church music, especially in the Episcopal Church, was unwavering and time-sensitive. Her zeal was contagious and her love of serving God was simply boundless. She wanted to be the best she could be, and she was willing to work hard to accomplish her goal.

Offered for You

My aim in bringing this book to life was to provide a resource that, above all, would be helpful to those serving in Episcopal churches, leading congregational song, building music programs, and working together in the mission and ministry of the church, such as:

- musicians from other denominations now serving in an Episcopal church who need an overview of the specifics of the Episcopal Church, information about liturgy, *The Book of Common Prayer* (1979) and liturgical supplements, *The Hymnal 1982* and music supplements, resources for planning, an awareness of the Anglican tradition, past and present

- young church musicians who are recently graduated from university or conservatory and employed in Episcopal churches, who seek an understanding of the ministry of music in general, the traditions and music of the Episcopal Church, and the resources needed to develop an effective music program

- organists, choir directors, and cantors presently engaged in music ministry in Episcopal churches for however long, who desire to expand their own knowledge, renew their creative energy, and share resources and information with others, as mentors have to countless church musicians through the ages

- clergy who have an appreciation for church music and want to learn more, who desire a cooperative and mutually respectful relationship with the musicians with whom they serve

- choir members, wardens and vestry members, and parishioners supportive of music and musicians, who would appreciate and benefit from understanding the scope of knowledge and skills required to develop and sustain music ministry in the church

Inspiration for This Resource

In 1989, *A Guide to the Practice of Church Music* was published and was quickly appreciated as the most comprehensive resource for church musicians and liturgical planners in the Episcopal Church, if not beyond. The author, Marion J. Hatchett (1927–2009), was an Episcopal priest, professor of liturgical and church music at The School of Theology of the University of the South (Sewanee) for thirty years, and one of the primary liturgists who helped shape *The Book of Common Prayer*.[1]

A Guide to the Practice of Church Music and several more of Marion Hatchett's books were either on my desk or only an arm's length away. They provided the detail, almost an etiquette, I needed on a daily basis in my vocation. Filled with ideas and historical notes, the appropriate ways of planning and carrying out liturgical and musical detail, the options and resources that existed at the time, *A Guide to the Practice of Church Music* provided knowledge, and knowledge gave me confidence.

Since that publication, new resources, including alternative rites to expand our liturgical language, the *Book of Occasional Services* (2003), *Enriching Our Worship*, and a wealth of hymnals and supplements, including *Lift Every Voice And Sing II*; *Wonder, Love, and Praise*; *El Himnario*; *Voices Found*; and *Enriching Our Music I* and *II* have changed the scope of our worship offerings. The hymnody of other cultures, including Native American, Asian, African, African American, gospel, South American, and the music of the Iona (Scotland) and Taizé (France) communities have had a profound and lasting influence on the music of our church. New and inspiring settings of the psalms have encouraged more congregations to sing, rather than say, the sacred texts of the Hebrew faith. Alternative and emergent styles of worship are increasing and creating a unique musical and liturgical presence. The use of the Revised Common Lectionary has made somewhat obsolete the well-known liturgical and music planning texts we have known and makes necessary the writing and publishing of new resources.

By no means do I consider this book a sequel to the scholarly work of Marion Hatchett. Instead, I offer this as a supplement with the best of intentions.

---

1. Marion Hatchett, *Commentary on the American Prayer Book* (New York: The Seabury Press, 1980), biographical information on flaps.

An Overview of the Book

- Each chapter epigraph is a verse or more from the Psalms, some of the oldest songs we know, and ones that surely Jesus sang in temple worship. In psalms of anger, rejoicing, fear, confidence, lament, prayer, praise, atonement, cursing, suffering, and thanksgiving we hear the people of Israel crying out to God. How appropriate to hear the psalms at all our beginnings as we strive to lead congregational song wherever we are planted.

- For many topics included in this resource, only the essence is addressed. In some cases, papers, chapters, or even books have been written on the subjects. This is not to diminish the scope of the subject, but to be aware of the breadth of knowledge needed for effective music ministry and the limits of time and space here.

- At the end of each chapter is a list of recommended resources. For the most part, these are not lists of books, but articles or chapters worthy of reading within books listed in the bibliography. I encourage you to seek other information and avenues of learning to find what you need for the work that you do.

- With very few exceptions, the books listed in the bibliography are in my personal library. I have not provided lengthy lists of books in each section to overwhelm the seeker, only to provide a beginning for exploring and understanding the Episcopal Church, music ministry, liturgical and musical planning, and those areas of knowledge needed to be an effective leader in the church. If some books are listed but out of print, find them from other sources; they are in the bibliography because they are informative classics and should be known and used.

- A glossary appears at the end of the book. Unlike other glossaries in which all the terms are listed in alphabetical order, these are listed alphabetically within sections: 1) church structure and government; 2) clergy and lay participants; 3) *The Book of Common Prayer* and liturgical terms; 4) sacraments; 5) liturgical traditions and customs; 6) vestments; 7) liturgical year; 8) music terms; 9) altar vessels, linens, hangings, supplies, and liturgical symbols; 10) architecture and church furnishings. Episcopalians have a language that may seem peculiar to others, daunting, or even mysterious. For those who are new to the church, a glossary in sections might simplify the learning process. Imagine going into the sacristy or vesting room with the lists and coming out with knowledge in hand. Imagine sitting down in the nave and learning the names of the church furnishings within the architectural setting. Imagine perusing *The Book of Common Prayer* and associating terms with the actual contents or sitting down with lists of sacraments, customs, and details of the liturgical year and experiencing greater clarity.

Downloadable Appendices

A significant feature of this resource is access to sixteen downloadable lists containing approximately one hundred pages of additional information, which may be quite useful to those involved in music ministry and leading worship in the Episcopal Church. The appendices may be found at *www.churchpublishing .org/AllThingsNecessary* and include these topics:

1. *A Timeline of Events in the History of Christianity, the Anglican Church, and the Episcopal Church.* A succinct listing of dates and events, people, and historic actions that formed the Episcopal Church we experience today. (Chapter 1)

2. *A Guide to The Book of Common Prayer (1979).* The contents of *The Book of Common Prayer* organized by liturgies for which you will regularly and occasionally plan music; liturgies that occur once a year; the lections of holy days, common of saints, various occasions, and the Daily Office; historical documents; a listing of prayers and thanksgivings; information not listed in the table of contents. (Chapter 1)

3. *Hymns with Refrains, Chords, Descants, Instruments, Alternate Accompaniments.* An extensive list of hymns from *H82*, *WLP*, *VF*, and *LEVAS II* containing unique musical elements that enrich congregational song and inspire creativity for music leaders to emulate and incorporate as hymn anthems. (Chapter 2)

4. *Hymns for Use as Anthems.* A suggested list of hymns from *H82*, *WLP*, *VF*, *LEVAS II*, and *MHSO* for special occasions and all liturgical seasons that might serve well as anthems for adult, children, and youth choirs. (Chapter 2)

5. *Plainsong Hymns.* Information on accompanying plainsong, the benefits of singing plainsong hymns, and a listing of all plainsong hymns, tune names and modes in *H82*, *WLP*, and *VF*. (Chapter 2)

6. *Hymn Writers and Composers, Late Twentieth Century to Present.* A partial list of authors and composers who have had a profound influence on hymnody, examples of their hymns, and suggested collections of hymns. (Chapter 2)

7. *Music Appropriate for Cantors.* Specific selections in the Daily Offices, canticles, music for Holy Eucharist, Holy Week services, Burial of the Dead, and the Great Litany for a cantor to sing. (Chapter 3)

8. *Professional Organizations: Journals, Articles, and Websites.* Principal organizations, publications, descriptions, and contact information for musicians serving in Episcopal churches, denominational resources, organizations in which to participate and from which to learn. (Chapter 3)

9. *Music for the Daily Offices.* A complete listing of music for preces, invitatory antiphons and canticles, salutations and suffrages, collect tones, morning and evening canticles, anthems at the candle lighting, and sung Scripture for the Daily Offices. (Chapter 5)

10. *A List of Canticles.* Canticles 1–21 and A–S with all settings included from *H82, WLP, VF, EOM 1* and *EOM 2.* (Chapter 5)

11. *Canticles—Suggested Use in the Daily Offices.* A chart of canticle suggestions for daily Morning Prayer and Evening Prayer by day, season, and appropriateness after Old and New Testament readings. (Chapter 5)

12. *Music Selections for Holy Eucharist.* A complete listing of music for the opening acclamations, Kyrie, Trisagion, Gloria in excelsis, and songs of praise settings, Gospel and Gospel acclamations, Nicene Creed, prayers of the people, peace, sursum corda and prefaces, Sanctus and Benedictus, eucharistic prayers, memorial acclamations, Amen, Lord's Prayer, fraction anthems, music at the communion, blessings, and dismissals from *H82, WLP, LEVAS II, MHSO, EOM 1, EOM 2,* and AB. (Chapter 7)

13. *Service Music with Instruments.* Specific selections of service music from *H82, WLP, EOM 1* and *2* that include notation for handbells, flute or oboe, percussion, and piano. (Chapter 7)

14. *Church Websites.* A sampling of church websites from Regions 1–8 of the Episcopal Church that offer information about anthem selections, descriptions of choirs, concert ideas, information about children's

and youth choirs, guidelines for wedding and funeral music, recordings of choir and congregational hymn singing, and additional useful
information. (Chapter 8)

15. *Composers of Choral Music for the Church.* A partial list of choral com-
    posers of church music from the sixteenth to twentieth centuries and
    a list of present-day composers, to offer a glimpse of the Anglican
    musical heritage and the rich offerings of Episcopal church music
    today. (Chapter 8)

16. *Seek and You Will Find.* An extensive listing of topics with sources
    and information on websites, choral music, contemporary worship
    and music, alternate and emergent worship, global music, Holy Week
    music for priests and deacons, hymns and hymnals, instruments, litur-
    gy and planning, professional organizations, organ and instruments,
    publishers and distributors for church music, all and more needed for
    music and worship leadership. (Chapter 8)

In the Ending, a Beginning

While writing this book, one idea or recall led to another and the list of topics grew. What should be included or excluded? How much detail is needed?
What will be the most helpful to those who are new to the Episcopal Church?
What is needed for the young person just out of college or seminary? What
will benefit those who have already served the church, or those who could
serve as mentors? Will clergy be able to use this, too?

I am keenly aware that there is a tremendous amount of information one
needs to know to serve effectively as a church music leader in the Episcopal
Church. How did I learn all of what I have written? Definitely not in under-
graduate and graduate school where I earned degrees in organ performance
and where no course was ever offered on hymn playing, conducting from the
console, working with a volunteer choir, or liturgical and music planning,
much less all the other subjects necessary for the profession.

I am certainly not an authority in the field of church music, only long-
serving. Through the years I have read the words of others, attended workshops and conferences, talked with colleagues, participated in liturgy and
music commissions, taken seminary courses, helped plan diocesan events, and
played the organ in churches for over fifty years. In every event, every organization, every resource, every service, I learned something, either from what

went well or from that which humbled me to do better the next time. Every church musician could say the same and have enough stories to fill many more books.

Initially, I was somewhat skeptical of the title, *All Things Necessary*, given to this book. To me the title seemed somewhat overconfident, as if any one resource could possibly provide all that we really need to do our jobs. Yet, all that we need, all that is necessary, is available to us through resources like this, instruction, study, practice, collegial relationships, time, practical application, experience, and understanding. In some ways I am hesitant to complete this book, knowing there is always more information to gather and make available. But the next step is yours—your beginnings, your growth in knowledge and wisdom, your continuing service to God in the Episcopal Church or wherever you follow your vocation, adding your own voice to all things necessary.

Thank you for all that you do to bring your congregations into the Holy, support their song, and send them out with strength for the journey. By the grace of God you are blessed beyond measure and loved beyond the telling.

Abbreviations

AB—Altar Book
  Music selections for the celebrant and deacon are marked as AB/page.
BCP—The Book of Common Prayer (1979)
BOS—Book of Occasional Services (2003)
EOM 1—Enriching Our Music 1
  Canticles A-K and music for the eucharist are marked as EOM 1/page.
EOM 2—Enriching Our Music 2
  Canticles L-S and music for the eucharist are marked as EOM 2/page.
EOW—Enriching Our Worship
  Music selections for eucharist are marked as EOW/page.
H82—The Hymnal 1982
  Hymns are marked as H82/page. "S" before a number (S/page) refers
  to Service Music found in the Service Music, Accompaniment Edition
  Volume 1 of *The Hymnal 1982.*
LEVAS II—Lift Every Voice and Sing II
  Music is marked as LEVAS/page.
MHSO—My Heart Sings Out
  Music is marked as MHSO/page.
RCL—Revised Common Lectionary
VF—Voices Found
  Music is marked as VF/page.
WLP—Wonder, Love, and Praise
  Music is marked as WLP/page.

CHAPTER ONE

The Episcopal Church and The Book of Common Prayer

All the paths of the Lord are love and faithfulness
to those who keep his covenant and his testimonies.
(Psalm 25:9)

A Brief History of the Church

Our history is important. We are who we are today because of the faithful witness of those who, through the ages, have been called to follow the teachings of the crucified, risen, and ascended Jesus Christ. From the Day of Pentecost, when over three thousand people were baptized, followers of Christ devoted themselves to the apostles' teaching and fellowship, to the breaking of bread and the prayers.

The early church grew in size and authority and survived even when the Roman Empire collapsed. In the midst of political and economic changes, struggles between the old order and newer cultures created by emerging and growing nations in Europe, the church clung to its authority and power rather than embracing change.

As the Reformation was taking shape under the leadership of Martin Luther and John Calvin on the continent, in England, removed from the growing conflict in Europe, Henry VIII ruled (1509–1547), and, for most of his reign, challenged the authority of Rome. The beginning of the end of the relationship between Rome and England was Henry's desire for a forbidden divorce, pitting the formidable king against the pope and the church.

The Reformation that ensued in England was not as radical or fast-paced as on the continent. Worship was offered in English rather than the Latin of the church. Bishops continued as overseers, but at the pleasure of the king.

Like the reformed churches in Europe, the doctrine of salvation through faith and God's grace replaced salvation through successes or worth alone. The church in England created a prayer book for all people, continuing to worship in a manner that remained similar to that of the Roman church.

With exploration beginning in a "new world" across the ocean, persecution and dissent in England and on the continent, settlers and missionaries from this reformed catholic church went to the new land to pursue religious freedom. The first permanent English settlement was built in Jamestown, Virginia, in 1607 and the chaplain to the colonists, Robert Hunt, preached and officiated.

Without bishops to ordain priests and without enough priests for each parish, communities in Virginia established a democratic style of church leadership. Lay people were chosen to serve on a vestry and make administrative decisions for the parish. Lay people led Morning Prayer (Matins) in the absence of a priest to consecrate bread and wine for communion. Meanwhile, a governor and representatives in the House of Burgesses made decisions for the people that only the king, bishops, and parliament would make in England. A foundation of democracy was established and appreciated.

During the American Revolution many Anglicans in the northern colonies fled to Canada. Those who remained were persecuted for their allegiance to the king, if only in using the prayer book of the Church of England or offering prayers for the royal family. The independence gained by the American Revolution brought separation of church and state to the new country.

When the war was over, those in New England knew changes were inevitable, but they believed they needed bishops. Samuel Seabury, a Loyalist from Connecticut, was selected to go to England to be consecrated a bishop, but the bishops of the Church of England refused. Seabury went to Scotland, was ordained in 1784, and returned to the United States with the daunting task of uniting the colonies in one new church. Virginia was used to being governed by lay people without the presence of bishops. Those in New England had been governed by the clergy without the presence of laity.

By 1789 the Bill of Rights granted freedom of religion to all. The first General Convention of the Episcopal Church met in Philadelphia, the House of Bishops and House of Deputies were established, and *A Book of Common Prayer and Administration of the Sacraments, and other Rites and Ceremonies of the Church* was revised and adopted.

The General Convention of 1835 declared that its mission field was the world and sent missionaries throughout the Midwest and to China, Japan, and Africa. For the first time, bishops were sent to regions to establish churches where no church existed at the time.

Another area of growth came when Absalom Jones founded the African Episcopal Church of St. Thomas, the first black parish in Philadelphia, after being poorly treated in his own parish. Jones was ordained a priest in 1802, and was the first African American priest in the Episcopal Church.

The Oxford Movement, recalling the church's Catholic heritage, began in England and America in the early 1830s. Controversial in both countries, the Oxford Movement resulted in more "high church" style of worship, including the use of vestments, attention to liturgy and ceremony, and the centrality of the Eucharist to worship.[2]

In 1886 the Chicago-Lambeth Quadrilateral adopted a statement that the Episcopal Church and the Church of England should be united by these four principles: the Holy Scriptures of the Old and New Testament as the revealed Word of God, the sacraments of Baptism and the Supper of the Lord, the Nicene Creed as the sufficient statement of the Christian Faith, and the historic. The bishops of the Anglican Communion adopted the statement in 1888.[3]

During the twentieth century, the Episcopal Church continued to develop its national identity. In the second half of the twentieth century the denomination took a public stand against the death penalty, came to support the civil rights movement and affirmative action, increased the role of the laity in its governance, revised the prayer book, and began to ordain women to the priesthood and episcopate.[4] In 2006 Katharine Jefferts Schori was elected and consecrated the first female presiding bishop of the Episcopal Church.

In 2003, the election and consecration of Gene Robinson, an openly gay and non-celibate priest, as bishop of New Hampshire created much controversy throughout the Anglican Communion. Some conservative bishops and parishes opposed to Robinson's election chose to align themselves under alternative oversight within or outside the Anglican Communion.

While the denomination has been speaking out against the discrimination of gays and lesbians for many years, gender and sexuality issues con-

---

2. Christopher L. Webber, *Welcome to the Episcopal Church: An Introduction to Its History, Faith, and Worship* (Harrisburg, PA: Morehouse Publishing, 1999), 2–18.

3. *The Book of Common Prayer* (New York: The Church Hymnal Corporation, 1979), 876.

4. Robert Prichard, *A History of the Episcopal Church, Revised Edition* (Harrisburg, PA: Morehouse Publishing, 1999), 251–300.

tinue to divide the Episcopal Church. The General Convention of 2009 voted that "any ordained ministry" be open to gay and lesbian persons. The 2012 General Convention authorized provisional use of a rite for blessing same-gender unions, recognizing that under existing canons clergy can decline to preside at a blessing liturgy without penalty for objecting to or supporting Convention's action on blessings. The Episcopal Church of the USA (ECUSA) became full communion partners with the Evangelical Lutheran Church of America (ELCA) in 2000 and the Northern and Southern Provinces of the Moravian Church in 2009. Full communion is a relationship between distinct bodies in which each recognizes the other as a catholic and apostolic church holding the essentials of Christian faith. Denominations become interdependent, fostered locally, while remaining autonomous. Diversity is preserved while unity is visible in common confession of the one faith, in sharing the sacraments, in being open to the gifts of the other as each seeks to be faithful to Christ and his mission.[5] As of this writing (2011) ECUSA has an interim eucharistic sharing with the United Methodist Church and a covenant partnership with the Presbyterian Church USA. ECUSA is also in full communion with the Old Catholic Churches of the Union of Utrecht, the Philippine Independent Church, and the Mar Thoma Syrian Church of Malabar, India.

A Timeline of Events in the History of Christianity, the Anglican Church, and the Episcopal Church may be found online at *www.churchpublishing.org/AllThings Necessary*.

An Episcopalian

The word *episcopal* comes from the Greek word *episcopos* meaning *bishop* or *overseer*. The Episcopal Church has an organization or government with bishops as overseers. We are Episcopalians because we have bishops, successors to the apostles, who are central to our common life in the church.[6] An Episcopalian is a member of the Episcopal Church, which is descended from the Church of England. There are some issues on which we differ and many on which we are united. Our shared history has helped to shape and define us and our beliefs.

---

5. A Commentary on "Called to Common Mission" by William A. Norgren, March 1999. For more information, see the website of the Episcopal Church at www.episcopalchurch.org.

6. Webber, *Welcome to the Episcopal Church,* 2.

The Catechism teaches, among other things, these beliefs:[7]

- Jesus Christ is fully human and fully God. He was crucified, died, raised from the dead, ascended into heaven, and is seated at God's right hand.

- The Trinity is one God: Father, Son, and Holy Spirit.

- The Bible, the Holy Scriptures, written by human authors inspired by God, are the books of the Old and New Testaments. God still speaks to us through the Bible with the help of the Holy Spirit.

- The two great sacraments are Holy Baptism and the Holy Eucharist.

- The Nicene Creed and Apostles' Creed are statements of our basic beliefs about God.

- The ministers of the church are lay persons, bishops, priests, and deacons. The ministry of a bishop is to represent Christ and his church, particularly as apostle, chief priest, and pastor of a diocese.

We are called to live out our Baptismal Covenant, to:[8]

- Continue in the apostles' teaching and fellowship, in the breaking of bread, and in the prayers.

- Persevere in resisting evil, and whenever we fall into sin, repent and return to the Lord.

- Proclaim by word and example the Good News of God in Christ.

- Seek and serve Christ in all persons, loving our neighbors as ourselves.

- Strive for justice and peace among all people, and respect the dignity of every human being.

We are called to a sacramental life:

- Sacraments are outward and visible signs of inward and spiritual grace, given by Christ as sure and certain means by which we receive that grace (*BCP*, p. 857). In addition to the sacraments of Holy Baptism and Holy Eucharist, other sacramental rites of the church include: Confirmation, Ordination, Holy Matrimony, Reconciliation of a Penitent, and Unction. Through the sacraments we encounter the invisible God in the visible world, through words and actions that acknowledge the presence of God in our lives.

---

7. Catechism of *BCP*, 845–862.
8. *BCP*, 417.

• A sacramental life is a life of service, a life of action, to proclaim, seek and serve, strive and respect, as promised each time our Baptismal Covenant is renewed.

An Anglican Tradition

The word *Anglican* means *English.* The Episcopal Church is a descendant of the Church of England and a member of the Anglican Communion throughout the world. If twelve people were asked to describe the Anglican tradition, there might be twelve different answers. Here is a thirteenth description:

• First and foremost, the Anglican tradition, like other Christian traditions, is founded upon the belief and truth that the praise of God, the creator and source of all that is, seen and unseen, is central to our worship; that Jesus Christ is the only Son of God, eternally begotten of the Father, God from God, Light from Light, true God from true God, begotten, not made, of one Being with the Father.[9]

• Much of our tradition is found in *The Book of Common Prayer;* this understanding is the foundation for the Anglican truism that "praying shapes believing."

• Holy Scripture provides a foundation for our life in the church and is an essential part of our worship. Hymns, service music, and choral anthems are selected and the sermon preached from the lessons and psalm appointed for each service. Lessons are provided for each day of the week, to be read in the Daily Office and for special occasions.

• Because of the centrality of the sacraments to Anglican worship, attention to the liturgy, movement within the service, vestments, focus on the Eucharist, and matters ceremonial are significant.[10]

• Within the Anglican Communion, ceremonies and the patterns of worship are similar. Whether high church (with the celebrant singing or chanting much of the liturgy and employing the use of incense or sanctus bells) or low church (where such ceremonials are not utilized) or somewhere in between, the structure of the liturgy is the same.

• What unites us every week is the celebration of the Holy Eucharist. On any given Sunday, Anglican parishes all over the world will be celebrating the Holy Eucharist using a similar *ordo,* or liturgical pattern.

---

9. *BCP,* 358, Nicene Creed.
10. Webber, *Welcome to the Episcopal Church,* 16.

An Anglican Music Tradition

Church musicians and clergy alike will express diverse and, perhaps, nostalgic opinions about an Anglican music tradition today, especially as the term applies to the churches they serve. Regarding choral repertoire, for instance, some will say that only choral music written specifically for the Church of England should be sung, or only music from the sixteenth century, or only unaccompanied anthems or accompanied choral music from the seventeenth to eighteenth centuries or nineteenth to twentieth centuries. Others will express the desire to combine the best of the past with the best of the present. Others will choose only contemporary music. Diversity has no bounds.

From its inception, music was created for the liturgy in the Church of England. Anthems and motets were composed and sung by cathedral, collegiate, and parish choirs and hymns were written for use by congregations. Psalms were set to chant for choirs and/or congregation. Choral settings of the ordinary of the Eucharist (*Kyrie eleison, Gloria in excelsis, Credo, Sanctus, Agnus Dei* and *Benedictus*) and canticles for Matins and Evensong were composed, as well as preces and responses for the priest/cantor and choir.[11] Anthem and hymn texts were based on scriptural passages, telling the story of God from the time of creation through the crucifixion and resurrection of Jesus Christ, the mission and ministry of the apostles, and the emerging Christian church. The music composed may have been simple or elaborate or somewhere in between, but the words represented a portion of the biblical narrative. The Holy Scriptures were important from the beginning and continue to be so today.

A golden age of language blossomed in the church after the Reformation, as music was permitted to be sung in English instead of the Latin of the Roman church. The choral repertoire was greatly expanded by such composers as William Byrd, Thomas Tallis, Christopher Tye, Orlando Gibbons, Thomas Morley, Adrian Batten, and Thomas Weelkes. Anglican choral music was written for some combination of S (soprano/treble), A (alto/countertenor), T (tenor), and B (bass), either accompanied by organ or sung without accompaniment. New styles of choral music were developed, including the *verse-anthem*, a distinct Anglican form of composition based on a verse from Holy Scripture or a text from *The Book of Common Prayer*, in which the music alternates between sections for a soloist or small group of singers and full choir. Byrd, Gibbons, Weelkes, Thomas Tomkins, and John

---

11. Andrew Wilson-Dickson, *The Story of Christian Music*, (Minneapolis: Fortress Press, 1996), 30, 41–43.

Bull were particularly notable for this form of composition.[12]

From the middle of the sixteenth century, congregations sang metrical psalms, canticles, hymns, and translated tunes from the continent first as unison melodies and eventually in four-part harmony. This way of singing developed into the English hymn, one of the most lasting and important music styles in Western Christian worship.[13]

Anglican music flourished in the nineteenth century and well into the twentieth century with such renowned composers as Herbert Howells, John Ireland, Harold Darke, Edward Elgar, C. H. H. Parry, C. V. Stanford, Herbert Sumsion, Ralph Vaughan Williams, William Walton, and Harold Friedell providing an exceptional quality of choral music for the church.

Music in cathedrals was performed by choirs of men and boys, selected and highly prepared in pursuit of musical excellence, often in residence at the cathedral where there were multiple rehearsals for the preparation of anthems and music to be sung for services each week. Hymns and simple settings of the psalms, canticles, and ordinary of the mass were more characteristic of music in the parish church, where choirs were more likely to be smaller and less well-trained.

Of such is the Anglican musical tradition of our past.

An Episcopal Music Tradition

Since the mid-twentieth century, the Episcopal Church has experienced renewal and revitalization in its hymnody, liturgy, and music. Political decisions, socioeconomic changes, wars, social justice concerns, the shrinking of the world through high-tech communications, and the economy have shaped who we are as Episcopalians. Can we concisely define the Anglican tradition of music in the Episcopal Church today? I think not. We are complicated in our diversity, simpler in our goals.

Our congregational song may be supported by organ, piano, guitar, praise bands, synthesizers, hammered dulcimer, Native American flute, wind or string instruments, Japanese bells, African drums, voice, or the absence of accompaniment altogether. Our songs may include plainsong chant, songs from

---

12. Donald Jay Grout, *A History of Western Music* (New York: W.W. Norton & Company, Inc., 1960). 236–237, 331.

13. Wilson-Dickson, *The Story of Christian Music*, 110–111.

the Iona (Scotland) and Taizé (France) communities, Anglican chant, hymns, metrical psalms, popular religious song, music from other cultures, gospel music or spiritual in a traditional, blended, alternative, or emergent-church style. Our congregations balance prayer book, hymnals and supplements, and service leaflet—or view the words and music on a screen or see and hold nothing at all, praying and singing by memory and call-and-response. Our worship may include incense, flowers, bells, processions, pews, stations of the cross, icons, vestments, banners, choirs, or none of the above. We may worship in structures designed for communal devotion or sitting on the floor in a home to speak of the love of God and break bread together. Our liturgy may be sung or said. Our services can include quiet dignity or exuberant singing, even dancing. Our music selections may come from centuries past or from a new text set to a tune written just last week; from the music and traditions of our sisters and brothers in Christ in Africa, South America, Asia, Eastern Europe, and elsewhere throughout God's kingdom.

Regarding an Anglican tradition in our music, however, I do believe that music in the Episcopal Church today can be guided by some of the same principles that shaped the tradition in the past.

- Music, including selection, practice, and performance, should always be directed toward God, to honor the creator of our song in all ways good and possible. Music should bring the worshiper into a sense of the presence of the divine.

- Music in the liturgy should be chosen primarily from scriptural passages, authorized texts, and with an understanding of its theology.

- Music should have integrity within the service, chosen to engage the congregation in participation, not for entertainment.

- Musical excellence is a worthy goal, one which can and should be obtained. Musicians are a people who practice, whether an instrument, voice, conducting, or in a group.

The Episcopal Church strives to honor the foundations of the Anglican tradition while embracing diversity in people, cultures, languages, the ways we worship and the songs we sing. The church is called to mission within and outside the church and to bring people to the presence of God through the ways we worship. Music is integral to the tradition and integral to the liturgy, mission, and story.

For Music Leaders in Episcopal Churches

Arm yourself with knowledge and be patient with gaining experience, which will be yours with time and commitment.

Know thoroughly, nay intimately, *The Book of Common Prayer*. Know where to find the liturgies of the Daily Office, Holy Eucharist, litanies, collects, prayers, sacramental liturgies, rubrics, and more.

Know thoroughly *The Hymnal 1982* and the hymnal supplements. Acquire knowledge of hymns and service music from different time periods, cultures, and styles. Discover the hymns that the congregation treasures and those that should remain in the domain of the choir for a while.

As a teacher and leader of the choirs, you will find that knowledge of Episcopal history, music, and traditions will inform those involved in music ministry, and that their offerings will be more finely presented because of their increased awareness and affection for the church. The more you learn, the more you will be able to teach. The more you teach, the more you will learn.

Increase your knowledge of the history and beliefs of the Episcopal Church. Your employment should not be based on membership in the church, but an understanding of the church and the rich offerings in *The Book of Common Prayer* will serve you well. Read and consider "An Outline of the Faith" (Catechism), *BCP*, pp. 845–862. Read through the "Historical Documents of the Church," *BCP*, pp. 864–878.

Know enough of the church's history to teach your choirs and congregation as the history relates to music and liturgy choices. Write articles for the church newsletter, lead adult forums, teach, and learn. All these things will strengthen your position and you.

History of the Prayer Book

The Anglican Church was established in the colonies in 1607 but did not separate from the Church of England until 1789. The Episcopal Church was formed in response to independence from England after the Revolutionary War. The first American prayer book was published in 1790 and used language and rites from the English *Book of Common Prayer* (both the 1549 and 1662 versions) and the *Scottish Communion Office* of 1764. The Preface to *The Book of Common Prayer* (1789) contained a respectful declaration of independence from the Church of England and the "necessity and expediency of occasional alterations and amendments in her Forms of

Public Worship . . ." The Preface also declared "that this Church is far from intending to depart from the Church of England in any essential point of doctrine, discipline, or worship; or further than local circumstances require." (*BCP*, pp. 9–11) Further revisions to the Episcopal prayer book occurred in 1892 and 1928 before the current edition.

The most substantial revisions came in *The Book of Common Prayer* (1979), which was first published in 1977 as a proposed book. The traditional language of the 1928 edition was retained in Rite One services and the services in contemporary language, some of which were newly written and some adapted from older language, were considered Rite Two.

The principles which the 1549 prayer book followed also guided the 1979 revision: fidelity to the Scriptures and the liturgy of the early church, the unifying of the realm (i.e. the church), the edification of the people. The revisers of *The Book of Common Prayer* (1979) based their work on Scripture and historic liturgies, added flexibility in rubrics for specific groups and worshiping communities, and composed prayers and litanies to meet missionary, pastoral needs, and social concerns of the day.[14] The official name of our prayer book is *The Book of Common Prayer and Administration of the Sacraments and Other Rites and Ceremonies of the Church, Together with The Psalter or Psalms of David*, commonly known as *The Book of Common Prayer* or just *BCP*.

In 1001 pages you will find rites for Holy Eucharist and the Daily Offices (Morning Prayer, Noonday Prayer, Order of Worship for the Evening, Evening Prayer, Compline), baptism, confirmation, weddings, funerals, and ordination; the Great Litany, prayers and other litanies, forms for special days, and the psalms in language of great beauty and pastoral sensitivity. In addition there are historical documents, a catechism that helps define our faith, lectionaries, collects, the church calendar, and tables for finding Holy Days and even the date of Easter through the year 2089. This is not just any book of common prayer, but *The Book of Common Prayer*. This is the official prayer book of the Episcopal Church.

I hope you will come to know and treasure the contents of this extraordinary book. As a team player in planning worship services, familiarity with *The Book of Common Prayer* is an absolute necessity, and knowing the contents will assist you throughout your ministry. The Rites of Holy Eucharist, along with the Baptismal Liturgy, Confirmation, and the Daily Offices, may be those most used in your ministry in an Episcopal parish.

---

14. Hatchett, *Commentary on the American Prayer Book.*, 13.

More information about those rites—and all the resources of *The Book of Common Prayer* may be found online at *www.churchpublishing.org/AllThings Necessary, A Guide to The Book of Common Prayer.*

The Revised Common Lectionary (RCL)

First, a *lectionary* is an ordered system for reading Scripture at the Daily Offices and services of Holy Eucharist. The lectionary contains references for psalms and readings for various days of the liturgical year. Generally, a Christian lectionary will include a reading from Hebrew Scriptures (Old Testament), an epistle reading (New Testament), and a Gospel reading in addition to a psalm. The Sunday lectionary cycle will include readings from all four gospels and significant portions of both Testaments over the three year cycle. The *BCP* contains a lectionary for the Sunday services of Holy Eucharist in a three-year cycle: Years A, B, and C (887–921), Holy Days (921–925), Various Occasions (927–931) and a two-year Daily Office lectionary (934–1001). Be aware that *BCP*s printed before Advent 2010 will include a lectionary no longer used by the Episcopal Church.[15] The Common Lectionary, also referred to as the *BCP* Lectionary (887–931) and published in 1983, is a revision of that adopted by the Roman Catholic Church after the Second Vatican Council. The Common Lectionary was an ecumenical project of several American and Canadian denominations, developed out of a concern for the unity of the church and a desire for a common experience of Scripture, a harmonization of many different denominational approaches to the three-year lectionary.[16]

The Revised Common Lectionary, published in 1992, was also an ecumenical project of several American and Canadian denominations. In addition to the Episcopal Church, the RCL is now in use in the Evangelical Lutheran Church in America, American Baptist Churches in the USA, Disciples of Christ, Presbyterian Church in the USA, United Church of Christ, United Methodist Church, Christian Reformed Church in North America, the Evangelical Lutheran Church in Canada, the United Church of Canada, the Anglican Churches of Australia, Canada, and South Africa, and the Church of England.[17]

---

15. Don S. Armentrout and Robert Boak Slocum, eds., *An Episcopal Dictionary of the Church, A User Friendly Reference for Episcopalians* (New York: Church Publishing, 2000).

16. Hatchett, *Commentary on the American Prayer Book,* 326.

17. Armentrout and Slocum, eds., *An Episcopal Dictionary of the Church.*

Among the features of the Revised Common Lectionary are the option of semi-continuous reading of Old Testament narratives or lections in thematic harmony with the Gospel of the day for the Sundays after Pentecost, and the inclusion of stories of women and their role in salvation history, offering texts about women never before used in the lectionary for Sundays.[18]

Readings are prescribed for each Sunday: a passage from the Hebrew Scriptures, including the books of the Apocrypha, or the Acts of the Apostles; a passage from one of the Psalms; another from either the Epistles or the Book of Revelation; and finally a passage from one of the four Gospels. The Gospel readings in Year A are taken from Matthew, Mark in Year B, and Luke in Year C. Portions of the Gospel of John are read throughout Easter and other liturgical seasons, including Advent, Christmastide, and Lent.[19]

Year A begins on the first Sunday of Advent in 2013, 2016, 2019, 2022, etc.

Year B begins on the first Sunday of Advent in 2014, 2017, 2020, 2023, etc.

Year C begins on the first Sunday of Advent in 2012, 2015, 2018, 2021, etc.

Supplemental Liturgical Materials

Since the publication of *The Book of Common Prayer*, supplemental liturgical materials have been prepared by the Standing Commission on Liturgy and Music and published by Church Publishing Incorporated. Supplemental materials are intended to expand the *BCP* rites to reflect diversity and develop inclusive and expansive language, new prayers and rites for ministry, and to enrich our prayers.

Enriching Our Worship (1998)

- Supplemental texts for Morning Prayer, Evening Prayer, and Order of Worship for Evening (18–43), the Great Litany (46–49), the Holy Eucharist (50–71)

---

18. *Revised Common Lectionary: Years A, B, C, and Holy Days according to the use of The Episcopal Church.* (New York: Church Publishing, 2007).

19. Armentrout and Slocum, eds., *An Episcopal Dictionary of the Church.*

- Includes canticles A–S (30–40), taken from the Old Testament, New Testament, Apocrypha, and texts from Anselm of Canterbury and Julian of Norwich
- Suggested canticles for Morning and Evening Prayer (44–45)
- Three Eucharistic Prayers (57–65) and two forms for the Eucharistic Prayer (65–67), for use with the Order for Celebrating the Holy Eucharist, *BCP*/400–401
- Music for opening acclamations, three prefaces with concluding doxologies, and fraction anthems (80–88)
- Note: music options for EOW come from EOM 1 and 2. These settings may also be used with the BCP Holy Eucharist Rite Two service; and the settings for BCP Holy Eucharist II may also be used with EOW liturgies.

Enriching Our Worship 2: Ministry with the Sick or Dying and Burial of a Child (2000)

- A public service of healing, prayers, psalms, canticles, litanies, scriptural suggestions, order for Eucharist, prayers and rites at the time of death
- Appropriate hymns for ministry with the sick (42–45) and burial of a child (146)

Enriching Our Worship 3: Burial Rites for Adults, Together with a Rite for the Burial of a Child (2007)

- Includes vigil rites before a funeral, rite for receiving the body, committal at a crematory, service of remembrance
- Prayers for those who die in military service, of unknown faith, unbelievers, collects, prayers and reading selections
- Suggested songs and hymns for burial rites (89–90)

Enriching Our Worship 4: The Renewal of Ministry and the Welcoming of a New Rector or Other Pastor (2007)

- A downloadable resource
- A revision of the *BCP* Celebration of a New Ministry rite (*BCP* 559) placing ordained ministry within the context of baptism
- Includes texts for the gathering of the community with bishop presiding, ministry of the word, renewal of baptismal vows, prayers of the people, holy communion, and the presentation of a symbolic gift from the people to the new pastor

Enriching Our Worship 5: Liturgies and Prayers Related to Childbearing, Childbirth, and Loss. (2010)

- Liturgies for blessing and healing, litanies and prayers, Scripture readings, and hymn suggestions

- Canticle suggestions (78) and suggested songs and hymns from *H82* and supplements (79–83). Songs and hymns from other denominations and sources (83–85), suggested anthems (86), and sources for prayers, liturgies, and music (86–87)

- Specific for blessing of a pregnant woman, loss of pregnancy, reconciliation for an abortion, difficult decisions, unexpected or unwanted pregnancy, loss of a child, termination of pregnancy, infertility, sterilization, and adoption

If you have found customs, whether they be Roman, Gallican, or any other Churches that may be more acceptable to God, I wish you to make a careful selection of them, and teach the Church of the English, which is still young in the faith, whatever you can profitably learn from the various churches. For things should not be loved for the sake of places, but places for the sake of good things. Pope Gregory the Great to Archbishop Augustine, 597

Recommended Resources FOR CHAPTER ONE

- Black, Vicki K. *Welcome to the Book of Common Prayer.* Harrisburg, PA: Morehouse Publishing, 2005.
  - —Chapter 1: Discovering the Book of Common Prayer, pp. 1–22.
  - —Chapter 2: Becoming Christian: Holy Baptism, pp. 23–36.
  - —Chapter 3: Sharing a Common Meal: The Holy Eucharist, pp. 37–59.
  - —Chapter 4: Praying throughout the Day: The Daily Office, pp. 61–77.
  - —Chapter 8: Tools for Prayer and Study: The Lectionary, Prayers, Catechism, and Historical Documents, pp. 127–142.
- Doran, Carol A. *Popular Religious Song.* The Hymnal 1982 Companion, Volume One, p. 13. Raymond F. Glover, editor. New York: The Church Hymnal Corporation, 1990.
- Lehman, Robert W. *American Sarum: Our Anglican Liturgical and Musical Heritage.* Journal of the Association of Anglican Musicians, November 2010.

• Webber, Christopher L. *Welcome to the Episcopal Church.* Harrisburg, PA: Morehouse Publishing, 1999, p. 1–23.

• Westerhoff, John. *A People Called Episcopalians: A Brief Introduction to Our Peculiar Way of Life*, St. Luke's Episcopal Church, Atlanta, GA, 1998, pp. 3–15, 29–31.

CHAPTER TWO

Hymns, The Hymnal 1982, and Hymnal Supplements

Hallelujah! Sing to the Lord a new song:
sing his praise in the congregation of the faithful.
(Psalm 149:1)

A Hymn

"A hymn is the praise of God by singing. A hymn is a song embodying the praise of God. If there be merely praise but not praise of God, it is not a hymn. If there be praise and praise of God, but not sung, it is not a hymn. For it to be a hymn, it is needful, therefore, for it to have three things: praise, praise of God, and these sung." (Attributed to Saint Augustine)

What is more joyful than a congregation expressing its faith through singing? People may remember portions of a sermon upon leaving a service, but often the music will still be in their hearts and minds, if not on their lips. When a loved one dies and family members gather to plan a service, hymns are selected that were meaningful to the departed or that help those remaining cope with their loss. Imagine Christmas Eve without "Silent night" or "O come, all ye faithful." Imagine Easter Day without "Jesus Christ is risen today." Hymns help shape our faith. They express emotion and hold a wondrous power to heal, convert, strengthen, and embolden the faithful. If the average congregation sings just three hymns in a worship service and not one is repeated during the course of a year (not counting Christmas Eve and other non-Sunday services), that congregation would sing just 156 out of 720 hymns in *The Hymnal 1982*. For the moment, we will consider only *H82*. How many congregations really know 156 hymns? How many know 300 hymns or more?

If there is interest in teaching new hymns and the congregation is willing to learn, then choices should be made with great consideration. What constitutes a good hymn, one that will become part of the congregation's song, one that is worthy of the praise of God, one that you want a chorister in your charge to still be singing in twenty years? Here are some suggestions:

- Choose texts that reflect God's redeeming love, grace, and presence in word and sacrament; tell the story of Jesus Christ, his life and ministry, death, resurrection, and ascension; reflect sound Anglican theology; aid in drawing worshipers closer to God and promote praise and worship by the community.

- Choose tunes that are within a comfortable range for high and low voices; melodies that help, not hinder, the shape of the text; rhythms that are not difficult but that enhance the hymn; melodies that are fairly easy to sing and memorable; harmonies that are rich and varied with an occasional "aha!" note or chord to lend interest and delight to the singing.

- Choose hymns that are well-crafted and that are a good marriage of text and tune, each being a partner in strength for the other.

Hymns for any liturgy, Sunday or special service should be chosen to reflect the lessons assigned for the day or the season. There are multiple resources to assist in this process. Specific planning considerations might include:

- The entrance hymn should be familiar, to unite the gathered in their first act of corporate worship. Some musicians consider only hymns in 4/4 time, where there are two pulses in each measure, on beats one and three, (much like a march) for ease of processing; hymns in 3/4 time might feel more like a waltz rhythm, less easy for walking. I consider the appropriateness of the hymn, first and foremost, and I am most certain God will plant our feet, one foot in front of the other, with any music we sing.

- A sequence hymn, ideally, would reflect the lessons and psalm already heard.

- A hymn during the offertory could reinforce the lessons or prepare for the communion that will follow.

- Hymns at the communion may be selected from a wide range of music designated for communion or other hymns and songs based on the propers of the day. Many congregations enjoy singing the music of the Taizé Community in France, music from the Iona Community in Scotland, and other simple songs that are easily repeated and memorized while they move to and from communion. (Note that some worship leaders will not consider using music chosen from sources other than the authorized hymnals of the denomination.) The post-communion hymn should also be based on the propers of the day, but ideally be a familiar hymn for the people to be sent forth rejoicing in the power of the Holy Spirit.

Understand that, even with extensive knowledge of hymnody and dedication to choosing hymns appropriately, you simply will not please everyone. For many years I played and directed services at 5 pm, 7 pm, 9 pm, and 11 pm on Christmas Eve, each with a half-hour prelude of congregational carol-singing, organ, handbell, instrumental, and choral music. There were four different choirs at the services, three handbell ensembles played at three services, a brass group played at two services, and solo instrumentalists at all the services. Not one anthem or organ selection was repeated throughout the evening. Hymns and carols were selected weeks in advance so that, except for "Silent Night," each service had a rotation of all the carols, usually ten or eleven in each. At about 12:45 am one year, as I was cleaning up from Christmas Eve and preparing for the Christmas Day service, before going home to tidy the house, prepare breakfast casseroles, fill stockings, take gifts out of hiding for the wonderment of the little ones, and sleep for an hour or two after an evening of glorious music-making, a woman came up to me and said, "You ruined my Christmas!" I took a deep and calming breath, looked her in the eyes, and said, "Please tell me more." She said, "You didn't play my favorite Christmas carol!" "Which carol is that?" I asked. "What Child is This." I told her that if she had attended the 5 pm or 9 pm service we would have sung her favorite carol. I suggested she contact me prior to Christmas the next year and I would be glad to tell her in what service that carol would be sung. Then, I forgot. The next year she came up to me at the same time and with the same complaint. Then, I remembered. "But, we did sing 'What Child is This.'" She said, "That's not my favorite carol. My favorite carol is 'It Came Upon a Midnight Clear'!"

Surely there are people in this life whose happiness is derived from making other people unhappy. Just as surely there are people who struggle with maintaining a positive Christmas spirit throughout December, just waiting for Christmas to be over so they can get back to normal. My saintly grandmother had an expression that I have said many times in my work in the church: *Thank God we are all not constipated the same!* Perspective and humor work wonders.

Choose hymns with knowledge and integrity, compassion and strength, always balancing the goals of praising God with inspiring the congregation.

History of *The Hymnal 1982*

The General Convention of 1982 approved the texts submitted by the Standing Commission on Church Music (SCCM), thus the title of *The Hymnal 1982*, and then charged the commission with completing the hymnal with appropriate music. The hymnal was published in late 1985 and dedicated in a glorious service at Washington Cathedral on January 10, 1986, with members of the Standing Commission on Church Music and consultants to the commission present. At the singing of the first two stanzas of *H82* 413, Erik Routley's text "New songs of celebration render" sung to the tune *Rendez à Dieu*, the Standing Commission stood and moved to the crossing. Presiding Bishop John M. Allin led the liturgy, and when Bishop Allin, the SCCM, the Choir of Washington Cathedral, vested participants, and the entire congregation held their hymnals high for the dedication, there was palpable excitement, not only for a job well done but for a new beginning in the worship life of this people of God. How appropriate that the hymn selected for the ending of that portion of the dedication was *H82* 420 (stanzas 1–3), Fred Pratt Green's text "When in our music God is glorified," set to C.V. Stanford's tune *Engelberg*.

The SCCM had developed a statement that expressed the commission's commitment to maintain and enhance the rich repertoire which constituted the singing tradition of this people of God. That commitment led to the development of these objectives:

- To prepare a body of texts that presents the Christian faith with clarity and integrity;

- To restore music that has lost some of its melodic, rhythmic, or harmonic vitality through prior revision;

- To reflect the nature of today's church by including the works of contemporary artists and works representing many cultures;

- To strengthen ecumenical relationships through the inclusion of texts and tunes used by other Christian traditions;

- To create a hymnal embodying both practicality and esthetic excellence.[20]

---

20. *The Hymnal 1982*, Preface.

In the Preface to *The Hymnal 1940*, the suggestion was made that the average lifetime of a hymnal is twenty-five years.[21] Clearly, *The Hymnal 1982* was published more than twenty-five years later. However, beginning in 1972 other resources were published to supplement *Hymnal 1940* as the work of prayer book revision continued, resulting in *The Book of Common Prayer* (1979). You may find some of these supplements in your church or choral library and wonder whether to keep them or not. If you have enough copies for the choir, then find room for them, for many of the hymns, songs, and canticles not included in *The Hymnal 1982* can so appropriately be used as anthems, especially with a less experienced church choir, a small choir, or a choir of young people. These supplements include *More Hymns and Spiritual Songs*; *Songs for Liturgy*; *Five Settings of the Eucharist (Rite II)*; *The Book of Canticles*; *Hymns III* (almost 60 percent included in *The Hymnal 1982*); *Songs for Celebration* (hymns and songs from the renewal movement); *Eucharistic Music for the Liturgy* (more Rite Two settings); *Gradual Psalms, Alleluias and Tracts for the Three-Year Lectionary and Special Days and Holy Days*, *Lift Every Voice and Sing*; and the *Hymnal Studies Series*.

The Hymnal 1982 and *The Book of Common Prayer*

In the first chapter I suggested you should know thoroughly, nay intimately, *The Book of Common Prayer*. Now I exhort you to know *The Hymnal 1982* with equal thoroughness and zeal. These two treasures are the most important resources you need and have the privilege to know and use in your ministry as a music leader in the Episcopal Church.

Before continuing, make sure you have copies of both volumes of the keyboard edition of *Hymnal 1982*. Service music and other accompaniments are found in Volume 1; hymns and their accompaniments are in Volume 2. These two books are sold as a set and must be in the hands of every musician serving in an Episcopal Church.

Church Publishing, Incorporated has three other formats for *The Hymnal 1982*:

- *Hymnal 1982 Selections in Large Print*: contains one hundred hymn texts, spiral binding

- *Hymnal 1982 Basic Singers Edition*: the pew edition that contains all the hymns and service music but not the accompaniments to unison hymns, canticles, or service music settings

---

21. *The Hymnal 1940* (New York: The Church Pension Fund, 1940), iii.

- *Hymnbook 1982*: contains all the hymns with accompaniments but does not include service music; good resource for home use and for other denominations

A major consideration for *The Hymnal 1982* was that the "hymnal should be a companion for use with *The Book of Common Prayer*. A new edition of the hymnal should support *The Book of Common Prayer* with its expanded lectionary, its revised calendar (which includes additional feasts and other emphases), its renewed emphasis upon Holy Baptism as a public rite, its enrichment of the Daily Office, the proper liturgies for special days, the rites for Holy Eucharist, the pastoral offices, and the Episcopal services."[22] For the purpose of this next exercise, take a copy of *The Book of Common Prayer* and a copy of the pew edition of *The Hymnal 1982* and lay them side by side on a table, both open to the Table of Contents/Contents in the front of the books. Notice how the contents mirror one another. Just as the Daily Offices of Morning and Evening Prayer appear first in the *BCP*, so also does the music for those rites appear first in *H82*, service music followed by hymns. Then the order of hymns in the *H82* begins with those for Sunday, followed by the order of the liturgical year, Advent through the Day of Pentecost. Hymns for Holy Days, the Common of Saints and Various Occasions are then followed by those of Baptism and Eucharist, followed by the Pastoral Offices of the Church: Confirmation, Marriage, Burial of the Dead, Ordination. Hymns for the Consecration of a Church and General Hymns under eleven categories continue, followed by those for the Christian Life, Rounds and Canons, finishing with National Songs. The last hymn, *H82* #720, is our national anthem.

Essential Information about *The Hymnal 1982*

- Numbers in the hymnal preceded by the letter "S" indicate Service Music, found in the front of the pew edition of *H82*. Service music includes sung versicles and responses, canticles, and music for the Holy Eucharist, such as *Kyrie, Trisagion, Gloria in excelsis, Sanctus,* and Fraction Anthems.
- *Service Music, Accompaniment Edition Volume 1* contains an Appendix (Notes on p. 417, music S 289–S 449) and includes settings not found elsewhere in the hymnal: Invitatory aniphons, including pointings for An-

---

22. Alec Wyton, *Journal of Church Music*, February 1986.

glican chant, music for the services of Noonday and Compline, litanies, proper liturgies for special days, settings for the burial services, music for Eucharistic Prayer C, more music selections for the Daily Offices and Holy Eucharist, Anglican and plainsong chants, a collection of simplified Anglican chants, a psalm tone chart, and collect tones. Singers' parts, printed within the stylized boxes formed by heavy braces, may be reproduced by a congregation for its own use provided that the copyright notice is always given.[23]

- Each hymn in the *Accompaniment Edition Volume 2* comes complete with important information and directions:
  —In hymns of five stanzas or more, a line appears under number 3 to assist the singer in visually finding the correct stanza in each system of the music.
  —Over forty hymns have chords above each line of music suitable for accompaniment by guitar. Note the direction at the end of most of those hymns: *Keyboard and guitar should not sound together.* (Ex: 105) Occasionally a chord/capo indication will be given. (Ex: 304)
  —Words: author's and translator's birth and death dates are listed, sources of the text are given; credits and dates for individual stanzas written by other authors are also listed.
  —Music: the tune name is printed in italics; an index of tune names appears in most hymnals and is helpful for coordinating organ and choral music and identifying the hymn. Tune names have interesting origins, many of which you will find in *The Hymnal 1982 Companion, Volumes Three A and Three B.*
  —Directions for singing in rounds, different voicings, descants, and the addition of instruments for accompaniment may be present. (Ex: 43)
  —Metronome markings are usually given in the bottom right corner. (Ex: 150)
  —The meter of the hymn text is located in the bottom right corner beneath each hymn. Look at 330, *Tantum ergo Sacramentum,* a tune which may not be familiar to your congregation. The meter of the text is 87.87.87, which means there are three lines of text and those separated by periods. Each line is a phrase with two parts: the first has eight syllables and the second has seven syllables. Consult the Metri-

---

23. *The Hymnal 1982*: Service Music, Accompaniment Edition Volume 1, 417.

cal Index of Tunes, p. 1039, for other hymns with the same meter. 58/*St. Thomas*, has the same meter and may be more familiar to the congregation, thus allowing the text to be sung with a tune that gives confidence to the congregation. The challenge in selecting a different tune is making sure text and tune are well suited for one another, so that a strong text has an equally strong tune, and that a weak syllable does not fall on a strong beat or vice versa.

— If a hymn tune is repeated with a different text elsewhere in *H82*, usually the music is in a different key. (Ex: 538 and 416) This permits the organist to choose a suitable key for congregational singing. Those indications are also given at the end of the hymn.

— Another harmonization may also be offered, giving the organist options for accompanying the hymn or different stanzas. Compare the accompaniments to hymns 48 and 616.

— Alternate tunes may also be suggested. (Ex: 441/*Rathbun* may also be sung to 442/*Tomler* or 571/*Charlestown*.)

— Two tunes in *H82* include an Amen: 403/*MacDougall* by Calvin Hampton and 296, 420, 477/*Engelberg* by Charles Villiers Stanford. In *The Hymnal 1940* and other denominational hymnals of that era and before, an Amen was sung at the end of almost every hymn. Why are they not included in *H82*? The word *Amen* translates to *so be it* or *it is so*. When a prayer is said by a priest, deacon, or lay person during a service, the congregation says *Amen* to literally say *I agree*, a corporate response to the prayers of one person. When the people stand to sing a hymn, however, they are already in a corporate mode, in community. To add an *Amen* would be redundant. In both *MacDougall* and *Engelberg*, the *Amen* brings the music to a conclusion.

Indices in the Accompaniment Editions of *The Hymnal 1982*

The indices in Volume 1 of the *Accompaniment Edition* provide additional and valuable information, including copyright acknowledgments (405), composers, arrangers and sources (407), index of service music (410), metrical psalms and hymns based on psalms (679), hymns based on canticles and other liturgical texts (680), hymns for use with children (682), liturgical and subject index (684), scriptural references (703), and hymns on the consultation on ecumenical hymnody list (712).

Indices in Volume 2 include copyright acknowledgments (1021), general performance notes (1026), authors, translators, and sources (1028), composers, arrangers, and sources (1033), metrical index of tunes (1039), tune names (1045), and index of first lines (1050).

Hymnals and Supplemental Hymnals

Lift Every Voice and Sing II

The intention of the editorial committee preparing *Lift Every Voice and Sing II* (*LEVAS II*), published in 1993, was to include spirituals, traditional and contemporary gospel songs, adapted Protestant hymns, missionary and evangelistic hymns, service music and mass settings in both traditional and gospel settings, and hymns for African American saints on the church's calendar.[24]

The arrangement of musical pieces is first according to the liturgical year, then those of Black Saints, followed by general categories of Praise to God, Jesus Christ our Lord, the Holy Spirit, then Baptism and Conversion, Communion, Evangelism, Prayer, Assurance, Children, Social Justice, and Benediction. The first hymn in *LEVAS II* is the title hymn, which is also found in *H82* at 599.

Musical compositions of the parts of the mass (*Kyrie, Gloria, Sanctus,* and Fraction Anthems) provide alternative and uplifting choices for use in our worship services. Additionally, there are Songs of Praise, music for the Memorial Acclamations, the Lord's Prayer, Prayers of the People and Responses, and Amen settings to know and sing. Of particular note are the arrangements of Psalm 126 and Psalm 23 and portions of Psalms 145, 104, 22, 27,100, and Psalm 24 with refrains and simplified Anglican chant for the verses; Psalm 27 makes use of the refrain, also, but the text is sung to Anglican chant.

For those who are hesitant to sing spirituals or gospel music, read "Hymns and Songs: Performance Notes and Service Music: Performance Notes" in *LEVAS II*, pages xvii and xxv, for a greater understanding of voice characteristics, rhythm, meter and tempo, improvisation, use of instruments, and even body rhythm, which might possibly be the last element employed in most Episcopal churches but which can also be the most freeing.

---

24. *Lift Every Voice and Sing II*, Preface, viii.

Wonder, Love, and Praise: A Supplement to The Hymnal 1982

The 1994 General Convention passed a resolution that the Standing Commission on Church Music be directed to continue preparing supplements to *The Hymnal 1982* which provide this church with additional service music, inclusive-language hymnody, additional texts in languages other than English including texts printed in more than one language, additional hymnody related to the lectionary and rites of the Book of Common Prayer, and texts and tunes written since the compiling of the present *Hymnal.*[25]

Wonder, Love, and Praise, published in 1997, is a supplement, not a replacement for the *H82*. The first hymn number is 721, continuing the line of numbers from *H82*. As in *H82*, hymns and spiritual songs are arranged by liturgical season and general hymns under the headings of Threefold God, Christian Pilgrimage, Eucharist, Baptismal Covenant, Burial of the Dead, The Church's Mission, Praise, Unity, The Christian Life, and Spiritual Songs. One other category is worthy of note: the four texts and five songs about healing, a topic not previously included as a section in *H82*.

At one parish, the rector was keenly interested in introducing *WLP* to the congregation. I asked the rector and other clergy on the staff to set aside one hour and invited them to the music room so that we could sing through many of the hymns and songs, in part to give them a better understanding of why this book is so valuable, but also to share my enthusiasm. As I spoke and we sang, one of the clergy, most likely more comfortable with *The Hymnal 1940*, leafed through *WLP* during the entire time we were together, never singing a single song. At the end of the session he looked at me and said: "There's not a hymn I know in this entire book!"

He was almost right. Except for approximately ten tunes that also appear in the *H82* with different texts, about an equal number of songs out of the African American and gospel heritages, and some music from the Taizé Community that may be familiar to some, the rest of the hymns and service music selections are new, as well they should be.

Inspiration did not cease with the publication of *The Hymnal 1982*. Poets and authors, composers and arrangers continue to be stirred to write texts and tunes for worshiping communities in a variety of cultures, songs that unite us as one body in Christ. Liturgical renewal and an expanding awareness of global hymnody changed perceptions of Anglican mission and musical styles.

---

25. *WLP*, Leader's Guide, Preface.

Wonder, Love, and Praise expresses an avenue of hospitality through a wealth of musical styles from many cultures. Songs and hymn tunes are from Africa, China, Japan, Finland, South and Central America, the Caribbean, Russia, the Iona Community in Scotland, the Taizé Community in France, as well as Native American tunes and early American hymnody. If a hymn or song is from another tradition and language, the native language appears first, followed by the English stanzas. Phonetic translations are provided in the Leader's Guide. In general, the book offers new texts and fresh tunes that encourage full participation by the congregation.

If you have in your library only a pew edition of *WLP*, order the Leader's Guide. While you could take the pew edition to your local office supply store and have a spiral binding put on, the Leader's Guide already has a spiral binding and will thus lay flat on the organ or piano rack. Far more important, though, is the information written for each hymn by the Rev. Dr. John L. Hooker, priest and church musician, author, and composer of hymn tunes and harmonizations. He offers biographical information and historical perspectives, sources for text and song, musical analysis of hymn and song structure, even tempo suggestions and registration considerations with his sparkling wit and gifted way with words.

If your congregation does not use *WLP* yet, consider purchasing enough copies for the choir, so that they can sing the hymns, songs, and canticles as anthems, thus introducing the music. Eventually the people will want to sing this most accessible music.

Service music includes modern settings of the parts of the mass (*Kyrie, Trisagion, Gloria in excelsis*, the Nicene Creed, *Sanctus*, and *Agnus Dei*/Fraction Anthems). In addition there are settings of *Alleluia* and verses for Gospel Acclamations, the Memorial Acclamation, the Great Amen, and the Lord's Prayer.

Additional settings of canticles, some paraphrased, add another dimension of richness to the people's song from this supplement:

881–882—The First Song of Isaiah, *Ecce, Deus*, Canticle 9

883—The Third Song of Isaiah, *Surge, illuminare*, Canticle 11

884–885—A Song of Creation, *Benedicite, omnia opera Domini*, Canticle 12

886–887—A Song of Praise, *Benedictus es, Domine*, Canticle 13

888—A Song of Penitence, *Kyrie Pantokrator*, Canticle 14

889–890—The Song of Zechariah, *Benedictus Dominus Deus*, Canticle 16

891—The Song of Simeon, *Nunc dimittis*, Canticle 17

892–894—A Song to the Lamb, *Dignus es*, Canticle 18

895—The Song of the Redeemed, *Magna et mirabilia*, Canticle 19

896–901—Glory to God, *Gloria in excelsis*, Canticle 20

902–903—You are God, *Te deum laudamus*, Canticle 21

904–905—A Song of Wisdom, *Sapientia liberavit*, Canticle A

906—A Song of Pilgrimage, *Priusquam errarem*, Canticle B

As in *The Hymnal 1982*, the indices provided in the Leader's Guide are extremely beneficial for your planning process. Note that the liturgical index is keyed to the *BCP* Eucharistic Lectionary and not the Revised Common Lectionary. Indices include copyrights (248), authors, composers, arrangers, translators, and sources of hymns and spiritual songs (249), authors, composers, arrangers, translators, and sources of service music (250), scriptural references (251), liturgical index (252), tunes (261), tune names (262), first lines (263).

Voices Found: Women in the Church's Song

Published in 2003, *Voices Found: Women in the Church's Song* is a collection of hymns and spiritual songs written by women, or for and about women. Some are familiar hymn tunes from other sources. Some are written in chant form, and some are arranged for two or more voices, ideal for use with treble choirs or small women's ensembles. Some names of women authors and composers are known: Fanny Crosby, Emma Lou Diemer, Delores Dufner, Hildegard of Bingen, Julian of Norwich, Jane Marshall, Alice Parker, Betty Pulkingham, Natalie Sleeth, Teresa of Avila, Catherine Winkworth, to name just a few. This collection continues the theme of diversity in our music, recognizing the gifts of women in the midst of the church's song.

The goals of *Voices Found* were to affirm women's quest for spiritual and social justice, to broaden the repertoire of music available to the church, and to continue a tradition of excellence in congregational singing.[26]

There are hymns and songs for morning and evening, the liturgical year, Holy Days and Various Occasions, and the sacraments. In addition, there are thirteen hymns on women in Scriptures, eleven psalm and canticle settings, and eight hymns for children.

---

26. *Voices Found, Leader's Guide*, Preface.

Voices Found: Leader's Guide, published in 2004, is a spiral-bound book, in the same format as the leader's guide for *WLP.* Marilyn Haskel and Lisa Neufeld Thomas gathered biographical data on poets and composers, wrote about the basis for the texts and the musical structure, for which Sunday or season they would be appropriate, and offered performance practice suggestions. The information included for each hymn in the *Leader's Guide* is simply invaluable.

Indices in the *Voices Found Leader's Guide* are very similar to those in the *WLP Leader's Guide:* Copyrights (208), Index of Authors, Translators, and Sources (210), Index of Composers, Arrangers, and Sources (211), Scriptural Index (212), and Topical Index (213). The Three Year Eucharistic Lectionary (214) is for the Eucharistic Lectionary in *The Book of Common Prayer,* not the Revised Common Lectionary; as many occasions are the same with both lectionaries, those unique to the RCL are so indicated.

El Himnario

This hymnal, published in 1998 by Church Publishing Incorporated, contains traditional hymnody translated into Spanish, some traditional Latino hymns, as well as religious folk songs, choruses, and psalms.

Song and hymn categories include: God, Jesus Christ, the Holy Spirit; liturgical seasons and special days; the church, mission, and church unity; sacraments and pastoral services; metrical psalm settings, canticles, and music for the Eucharist.

The texts are entirely in Spanish, no English translations. Chords are included for keyboard and guitar use.

El Himnario Selecciones, is a text-only collection of "selections" from *El Himnario.*

Indices include composers/authors and sources, biblical references, metrical, tune names, and topics, as well as an index by first lines.

My Heart Sings Out

Although compiled primarily for the benefit of children, *MHSO* is a collection of music for church musicians, teachers, clergy and liturgists to use for all-age worship in church, church school, children's chapel, religious schools, and vacation Bible schools.[27] Intergenerational services and programs will benefit from exploring and using this hymnal.

---

27. *My Heart Sings Out, Teacher's Guide,* 7. Fiona Vidal-White. (New York: Church Publishing, 2006).

The pew edition of *My Heart Sings Out* has been in use since 2004. The *Teacher's Guide* for *MHSO*, in addition to including the songs and hymns published for use in Episcopal churches and beyond, is a comprehensive source of information for choosing music for children, music leadership skills with information on the role of the cantor, and worship planning, compiled by Fiona Vidal-White.

Before each music selection, symbols suggest age group accessibility, accompaniment and additional instruments, liturgical use and seasonal or lectionary connections, teaching points (scriptural, historical, or biographical), preparation and performance tips, questions to ask children in a learning environment, and pronunciation guides for languages other than English.

Indices include the usual and helpful: Copyright Information (271), Authors, Translators, and Sources (274), Composers, Arrangers, and Sources (275), Scriptural (283), Liturgical (284), Topical (289), Tune Names (292), First Lines and Popular Titles (292).

In addition, there is a Glossary (273) and indices for: Accompaniment (276– unaccompanied, organ, piano or electronic keyboard, hammered dulcimer, steel drums, percussion, guitar, Orff instruments, handbells or hand chimes, strings, and wind instruments), Age Level (280), and Harmony (282—rounds, parallel harmonies, call and response, two parts, simple and advanced harmony parts).

Hymns for Use as Anthems

In your church music position, you may struggle to select appropriate anthems from a choral library that is limited in size, diversity, and quality. In times of restricted, or even non-existent, resources for financially supporting music programs, fund-raising to purchase new music, borrowing music from a neighboring church, or repeating anthems with frequent regularity are options. However, if you want to expand the music offerings of your choirs, look no farther than *The Hymnal 1982* and the church's hymnal supplements.

- The texts and tunes represent a wide variety and the best offerings of poets, hymn text writers, composers, and arrangers from the fourth century to present day.

- Plainsong hymns assist the choir in their unison singing and plainsong chant style.

- There are 720 hymns in *The Hymnal 1982* and, most likely, many are never sung by the congregation, as they may be considered too difficult to sing or not chosen in favor of more familiar hymns. The remaining number of hymns could provide anthem repertoire for years.

- The choir may need an anthem that is less strenuous or that follows a busy season or concert schedule. A hymn-anthem may match the message of the lessons exceptionally well, perhaps better than an octavo anthem.

- In some churches, where announcements are given after the prelude, the choir may sing an introit before the processional hymn. Introits can be taken from this list of hymns or from other sources.

- In a church that uses *The Hymnal 1982* alone, hymn-anthems from *Wonder, Love, and Praise, Lift Every Voice and Sing II, Voices Found,* and *My Heart Sings Out* provide a wealth of new music for the worship of God.

Hymn-anthems provide a teaching opportunity to present a new hymn to the congregation. The choir sings the hymn as an anthem, and the congregation sings the hymn in worship services in subsequent weeks. Children's and youth choirs are particularly effective at introducing new hymns; a congregation trusts that, if the children can sing the hymn, then surely they can, too.

To use a hymn as an anthem, add an introduction, varied accompaniment (using the harmony from another denominational hymnal), interlude, descant (using tenor and alto notes in appropriate range, if one is not included), varied voicings (e.g., men on one stanza/women on another, youth/adult, other), solo or rhythm instruments or handbells, and a codetta (a passage that brings the music to a conclusion).

Adult choirs can sing hymn-anthems with children's and youth choirs, alternating stanzas, including handbells, providing descants, adding rhythm or solo instruments, or just singing refrains. Hymn-anthems can explore global hymnody, less familiar spirituals, familiar texts set to new tunes. A short organ chorale, based on the hymn tune, can be played in place of a stanza of the hymn-anthem. An example would be to sing "Once he came in blessing" (*H82* 53) and incorporate J. S. Bach's chorale on *Gottes Sohn ist kommen*.

Recommended
Resources FOR CHAPTER TWO

• *The Hymnal 1982 Companion, Volume 1.* Raymond F. Glover, editor. New
York: Church Hymnal Corporation, 1990.
— "British Hymnody from the Sixteenth Through the Eighteenth
Centuries," p. 365. Robin A. Leaver.
— "British Hymnody, 1900–1950," p. 474. Robin A. Leaver.
— "British Hymnody Since 1950," p. 555. Robin A. Leaver.
— "Protestant Hymn Singing in the United States, 1916–1943:
Affirming an Ecumenical Heritage," p. 505. David Farr.
— "Hymnody in the United States from the Civil War to World War I
(1860–1916)," p. 447. Paul Westermeyer.
— "Hymnody in the United States Since 1950," p. 600. Russell Schulz-
Widmar.

• Appendices for this chapter may be found at *www.churchpublishing.org/*
AllThingsNecessary and include:
— *Hymns with Refrains, Chords, Descants, Instruments, Alternate Accompani-*
ments. An extensive list of hymns using musical elements that enrich
congregational song and inspire creativity for music leaders.
— *Hymns for Use as Anthems:* A suggested list from *H82, WLP, VF,* and
LEVAS II for special occasions and liturgical seasons.
— *Plainsong Hymns:* Information on accompanying plainsong, as well as
a listing of plainsong hymns with tune names and modes from *H82,*
WLP, and *VF.*
— *Hymn Writers and Composers, Late Twentieth Century to Present:* a partial
list of those who have had a profound influence on hymnody, ex-
amples and collections.

CHAPTER THREE

Music and Music Ministry

It is a good thing to give thanks to the Lord,
and to sing praises to your Name, O Most High;
To tell of your loving-kindness early in the morning
and of your faithfulness in the night season;
On the psaltery, and on the lyre,
and to the melody of the harp. (Psalm 92:1–3)

A Biblical Mandate for Singing

Our faith is a singing faith. "The morning stars sang together and all the heavenly beings shouted for joy" at the creation. (Job 38:7) At the exodus of the Israelites from Egypt through the Red Sea, Moses, Miriam, and the Israelites rejoiced with tambourines and dancing: "Sing to the Lord, for he has triumphed gloriously; horse and rider he has thrown into the sea." (Exodus 15:1, 20) King David appointed four thousand ministers of music for the Temple (1 Chronicles 23:5). Forty-nine of 150 psalms speak of song or singing or mention musical instruments. Jesus sang psalms in worship at the temples, for that was the custom of the time. There was singing after the shared meal and before the agony in the garden: "When they had sung the hymn, they went out to the Mount of Olives." (Matthew 26:30) Paul described an orderly worship in his first letter to the Corinthians: "When you come together, each one has a hymn, a lesson, a revelation, a tongue, or an interpretation. Let all things be done for building up." (1 Corinthians 14:26) Hymns were sung in worship to praise the living God, to express joy, to offer thanksgivings, to comfort the sorrowful, to give courage to the afflicted, and to unite the faithful. The mandate has not changed.

The Role of Music in the Church

Music is Integral to Worship

The selection of hymns, service music, psalm settings, anthems, and opening
and closing voluntaries must be based on the lessons of the day within the
liturgical season, should set an appropriate tone for the celebration, highlight
the design and flow of the liturgy, and offer elements of dignity, joy, and
beauty. Music must not dominate the liturgy.

> Music is not necessarily helpful in a service. It can, in fact, be destructive of a
> rite. This is the case when music is used for its own sake or only as a demon-
> stration of the virtuosity of the performers, when it is beyond the abilities of
> the performers, when it interferes with the basic movement of the rite, when
> it gives undue prominence to secondary elements in a rite, or when the mood
> is out of keeping with the day or occasion. [28]

Music Helps the Listener Encounter the Holy

Music communicates feelings that are not easily expressed in words. A text
can be more clearly understood when the music profoundly engages the
words, lets them soar beyond an imaginable realm, or hushes them into the
heaven of awe and mystery. Words speak to the mind; music speaks to the
heart and spirit, the very core of our being, and wraps them all together with
the emotions of boundless joy, deep pain, extreme gratitude, heavy grief, and
immeasurable love. Martin Luther said, "Nothing on earth is so well suited
to make the sad merry, the merry sad, to give courage to the despairing, to
make the proud humble, to lessen envy and hate, as music." Within all those
emotions is the presence of God.

Usually the first music heard in the worship service is a voluntary offered
by the organist. Prior to, or perhaps during, that music, the people arrive,
having awakened family members, helped them get ready for church, eaten
breakfast and cleaned up the kitchen, driven to the church, found a parking
place, entered the building and exchanged greetings, walked into the nave
to find a place to sit, and knelt for private prayers. The task of the musician
is to help the people make the transition into an awareness of the holy, a
great and worthy mission.

Before each service, offer your preparations to the glory of God and pray
that something unexpected and mystical will happen that was not planned

---

28. Marion Hatchett, *A Guide to the Practice of Church Music* (New York: The Church Hymnal
Corporation, 1989), 15.

or practiced so that you, too, can experience the reality of the sacred while you are trying to provide that for everyone else.

Music Builds Community

After the opening voluntary, the next music for the congregation is a hymn. The people stand and participate in the first corporate act of worship, singing.

Members of the congregation could belt out their favorite hymns in the privacy of their sound studio shower stalls or in their cars stalled in traffic, but a congregation, whether twenty or two thousand, singing the same hymn becomes one voice. Attend a church convention or a conference of church musicians and be inspired by the singing, when a corporate breath is in absolute unison, collective attention to phrasing, harmony, and text is spontaneous and wondrously accurate, passion and faith are palpable. Your spiritual life will be forever changed.

There will be some voices that rise with the angels, others that are comfortable singing in a much lower register, some provide foundational singing, others are hardly heard, some have just a few notes to sing and others have a wide range, some are accurate in pitch, others have been probably told since early years not to sing but to mouth the words. All parts are needed to build up the body of Christ. All voices are needed to be part of the whole congregation, the sum of many voices. The psalmist did not command us to sing in perfect four-part harmony but to "Shout with joy to the Lord, all you lands; lift up your voice, rejoice, and sing." (Psalm 98:5) A beautiful voice may be admired, but God is the one who gave the gift. Good congregational singing may bring satisfaction, but did the honor and praise go to God? Did we all put forth an effort in this praise or let others do the work for us? The source of our song and the reason for singing is the One who is present through the Holy Spirit, breathes through us, and makes us want to sing.

> Singing is the most human, most companionable of the arts. It joins us together in the whole realm of sound, forging a group identity where there were only individuals and making a communicative statement that far transcends what any one of us could do alone. It is a paradigm of union with the creator. It is what the words talk about. We need to sing well.[29]

---

29. Alice Parker, *Melodious Accord: Good Singing in the Church* (Chicago: Archdiocese of Chicago, Liturgy Training Publications, 1991).

Music is an Instrument for Evangelism

I played the organ and led adult, youth, and children's choirs at a funeral for a former chorister, a twenty-year-old woman who was murdered by her eighteen-year-old brother, also a former chorister. That was a tough one. The service was a tribute to her life, not an honoring of her death. Anthems, hymns, and organ music of resurrection triumph, a sermon of reflection and strength, prayers of hope, comfort, and the promise of eternal life made the service one of thanksgiving for her brief life and ministry. Among the hundreds in attendance was a group of reporters. Several spoke to me during the reception and asked: "Is this your normal kind of funeral? I expected to be moved to tears of sadness but I was moved to tears of joy. The message of God's love was more than words—I could feel it. If it is okay, may I come back and attend a Sunday morning service?"

The word *evangelism* simply refers to the practice of sharing the beliefs of a faith with those who do not share those same beliefs. Evangelism often gets a bad reputation from those who force their views in emotionally-charged and public settings, with a black and white agenda of their way or no way. When music, whether at a funeral or a Sunday morning service, enables the visitor or an un-churched family member or friend to experience the awe, majesty, depth, breadth, and power of the love of God, that is evangelism in a most positive setting.

Music is Sacramental in Nature

The sacraments and sacramental rites of Holy Baptism, Holy Eucharist, Confirmation, Holy Matrimony, Ordination, Reconciliation, and Unction (ministration to the sick and dying) are outward and visible signs of an inward and spiritual grace. These are rites which convey a divine grace or blessing. "Sacraments and sacramental actions make Christ present to us, make us aware of God's presence and action in our lives."[30] Music is sacramental as it makes us aware of God's presence and God's action in our lives.

The church has come to understand that if the sacraments are important, then how we celebrate them should reflect that priority. Dignity, beauty, significance, and appropriate ceremony have been essential to those celebrations. So, too, in our music should there be beauty, meaning, and excellence.

---

30. John H. Westerhoff, *A People called Episcopalians: A Brief Introduction to Our Peculiar Way of Life* (Atlanta, GA: St. Luke's Episcopal Church, 1998).

In all ways we should strive to offer our absolute best—in our singing, in our accompanying and conducting, in our planning and preparations for worship, in our relationships with choirs, clergy, and congregations, in our many and vital offerings.

Music Expresses Diversity

The broadness of the Episcopal Church is expressed in a wide-ranging diversity of musical styles. A service may be led by or include a traditional choir with organ, piano, or other instrumental accompaniment; praise band with guitars, bass, drums, other instruments, and soloists or vocal group; popular religious song for music ensemble and/or congregation; organ with accompanied or unaccompanied choir; the music of the Taizé and Iona communities, sung with simplicity of sound; world music, accompanied with authentic instrumentation; or the music of the emergent church, sung to live accompaniment or recordings in more intimate settings.

The People, the Participants

"In all services, the entire Christian assembly participates in such a way that the members of each order within the Church, lay persons, bishops, priests, and deacons, fulfill the functions proper to their respective orders, as set forth in the rubrical directions for each service." (*BCP*, p. 13) The lay persons involved in the music of the services are congregation, choir, cantors, instrumentalists, organists or pianists, and choir directors. By rubric and by tradition, some of the musical portions of the rites are reserved for the people.

The Danish writer and philosopher Søren Kierkegaard (1813–1855) compares the church to a theater with conventional roles switched around. In essence, Kierkegaard said that God is the audience, those who sit in the pews are the participants, and those who are vested serve as the prompters.[31]

> God is the audience, the one who evaluates what is done. The people in the congregation are the listeners, the actors on stage, the ones who act out the drama, who participate actively. The speaker (preacher) is not the center of attention, but the one who prompts the listener, the congregation. Others

31. *Purity of Heart is To Will One Thing*, Douglas Steere, trans. (New York: Harper and Brothers, 1948), 180–181.

who are vested, assisting ministers, lay people, and the choir, are also prompters, encouraging the people to be involved and do their part.[32]

Unfortunately many church architects are not familiar with this understanding, for over the years they have designed churches where the vested participants are separated from the congregation by risers or brick walls or iron gates or lofty pulpits. They have costumes in the form of vestments, special lighting, and all the symbols, flowers, and beautiful appointments are on their stage. Thus the congregation expects to be prayed for, sung to, preached to, entertained, and kept at a distance. No wonder some congregational singing is so deplorable!

Charles Fulton and Juan Oliver, in their article "A Place of Good News: Liturgical Space and the Proclamation of the Gospel," suggest ways in which one can tell a church building is a "Good News" place. Some of these include: you are invited in; you are expected; your thoughts and modes of expression are valued; you can see and hear everything that is happening; you can move around to greet, talk with others; the distinctions in liturgical roles are articulated without the implication that some are more worthy than others; the space is sturdy and can handle being used by people; architecturally it is crafted with care and professional artistry; it looks best when full and being used.[33]

Some architectural settings may not be conducive to engaged participation or flexibility. Musicians and clergy must work diligently to overcome the erroneous concept that the clergy, choir, and other vested lay participants do the work for those sitting in the pews, and raise the attention and focus of the people to do what they are called to do—participate fully in the action of the liturgy with their hearts, minds, bodies, and their voices.

Congregational Song

Raymond Glover, editor of *The Hymnal 1982 Companion*, defines congregational song as "vocal music, usually in poetic form, sung by a gathered community (often with some sort of instrumental accompaniment), which

---

32. Source: Desiring Repetition: Søren Kierkegaard's Metaphor of the Theater in dialogue with Contemporary Worship Leadership Models by Andrew Thompson forum.sorenkierkegaard. nl, p. 4.

33. Marilyn L. Haskel and Clayton L. Morris, eds. *As We Gather to Pray: An Episcopal Guide to Worship*. New York: Church Hymnal Corporation, 1996, pp. 50–55.

is a statement of faith expressed in praise or prayer to God. Through its use the community retells the story of God's redeeming acts throughout history and expresses its faith as revealed through the personal encounters of its members with the living God, through scripture and through the historic teachings of the Church." [34] The hymns of our faith make up the greatest volume of our congregational song. Plainsong hymns, chorales, psalter tunes, folk tunes and carols, music from other religious traditions and from composers all over the world have been part of the culture of the Anglican and Episcopal Churches. More than ten years into the twenty-first century our hymnody continues to expand to represent our diversity, our socio-economic-political backgrounds, world customs, and varieties of worship styles. Congregational song also includes singing parts of the eucharistic liturgy, psalms, responses, and canticles. In the Daily Offices, the congregation adds the singing of canticles to their repertoire.

Follow the service of Holy Eucharist: Rite Two (beginning at *BCP* 355) and see the parts of the service which can be sung by the people. There are music settings in *The Hymnal 1982: Accompaniment Edition/Service Music* and the Altar Book for all of these parts.

- Response to the Opening Acclamation
- Song of Praise, sung or said (*Gloria in Excelsis, Trisagion, Kyrie eleison,* canticle, or hymn)
- Salutation (*BCP* 357)
- Acclamation at the end of Lessons
- Psalm or Psalm Antiphon
- Acclamations before and after the Gospel
- The Nicene Creed
- Responses in the Prayers of the People
- Response to and Passing of the Peace
- Offertory Hymn
- *Sursum Corda* (*BCP* 361)
- *Sanctus* and *Benedictus qui venit*
- Memorial Acclamation
- Lord's Prayer

---

34. Raymond F. Glover, "What is Congregational Song?" *The Hymnal 1982 Companion, Volume One*, 3.

- Response at the Fraction **or** Fraction Anthem
- Response to the Dismissal
- Hymns, all
- Amen, wherever it occurs in the liturgy

Follow the Daily Morning Prayer: Rite One (beginning at *BCP* 42) and note the parts of the office which can be sung by the people. There are music settings in *The Hymnal 1982 Accompaniment Edition / Service Music Volume 1* for all of these parts.

- Preces (Invitatory)
- Antiphon and Invitatory Psalm
- *Venite* or *Jubilate* or *Christ our Passover* during the Easter season
- Psalm(s)
- Canticles (after the Lessons)
- Salutation and The Lord's Prayer
- Suffrages
- Amen (after each sung Collect or Prayer)
- Hymn (optional)
- Concluding Versicle and Response

If the congregation cannot sing the responses or a particular music selection easily, either from lack of repetition or effective teaching or the choice of music is too difficult, then another setting should be chosen or the text should be spoken rather than sung. Striving for excellence requires both confidence and wisdom.

This question frequently arises: In the Episcopal Church, may the choir sing settings of the *Gloria, Kyrie,* Creed, *Sanctus, Agnus Dei* without the congregation? Sure, they may, and occasionally that would be a lovely offering. But asking how often would be the better question. If the community is called to participate and the choir participates for them, have we denied them their voice? Consider the people first. After all, these are their songs.

Essentials for Good Congregational Singing

- The organist should provide confident and effective leadership through competent organ technique, understanding of hymn texts, use of organ registrations, and sensitivity to the singing ability of the congregation. Pianists and other instrumentalists should provide the same effective leadership, employing the best of their skills and effective instrument placement.

- A quality organ (or piano or other instrument) that speaks clearly in the worship space and is capable of both the quiet support needed to lead a Christmas lullaby as well as the triumphal hymns of Easter is both desired and necessary.

- In most settings, a congregation is well served to eliminate carpets, pad-ded pew cushions, excessive banners, and anything else that would soak up sound and deaden the acoustic in the worship space. Reverberation is needed to permit people to hear the sound of the entire congrega-tion, rather than individual voices immediately around them, so they have more self-assurance to do their part in singing. Of course, in the Episcopal Church one occasionally has to deal with the struggle between improving the sound and quality of the music in an acoustically dead setting and the seeming desecration of a memorial gift given by a long-departed, no longer known, formerly faithful parishioner.

- Know your congregation, what they sing well, what they have not yet tried, what has worked in the past, and what has failed to suc-ceed. Build a trust relationship with them. When considering trying new music, assess their development as a singing body and whether what you want to do is for you or for them or for the greater good. If people in your congregation are still calling *The Hymnal 1982* the "new hymnal" then achieving your goals for teaching new music may be extremely challenging.

- Use every educational tool possible in every place possible: teaching fo-rums, articles and newsletters, choir rehearsals, meetings, notes in Sunday service leaflets.

- For a dose of reality, go online and find John Wesley's "Directions for Singing Hymns" from his preface to *Sacred Melody*, 1761.

Music and Ministry

Many times in my career I have been told by well-meaning people that I should become a minister. My response to them is always: "But I am a minis-ter." I do not mean to be impertinent with my response, only open and honest.

Although these exact words were not spoken at my baptism so long ago, I renew them with regularity in services of baptism: "I will continue in the apostles' teaching and fellowship, in the breaking of bread, and in the prayers. I will persevere in resisting evil, and, whenever I fall into sin, repent and return to the Lord. I will proclaim by word and example the Good News of God in Christ. I will seek and serve Christ in all persons, loving my neighbor as myself. I will strive for justice and peace among all people, and respect the dignity of every human being. I will continue to confess the faith of Christ crucified, proclaim his resurrection, and share in his eternal priesthood." (*BCP*, pp. 304–305, 308) If that is not what ministry is about, what is? Without a moment of hesitation, I believe I was ordained to ministry at my baptism. In truth, you were, too.

In general, most people would agree that a minister is someone who is authorized by a religious organization to lead worship in the church, to teach, and to be a spiritual presence within the congregation. In the Catechism of *The Book of Common Prayer*, in the section on Ministry, the first question asked is: "Who are the ministers of the Church?" The answer is: "The ministers of the Church are lay persons, bishops, priests, and deacons." The next paragraph describes the ministry of the laity, which is "to represent Christ and his Church; to bear witness to him wherever they may be; and, according to the gifts given them, to carry on Christ's work of reconciliation in the world; and to take their place in the life, worship, and governance of the Church." (*BCP*, p. 855)

So, for those of us who serve as cantors, organists, pianists, instrumentalists, choir directors, or a combination of these, what does it mean to be a musician in ministry? How do we represent and bear witness to Christ? What are the gifts we bring to the life and worship of the church?

Pastors, Teachers, Performers

Alec Wyton (1921–2007), English-born organist, composer, teacher, and international church music leader, said: "Leaders in the church in whatever area are Pastors, Teachers, and Performers in exactly that order."[35]

Pastor

For their pastoral care and concern, the music leader may be approached by choir members with stories of losing a job and the financial stress of unem-

---

35. Alec Wyton, *The Function of Music in Corporate Worship*, The Journal of Church Music, December 1987.

ployment, strain of caring for a parent long-distance, a child's grief after the death of a grandparent, a personal illness, impending medical tests, and so much more. Perhaps the chorister thought their concerns were not important enough to take the time of busy clergy. But they know their director and trust an openness to listen and care.

Simple things like sending get-well cards signed by the choir, visiting choir members in the hospital, arranging for the choir to make and deliver meals to the homebound, and listening to people are pastoral matters and they are important.

I served a very long time in one church and got to know the congregation quite well. An unusual ministry developed for those who were grieving. After playing the organ at a funeral for a loved one, I would look for the family or friend to return to church for Sunday worship. After several weeks of absence I would call the grieving person and say how much I missed seeing him/her at church and then let them talk. Usually the reason for the absence had to do with music—that listening or trying to sing hymns brought them to such a deep place within, that the pain brought no sound, only tears. The effort to sing a hymn was simply unbearable. So, I offered this ministry: when you are ready, call me up and let us find a time when we can meet at church, sit on the organ bench together, play through all your lost love's favorite hymns, play your favorite hymns, and have a good cry. A box of tissues was always near the organ console. This is certainly not a required ministry in the Episcopal Church, just one of many examples of ministry other Episcopal musicians around the country could share out of their own experiences.

I believe people are yearning to have a spiritual life with God. While the choir is developing musically, help them to grow spiritually. If you are comfortable doing so, pray with them before and/or after rehearsals and before worship. Prayer is simply a conversation with God. Trying to find the perfect words is not necessary; the words that come out of your mouth are the right words. Give thanks, allow time and silence for petitions from the choir, offer special concerns, and send them forth. If you are not comfortable praying without a text, use prayers in *The Book of Common Prayer* or prayers from numerous other sources, some of which are listed in the bibliography.

Schedule the evening service of Compline, a simply lovely service in *The Book of Common Prayer*, to be sung at the end of a rehearsal once a month or, at the very least, at the beginning and end of the choir year. Your lesson plans will need to be adjusted to provide the time, but the peace and beauty of the service will feed the hearts and souls of the choir, reminding them that the choir exists for a sacred purpose.

Teacher

For the choir to sing well, the music leader must train the choir in singing and music-reading skills and choral techniques, and instruct them in worship customs and liturgical detail.

The music leader can bring church music to the awareness of the congregation by writing informative articles for the parish newsletter, teaching adult education classes and forums, and working with Sunday School teachers to include positive music-learning opportunities for children. Information about the hymns, including interesting facts about the poets and composers, historical observations, sources of tune names, and the reasons particular hymns were selected for the day, could be included in the bulletin each Sunday. All of these opportunities for instruction connect the congregation, choir, and music leader and make known the value of music as an integral part of the liturgy and in the life of the church.

One of the most important jobs for the music leader is the teaching of new hymns, service music, and psalm settings, not only to the choir but to the congregation. I once served in a church where my repeated request to select *H82* 557, Richard Wayne Dirksen's music for the text "Rejoice, ye pure in heart!" was just as repeatedly refused. And each time I was given the same reason: "We don't know that tune." True, but when will the congregation ever learn this tune? *Vineyard Haven* simply transforms the text and makes every singer want to rejoice with an endless "Hosanna!" Every hymn in *The Hymnal 1982* was new to someone at some time. The job of teaching new music and changing minds and hearts is demanding at best, but one that must continue for the sake of the present church and the future. In so doing, you may even hear the seven last words in the Episcopal Church: "We've never done it that way before!"

One of the joys of teaching is having our students change our own lives with their honesty, openness, and wisdom. For a choir of boys and girls in grades four through eight, I included some teaching in each rehearsal, often focusing on the Scripture lessons assigned for the next Sunday and the hymns selected. At one rehearsal we looked at *H82* 491, a text of Christopher Smart set to music by Alec Wyton. I have never understood why this hymn was not included in the Christmas section of *The Hymnal 1982*, because the text is such a stunning reflection on the Incarnation. The word opposites in verse three are utterly profound: "O the magnitude of meekness! Worth from worth immortal sprung; O the strength of infant weakness, if eternal is so young!" After presenting the text, I asked the choristers to close their eyes and listen to the hymn played on the piano. The melody only spans the interval of a fifth, the accompaniment is uncomplicated, and the ending is neither an authentic nor a plagal cadence, but an F Major chord with passing notes in the tenor ending on G, providing audible and unresolved dissonance. As the final sound faded a chorister raised his hand and said: "Marti, there's something wrong with that hymn. The ending doesn't sound right." I took a breath to respond but noticed another chorister's hand in the air and called on him. "It's not supposed to end. It's like God's love. It never ends."

Performer

Imagine this posted job description for a church in need of a church musician: "Must demonstrate exceptional organ technique with wide range of repertoire and utmost proficiency at hymn playing, be adept at improvisation, skilled with choirs of all ages, a most capable conductor, a published composer and arranger, good with people." I know few people who would apply, fearful that they might have to walk on water for the audition—or at least know where the rocks are hidden beneath the surface. How do musicians become proficient, skilled, adept, or competent? They work hard.

An organist may have started playing the piano at an early age, then began organ lessons when they were big enough for their feet to comfortably rest on the organ pedals and still young enough to be oblivious to how complicated it is to play with feet and hands at the same time. Perhaps they went on to college to continue their study, practicing six or eight hours a day in addition to their course work, homework, and ensemble requirements. Perhaps they continued organ study for an avocation, while working another job to make their hobby financially feasible and to pay room and board. They learned how to use practice time effectively and they struggled to achieve goodness in performing the music. Pianists and instrumentalists may have also started at an early age, continued study at university or conservatory with countless hours devoted to developing their expertise, and pursued vocations or avocations in music while juggling the rest of life.

The person sitting in the pew may never know that a particular piece, less than four minutes in duration, might have taken an organist four months or more to prepare before playing as an opening or closing voluntary in church.

But the organist will strive to play the piece to the best of her/his abilities, not counting the time spent nor the technical struggles overcome.

I am aware that the word *performer* causes angst among the faithful. If a musician performs to satisfy self, bolster an ego, or seek applause, then that musician might wish to pursue a concert career, and surely God will provide an abundance of blessings. If a musician strives to perfect skills with the choir and on the organ and the offering of those gifts adds a beautiful presence to the liturgy for the glory of God and for the uplifting of the spirit, then the performance has been well done, and so be it. An *Amen* far surpasses applause.

Members of the altar guild polish silver, wash and iron linens, replace candles, dust, change numbers on hymn boards, make ready the bread and wine, and perform all the tasks required for the service. The flower guild designs the array of flowers for a particular liturgy, determines the appropriate vase(s), shops for the flowers, prepares them, then performs their tasks in arranging and placing the flowers for added beauty to the worship. Both groups strive to do their best to prepare for worship.

A preacher studies the lessons, does some research, prepares a sermon, perhaps even makes several revisions, practices saying the sermon in an empty nave. Then, at the appointed time in the service the preacher offers the sermon, desiring to do the best presentation possible, perhaps with a few hand gestures for emphasis, slightly louder voice with more pronounced diction than a normal speaking voice, maybe even a few dramatic pauses to deliver the message. The congregation focuses solely on the preacher and listens for content and meaning in their lives. Is this not also a performance, a fulfilling of a function, for which time and talent have been dedicated?

When I prepare to play the organ and direct choirs in worship, I work diligently and try to employ the skills I have developed over the years to offer my best to God, to the One who has given me many gifts, some of which I know and others which remain yet unknown. For me, this *is* a performance, for in this moment of service, which will never be repeated, my adrenalin will be pumping to be accurate, to strive for beauty, to be aware of timing and movement, to inspire and support the choir and congregation from the organ console, to be prepared if something goes awry, to help energize the liturgy if needed. Between the choir prayer and the first notes of the opening voluntary, I ask God to accept my human preparations, invite the Holy Spirit to direct and guide me, and then I let go and perform for God.

I fear there is much ado about something that matters little if our broader view is always on our praise of God. A portion of the prayer for church musicians and artists helps to maintain our vision: "Be ever present with your servants who seek through art and music to perfect the praises offered by your people on earth." (*BCP*, p. 819)

Role of the Choir

Just as music is integral to the liturgy, the choir is integral to the worship life of the parish. Just as the music leader is pastor, teacher, and performer, the choir also serves in the same capacities.

Since the fifth century the songs traditionally assigned to the choir have been the three processional songs of the eucharistic rite: the entrance song (a congregational hymn in much of Anglicanism), the offertory song, and the communion song. Other musical portions are integral to the rite, and the texts are normally read when they are not sung. These processional songs serve primarily to accompany actions and are not essential to the actions. Traditional liturgies have assigned the music at the three processions to the choir so that the people might be free to take part in the procession or to watch it progress. [36]

In its *pastoral* role the choir faithfully sings and leads congregational song; sings at sacramental rites: baptism, Eucharist, weddings, funerals, ordinations; provides confident musical leadership to inspire the congregation to sing their song; offers worthy texts and music to the glory of God; prays for absent and ill members; and practices hospitality to new choir members.

In one church choir I asked a member from each section to practice hospitality to new members, to help a new singer get a vestment, hymnal, anthem folder, and music, introduce the new person to other choir members, and pay attention to them for several weeks or until they were acclimated. The choir was growing and I was thrilled, but I noticed that we were unable to keep new altos in the choir. Each one would attend rehearsals and services for two or three weeks and then drop out. I called each one to invite them to return, but only one brave soul explained that the alto assigned to help them out would make comments that simply were not hospitable: "I'll find you a robe but you are going to have to find your own seat, because there are not enough seats for the altos now. You will

---

36. Marion J. Hatchett, *A Guide to the Practice of Church Music* (New York: Church Publishing, 1989), 25.

just have to read off of someone else's music because I'm sure there is not enough music for you. If you get to church before I do, do not take my seat." Needless to say, that volunteer was "fired" from her position, after lengthy pastoral sessions, of course.

As *teachers* the choir members teach new hymns, canticles, psalm settings, and service music to the congregation; lead in worship, offering an example of preparation and participation to those in the pews; and model good worship habits (kneeling, sitting, standing in unison, refraining from talking, being attentive, and actively participating in the liturgy).

As *performers*, the choir enriches congregational singing with descants and harmony; may upon occasion sing a text usually sung by the people, especially in a more challenging setting; performs anthems appropriate to the texts of the day, season, or special liturgy, and within their ability to sing well.

On one of those rare occasions when I was not engaged in full-time music ministry, I attended a Palm Sunday service with family members on the West Coast. Upon arriving at the church I was handed a bulletin but no palm branch or frond. At fifteen minutes after the appointed service time, after fifteen minutes of expectant silence, the rector, choir, Sunday School children, and other vested participants, slightly out of breath, came into the church and the organist started playing hymn 154, *All glory, laud, and honor*, all five verses, at about one pulse per second in a dead acoustic. Clearly the Liturgy of the Palms and parade were over and we were not invited to participate. The rector then announced the ushers would pass out the palm fronds and they did, as we sang all five verses of hymn 154, again, at the same tempo. The Old Testament, Psalm, and New Testament readings were omitted for sake of time, as we were told just after the hymn, so that the rector could offer his Palm Sunday homily, which consisted of fifteen minutes of chastising us in advance for not attending Holy Week services. Music at the communion was sung by two women, one accompanying on the guitar, both without needed amplification of some sort, or better placement, or stronger voices; hymn selections were replete with "Alleluias," entirely inappropriate. The Passion Gospel was read at the end of the service, almost as an afterthought, as just before the reading the rector took a few moments to go around and invite people to read the parts from within the congregation. At the Offertory, the choir of ten, average age about fifty-eight, moved out of the choir stalls and stood in a straight line on the chancel steps to sing the Allegri *Miserere Mei, Deus*. They looked miserable, their lack of comfort with Latin was agonizing, and their musical accuracy, in pitch and tonal quality, was beyond the telling. My heart ached for the choir. This was not their choice and, with this extraordinarily beautiful and difficult anthem, they simply could not succeed. Their music offering was a sacrifice, not a gift. How much better it would have been if they had sung an appropriate hymn or psalm or canticle, something within their capabilities and a blessing to the service.

Types of Choirs

The Gathered Community

First and foremost, the principal choir is the whole community of people gathered for worship. The psalmist commanded all of us, not just a select few, to sing a new song and to make a joyful noise unto the Lord. All of us have the responsibility to lift our voices to the God of love, the source of our song.

Volunteer Choir in a Small Congregation

As the majority of Episcopal Churches have fewer than one hundred people on their rolls, choirs in those churches are typically small in size. Each singer knows he or she is important to the whole and may even schedule vacations around the choir schedule. If there are six or eight singers in the choir, an absence of one may completely eliminate a section.

The organist may also be a volunteer and may not necessarily have had college or university training or even keyboard training beyond the piano. The mindset of many is that if you can play the piano, then surely you can play the organ. Ah, the mindset of some . . . If there is a choir director separate from the organist, the possibility exists that the director may have minimal conducting skills and neither time nor self-confidence to get some assistance. In small churches often there is very little or no money available for music, so the choir sings the same anthems repeatedly.

Some singers may have been in the choir forty years or more, know with historical clarity just how an anthem has always been sung, and are quite willing to inform the director. The choir may be an entity within the church that is indomitable before congregation, clergy, music leader, and potential new singers. In other places, a small and volunteer choir may be the heart and soul of the church, providing refreshments for Sunday coffee hour, taking care of church grounds, involved in mission and ministry, on the altar guild and vestry, volunteering to help the music leader, assisting clergy and church work as they can. Their fellowship is genuine and their commitment strong. Within those two models are countless more.

Music selection for the volunteer choir in a small parish is extremely important. Choose quality texts that are based on Scripture, texts that will inspire the choir and fit with the propers of the day. Avoid texts that are simply not worthy of any choir's offering to God. Choose music that is musically achievable for the choir, within vocal ranges that will not overstress the singers. There is nothing quite as disheartening as hearing a soprano who has refused to accept that age and gravity cause everything to sag, including the voice range, make a valiant effort to sing a high note and be more than a step off goal. Select anthems from hymns in *The Hymnal 1982* and supplements, using the many hymns that might prove too difficult for a congregation to sing.

Success in singing will boost confidence, and confidence will provide supportive choral leadership for the congregation. Rehearsals are really necessary, even though work schedules, distance from the church, night-time driving, and illness are always issues. If mid-week, evening rehearsals are not possible, consider rehearsing on Sunday morning, before and/or after the worship service. The inclusion of food and coffee is always a great enticement in any Episcopal church.

A small church choir can strive to sing unison well, not an easy task for a choir of any size, whether an anthem selection, plainsong hymn, or a hymn not yet known to the choir or congregation. Plainsong hymns are especially beautiful, a nod to the Episcopal Church's rich musical heritage, and an opportunity to provide reachable beauty in the worship service. Anthems written for two and three equal parts or SAB are excellent choices for the choir. Four-part anthems may be scheduled occasionally, depending on the skill of the choir and adequate rehearsal time. If too much difficult music is planned for a particular season, the choir will feel confident singing some of the anthems and will have that deer-in-headlights look otherwise. Fortunately, their salvation is not dependent on singing Latin motets each Sunday.

Honor the choir with your expectations and direction. They are who they are, all that they are, and all that God intends them to be. They should not be made to feel inadequate because they do not sound like the big church choir down the street. They should be affirmed for being in the choir in their church, doing what they are called to do, singing their offering, and striving to do their best in the leadership of congregational song.

I started off in a small church, where I was the youngest person by at least four decades on Sunday morning. There were eleven in the choir, if they all attended a rehearsal or service at the same time. I played a Minshall-Estey organ, a single extended keyboard, no pedals, twelve stops, two of which worked. And when I floored the expression pedal to get some sound out of the instrument, dust filtered out from the speaker over the choir and fluttered down upon them like angel dust. They did not mind. They always had smiles and lots of compliments for my efforts, and were simply glad to be at church with one another, glad to sing for as many years as God gave them voice, glad to be. They captured my heart with their faith, joy, and sense of service; I am ever grateful to have had that foundational experience in my vocation.

Volunteer Choir in a Larger Parish

A larger parish (one hundred to two hundred active members) may have a larger choir. That would seem to be logical; many conditions might prevent that, however, including church location, commitment issues involving family and work-related activities, rush hour complications for rehearsals, and choir members who have frequent travel and/or family commitments on weekends. As the choir grows and there are three or four, or even five and six, people singing on each part, confidence grows as less-strong singers are supported and encouraged by the presence of voices they can hear around them singing accurately.

Weekly rehearsals are important and commitment to the choir and the much-needed rehearsals become stronger. Vocal and choral skills, music reading abilities, and an understanding of musical styles in a wide range of repertoire are developed. A half-hour class offered before rehearsal each week could provide a time for some singers to improve their music and sight-reading abilities and thus greatly enhance the sound of the choir as well as efficiency of rehearsal.

The choir may develop an awareness of their integral role in the leadership of congregational song and the spiritual life of the church. The volunteer choir in a larger parish may even have volunteer section leaders from within the choir who have music training and can encourage the rest of the section or even lead sectional rehearsals.

Auditions may not be required to sing in a volunteer church choir, but an audition-like, one-on-one time with the singer and music leader once a year may be helpful. During that time the singer is heard and the director might offer suggestions to improve the singing and even suggest that singing a different choral part might be more advantageous to the person and ultimately to the choir.

As churches grow, music programs may benefit from increased funding from the church to purchase more anthems, vestments, and program support. The musician(s) in a larger church may be part-time with training and experience, eventually full-time in some congregations. Volunteer assistance in administrative detail within the music department benefits the music leaders, as they become more involved in liturgy planning, meetings, rehearsal and worship preparation, and the constant struggle to find practice time.

Larger choirs can sing SATB anthems regularly, as well as the occasional offering of plainsong hymns and two or three part anthems. Sopranos and tenors can sing descants to hymns. The choir can teach new hymns, service music, and canticles to the congregation and upon occasion prepare and offer a larger choral work within the context of a service or concert.

Like the volunteer choir in a smaller church, they need to be honored and affirmed for who they are, not made to feel like they need to sound like a cathedral or professional choir.

Volunteer Choir with Paid Section Leaders

Section leaders within a choir, whether volunteer or paid, can provide an invaluable strength for the choir. Paid singers should be auditioned for singing talent and skill and the ability to blend with other singers to produce the sound desired. They are expected to be faithful in attendance at both rehearsal and services or, if an absence is needed, they are expected to find their own substitute from a list of your choosing. They usually sing solos in anthems and large choral works or serve as cantors to lead the congregation in psalm singing, versicles and responses, and service music.

Many churches of limited size but significant financial means hire singers to provide the core of the choir while the few volunteers appreciate their presence and support. There will always be parishioners who will value the fine music produced but complain about the cost. Will they also complain about the cost of the time and talents of administrators, directors of Christian education, sextons, bookkeepers, groundskeepers, spiritual advisors, and clergy, others who also serve God with their time, the gifts they have been given, and the skills they have developed?

Some churches are close to college and university campuses and benefit from the presence of young people in their worship services. Students may be hired to serve as section leaders or as a separate choir to sing when the parish choir needs a break. They appreciate the stipend, and learn more about the Episcopal Church and the historic legacy of music in the process. Perhaps they will even become future music leaders in the Episcopal Church. One challenge I have often seen is that of integrating the professional singers with the volunteers, so that the paid singers do not have an air of aloofness given their more highly-trained abilities. Think of the volunteer singer who parties late on Saturday night, awakens to a dreary Sunday and decides to sleep in, assured that the anthems will be sung well by the singers who are paid to attend and that his attendance is not needed. Clear understandings, verbal and written, with both the paid and volunteer singers could help unite the choir for a sacred purpose. Introductions, becoming acquainted with each other, social times, moments of laughter before or after rehearsals and services help ease division of any sort.

Youth and Children's Choirs

If you are fortunate enough to have children in your congregation, find some way to incorporate them into the music life of the congregation. They are not just the future of the church, they are the *now* of the church. Every ounce of energy invested in them has a worth far beyond gold. If you have only three children, offer them an opportunity to sing with the adult choir, if they are able to do so. Depending on their ages, they can sing parts with the adults or sing refrains of hymns or anthems or songs they alone are capable of singing.

If you have more than three children, begin a choir for them. Challenge them, treat them with respect, teach, and provide a positive and quality experience and the choir will grow. Resources for forming and directing choirs for children and youth are found in the bibliography. Consult the Royal School of Church Music (RSCM) website (www.rscm.com) or Choristers Guild (www.choristersguild.org) for more information on choirs and training schemes for choristers. Look at some of the church websites located in this resource, consider what exists in your congregation, dream big, and get started. Working with young people may be one of the greatest joys in your music ministry.

I am thrilled when I hear from former choristers, grown and with family, who say they want for their children what they had as choristers growing up in a graded music program at church. They say that no matter where they go they know the hymns and service music and they earnestly seek churches with a quality music program like they enjoyed. Former choristers serve in church leadership positions and sing in choirs all over the country. Thanks be to God!

In a choir, choristers learn about the elements of music and singing, hymnody, liturgy, history of the Episcopal Church, teamwork in singing, songs of other cultures, and the richness of our Anglican heritage in music. Young choristers understand they are an integral part of the life of the church when they sing on a regular basis in the church. Their confidence, knowledge, and sense of inclusion soar when they sing weekly, an attainable and worthy goal. If children learn a song, stand in front of the church to sing, are applauded for their efforts, and deemed "cute" by parents and parishioners alike, then I believe we have failed the choristers and the congregation, and perhaps even disappointed a higher being.

Young people have to juggle their time with the demands of homework, school activities, sports, family obligations, and other interests. Adding choir to the schedule may be more than they can handle. However, if young people have grown up in a choir program that provided rehearsals and teaching opportunities from pre-school through middle school, they already know commitment, excellence, and success. They will continue.

A high school choir, with choristers from seven area high schools, used to meet early in the evening on a weekly basis. Gradually, over several years, more and more demanding school activities and sports carried activities into the evening hours, causing a declining attendance at rehearsals. So the rehearsal was changed to Sunday at 7:30 am, requiring the singers to consider carefully what they did on Saturday evening. The choristers rehearsed until 8:30 am, ate breakfast provided by an assigned half dozen choristers each Sunday, sang the 9 am service and were done for the week. For us this worked well and the choir more than doubled in size. They wanted to sing together. They wanted to sing together in church. They made that possible.

The choice of a leader for youth and children's choirs is extremely important, for that person must have three very basic qualifications: 1) love of God; 2) love of church music; 3) love of working with children and young people. If a music leader possesses only the first two qualities, then another person should direct the children. With patience, keen commitment, and a lot of hard work, children's choirs can be formed and developed to the benefit of all.

Anthem choices are important. Choose quality texts that reflect the assigned lessons of the day and quality music that inspires singers to strive for excellence. Children and young people know when they are given music that is less good, but that others think they will enjoy. Young people can sing music with popular rhythms, but in twenty years they will still remember that they struggled to learn and sing a Latin motet in church or music from another culture. The rich heritage of music in the Anglican and Episcopal traditions offers choristers a quality repertoire. Children know when they are being placated. We need not dumb down the music selections because of the age of the choristers and what others think they are capable of singing. Instead we need to let our children far exceed our wildest expectations.

If children's and youth choirs are in their formative stages and the music library is inadequate, turn to *The Hymnal 1982* and the various hymnal supplements for a source of anthem material. Children can sing hymns that the congregation might not know or sing well. They can sing descants and hymns that are in round form to learn the fundamentals of two-part singing. A hymn can become an anthem by adding an introduction or instrumental part, interlude or codetta, select stanzas sung as solos. Youth choirs can progress from hymn-anthems to the music of the adult choir. If you seek a quality effort, give them quality music.

The Professional Choir

A choir of eight, twelve, sixteen or more professional singers, auditioned and rehearsed, can sing anything from Thomas Tallis to Morten Lauridsen, from plainsong to C. V. Stanford. They can sound like a quartet and they can sound like a forty-voice choir. They know how to adjust their voices for different styles of music, they sight-read quite well and learn notes and rhythms on their own time if they find inaccuracies during rehearsal. They are faithful in their attendance at rehearsals and services, some just because they want to be, all because they are paid to do so. They can add an extraordinary dimension of beauty and musical diversity to worship that inspires the people and offers strength to congregational song. They exist in churches with means that desire the highest quality of music and they provide that, and more.

The Cathedral Choir

Cathedral choirs may consist of men and women, men and boys or girls, women only, men only, or boys and girls. Whatever the combination, the choirs are usually selectively auditioned, enjoy the presence of paid/professional singers, and provide exemplary music for every service. They set a high standard, a model that is noticed throughout the diocese. Often, especially with the boys and girls, there are two or more required rehearsals each week, allowing for adequate preparation for the many services they sing. Some cathedrals offer a choir school where boys and girls attend daily rehearsals as well as their academic classes. Such regularity and requirements are not prevalent in most parish choirs and allow for the cathedral choirs to sing at a standard of excellence much like the professional choir.

The Occasional Choir

In many Episcopal congregations there are people who would like to sing in a choir but have neither the time nor the commitment to rehearse and sing weekly. The occasional choir is an opportunity to sing once a month or once in a liturgical season, for Christmas and Easter, for special services like All Saints' Day, Easter Vigil, Pentecost, patronal feast, and bishop's visitation, during the summer, for a cantata or concert, or for a regional, diocesan, or ecumenical gathering. There is always the hope that a positive singing experience in the occasional choir will encourage the singer to join the regular choir.

The Role of the Cantor

Paul Westermeyer, Lutheran pastor, author, teacher, cantor, and organist-choirmaster, provides a historical perspective and practical considerations about the various titles and the intrinsic meanings conferred upon church musicians in his book *The Church Musician*. Ultimately he argues that the word *cantor* best describes the many skills required to lead the song of the people.

- A *cantor* (from the Latin *cantare* meaning *to sing*) is one who leads the singing, as in the Jewish synagogue. Roman Catholics employ a *cantor* to lead the people in singing. In the German Lutheran tradition the *cantor* was in charge of music for the congregation, music and musical instruction in the school, and music for the city. Dietrich Buxtehude and Johann Sebastian Bach, among many others, were *cantors*.

- *Choir director* or *choirmaster* suggests only one aspect of a church musician's responsibility.

- An *organist* is a keyboard player who plays organ literature while the people listen, accompanies hymns and service music and, again, suggests only one aspect of the job.

- *Director of music* suggests one who coordinates a music program.

- *Minister of music* suggests a particular Christian, possibly but not necessarily ordained, who is responsible for the music, but it neglects reference to the people's song, which is what calls the church musician into being in the first place and defines his or her primary obligation.

- A *pastoral musician* may presume an office rather than the one who leads the people's song.[37]

A Cantor in the Episcopal Church

For many Episcopalians the word *cantor* implies the presence of a soloist in Jewish or Roman Catholic services, but not their own denomination. Yet cantors are providing music leadership in many Episcopal congregations today. They may be called by some other names, including *soloist* or *song leader*.

The cantor, male or female, need not be a trained singer, but must be someone who can read musical notation accurately, sing the words confidently and audibly, in tune and without loss of pitch, maintain visual contact with the congregation, and possess a voice that is pleasing and that invites the congregation to sing. An operatic voice does not always serve the congregation well, for the people will opt out of singing to listen to the trained voice or feel so insecure about their musical abilities in comparison that they decline to sing at all.

In small congregations that may not have a choir, a cantor can make possible the singing of many portions of the liturgy. The cantor may not sing anything assigned specifically to the presider or deacon.[38]

The cantor can also assist congregational song by teaching new music.

- Shorter texts, such as the *Kyrie eleison* (Lord, have mercy upon us), Memorial Acclamation, and Fraction Anthem can be sung by the cantor first, followed by choir, congregation, and clergy.

- A new piece of service music or psalm setting could be introduced and then sung by the cantor before inviting the congregation to sing.

- The cantor could teach the congregation a new hymn, before the beginning of the service or at an appointed time, by sharing information

---

37. Paul Westermeyer, *The Church Musician* (Minneapolis: Augsburg Fortress, 1997), 13–17.
38. *The Hymnal 1982, Service Music Edition,* 11–12.

about the text, poet, and composer, then singing the hymn phrase by phrase and inviting the congregation to sing in repetition.

- If a choir is insufficient in size and skill to comfortably sing some music assigned to them, the cantor can sing their part, thus not only teaching the choir but the congregation as well.

For a specific list of music appropriate for cantors, found in H82, EOM 1 and EOM 2, see *www.churchpublishing.org/AllThingsNecessary, Music for Cantors.*

The aim and final reason of all music should be nothing else but the Glory of God and the refreshment of spirit.

JOHANN SEBASTIAN BACH

Recommended
Resources FOR CHAPTER THREE

- Cronin, Deborah K. *O For A Dozen Tongues to Sing: Music Ministry with Small Choirs.* Nashville, TN: Abingdon Press, 1996.
- Haskel, Marilyn and Clayton L. Morris. *As We Gather to Pray: An Episcopal Guide to Worship.* New York: The Church Hymnal Corporation, 1996.
  —"A Place of Good News: Liturgical Space and the Proclamation of the Gospel" (Charles Fulton and Juan Oliver), p. 50
- Haskel, Marilyn L., ed. *What Would Jesus Sing? Experimentation and Tradition in Church Music.* New York: Church Publishing, 2007.
  —"What About Jazz? " (Richard Birk), p. 5
  —"What About Synthesizers? " (J. Owen Burdick), p. 15
  —"What About Handbells? " (Judith C. Dodge), p. 35
  —"What About Electronic Music? " (Isaac Everett), p. 45
  —"What About Contemporary Ensembles? " (Mark Glaeser), p. 57
  —"What About Instrumentalists? Young and Amateur Musicians" (Cynthia Holden), p. 71
  —"What About Instrumentalists? Using Professionals in Worship" (John Marsh), p. 87
  —"What About Guitars? " (Robert C. Laird), p. 97

—"What About Cantors? " (Joel Martinson), p. 105
—"What About Choirs and Organs? " (Robert P. Ridgell), p. 129
—"What About Unaccompanied Congregational Song? " (Donald Schell), p. 143

• MacDonald, Mark L., ed., for the Standing Commission on Liturgy and Music: *The Chant of Life: Inculturation and the People of the Land*, Liturgical Studies Four. New York: Church Publishing, 2003.
—"Singing for Life and Music in the Small Parish" (Marilyn Haskel)

Professional Organizations: Journals, Articles, and Websites, an Appendix listing principal organizations, publications, descriptions, contact information, and denominational resources, may be found online at *www.churchpublishing.org/ AllThingsNecessary.*

CHAPTER FOUR

Rubrics — The Rules of the Liturgy

The law of the Lord is perfect and revives the soul;
the testimony of the Lord is sure and gives wisdom to the innocent.
The statues of the Lord are just and rejoice the heart;
the commandment of the Lord is clear and gives light to the eyes.
(Psalm 19:7–8)

The word *rubric* comes from a Latin word meaning *red*, the color used in prayer books from the medieval period to highlight the conduct of worship, while black was used for the texts of the rites. Rubrics are rules that affect the order of the service, options for music and text, and the manner of performing the liturgy. They are essential.[39]

In the Episcopal Church *The Book of Common Prayer* and other liturgical resources are approved by General Convention. At the ordination of bishops, priests, and deacons promises are made to conform to the doctrine, discipline, and worship of the [Protestant] Episcopal Church [in the United States of America] (*BCP* 513, 526, 538). The worship is outlined in the *BCP* and the rubrics within assure a common vision for all Episcopalians, active roles for all participants in the liturgy, lay and clergy, a manner of celebration that has flexibility within structure, and doctrinal instruction. Rubrics offer hospitality to visitors by way of explanation and familiarity. Rubrics provide common actions for our common prayer.[40]

---

39. Armentrout and Slocum, eds., *An Episcopal Dictionary of the Church.*

40. Rev. Dr. Edward Kryder, *Essentials of Good Liturgy* (Alexandria, VA: Curriculum of the Leadership Program for Musicians Serving Small Congregations, 1995).

Rubrics appear in absolutely every service in *The Book of Common Prayer*. They tell us how to begin and end services, when to sit, stand, or kneel, what actions are designated for priest, bishop, or deacon, options that exist within the liturgy, and, most importantly for church music leaders, where music may be included in the service, music selections for different liturgical seasons, directions regarding hymn and anthem texts and the use of instrumental music, and choices for whether texts may be said or sung.

Space in this resource is given to rubrics because they are significant to our worship. Become familiar with the rubrics for your work in liturgy planning and for your music leadership in the worship services. Know the options and choices for music and refer to these lists and *The Book of Common Prayer* often in your work.

Rubrics in *The Book of Common Prayer*

There are *may* rubrics and *shall* rubrics, the first being optional and the second being mandatory. These are important to know for the music leader to fully prepare and effectively lead congregational song. For example, in the Holy Eucharist: Rite One, after the opening sentences (*BCP* 323), the rubric "The Celebrant says" is printed before the final paragraph, known as the Collect for Purity (the prayer beginning with the words "Almighty God, unto whom all hearts are open, all desires known, and from whom no secrets are hid"). Therefore that prayer is mandatory. In Holy Eucharist: Rite Two, however, in the same place, after the opening sentences (*BCP* 355), the rubric "The Celebrant may say" makes the Collect for Purity an option. If the organist does not know whether the presider is going to say the Collect for Purity, then the organist and the presider may be "speaking" at the same time, awkward and embarrassing moments that many organists have endured. Rubrics are important and should be observed.

Marion Hatchett offered a bit of humor regarding rubrics: "The prayer book committee had operated on the assumption, apparently mistaken, that clergy, lay leaders and church musicians could read italics. The word 'may' indicates that something is not normative. I once attended a Rite Two liturgy where all three opening sentences were said, followed by the Collect for Purity, followed by the *Gloria*, followed by the *Kyrie* in English, followed by the *Kyrie* in Greek, followed by the *Trisagion*. I was just glad that all six forms of the prayers of the people were not printed in the same place as the Eucharistic liturgy and that they did not opt for all four forms of the Eucharistic prayer."[41]

In addition to brief rubrics found within a service, there are pages of rubrics, most in the form of additional instructions, found throughout the *BCP*. It is necessary to know, or at the very least know where to find, these rubrics for worship planning and for optional considerations. Some of those that may be valuable include:

- Concerning the Service of the Church (*BCP* 13)
- Daily Office of Morning Prayer (36, 74)
- An Order of Worship for the Evening (108)
- Additional Directions for Morning and Evening Prayer, Order of Worship for the Evening (141)
- Proper of the Church Year (158)
- The Great Vigil of Easter (284)
- Holy Baptism (298)
- Additional Directions for Holy Baptism (312)
- Holy Eucharist: Rite One (322)
- Holy Eucharist: Rite Two (354)
- Prayers of the People (383)
- Additional Directions for Holy Communion (406)
- Confirmation (412)
- Marriage (422)
- Additional Directions for Marriage (437)
- Burial of the Dead: Rite One (468)
- Burial of the Dead: Rite Two (490)
- Ordination of a Bishop (511)
- Ordination of a Priest (524)
- Ordination of a Deacon (536)
- Additional Directions for Ordinations (552)

41. Rev. Bosco Peters, www.liturgy.co.nz, August 9, 2009.

• Celebration of a New Ministry (558)

• Additional Directions for New Ministry (564)

• Dedication and Consecration of a Church (566)

• Additional Directions for Dedication and Consecration
  of a Church (575)

• The Psalter (582)

• The Lectionary (888)

• Daily Office Lectionary (934)

Rubrics Regarding Silence

For many people silence is difficult to endure. People exercise with iPods loaded with their favorite songs. Music is played in factories and shopping centers to increase productivity and sales. Young people do homework and adults work with music. Music is imposed while waiting for a telephone connection with a business or doctor's office. Blaring music is heard from surrounding cars while waiting at stoplights. Music fills a void for some, reduces stress, eases pain and loneliness, and is simply enjoyable.

If you have had the experience of spending a retreat in a monastery or convent where silence is observed throughout the day except for one mealtime, you either entered into the silence fully, or kept your bags packed for a hasty exit. However, if you meditate regularly or even occasionally, you know the depth and beauty and peace that can be experienced in an abundance of stunning silence.

Silence is not merely the absence of sound, but an ambit where the presence of the divine is experienced in response to our prayers, the connecting of a body of people with their creator, the union of mystery and reality. A well-placed and appropriate silence can have a profound effect on a congregation.

There are scriptural references to worship and silence, perhaps the best known is from Habakkuk 2:20: "But the Lord is in his holy temple; let all the earth keep silence before him!"

There are sixty-six rubrics regarding silence in *The Book of Common Prayer*, some mandatory and some optional. Most of the optional silences occur before Confessions in Daily Offices and services of Holy Eucharist, Penitential Order, and at the Lessons in all services.

The mandatory silences take place before the laying on of hands by the bishop at Confirmation (*BCP* 417) and all ordinations after the *Veni Creator Spiritus* or *Veni Sancte Spiritus* is sung and before the Prayer of Consecration (Bishop/520; Priest/533; Deacon/544). All six forms of the Prayers of the People call for silence.

One mandatory silence occurs after the Breaking of the Bread in each Eucharistic Prayer, so the people have an opportunity to observe this silence with regularity. Prior to the beginning of a service, when I ask a celebrant how long to hold the silence after the Breaking of the Bread and before beginning the Fraction Anthem, the response ranges from "no silence" to "not more than five seconds." In one church I gently moved the congregation from no silence to ten seconds by adding one second of silence each month for almost a year. I listened carefully to the fidget factor during the silence to determine how the congregation was faring with this determined effort. Some time the next year, a guest preacher/celebrant was with this particular congregation. Although in our pre-service preparations I explained to him our custom of silence at the Fraction, he decided to do what was most comfortable for him. After the Fraction, while I waited to introduce the Fraction Anthem, he immediately spoke the words that were meant to be sung. During the coffee hour there was an outcry from the parishioners. Clearly, the silence had become important to their worship life.

At another church there was a custom during each week of the Easter season of inviting a class of the Sunday School children to stand behind the table while the celebrant offered the Eucharistic Prayer, after which they would receive the elements and then return to their pews. On the Sunday of this story, a class of first graders stood quietly behind the table, acutely aware of the vestments, frontal, paraments, candles, flowers so close to them, their eyes wide open with the awe of being in the middle of the action. At the conclusion of the prayer, the celebrant raised and held high the host. A loud snap was heard as the host was broken. In the moments of silence that followed, a young child took an audible breath and confirmed the inexplicable with an unexpected and resounding "Yes!" The silence was ended but the mystery and beauty and joy took on new life.

Rubrics Regarding Music

For the purposes of every music leader and liturgical planner, these rubrics are important to know:

Concerning the Service of the Church (BCP 14)

• Hymns referred to in the rubrics of this Book are to be understood as those authorized by this Church. The words of anthems are to be from Holy Scripture, or from this Book, or from texts congruent with them.

• On occasion, and as appropriate, instrumental music may be substituted for a hymn or anthem.

• Where rubrics indicate that a part of a service is to be "said," it must be understood to include "or sung," and *vice versa.*

• When it is desired to use music composed for them, previously authorized liturgical texts may be used in place of the corresponding texts in this Book.

Additional Directions for Holy Eucharist (BCP 406)

• The *Kyrie eleison* ("Lord, have mercy") may be sung or said in threefold, sixfold, or ninefold form. The *Trisagion,* "Holy God," may be sung or said three times, or antiphonally.

• *Gloria in excelsis,* or the hymn used in place of it, is sung or said from Christmas Day through the Feast of the Epiphany; on Sundays from Easter Day through the Day of Pentecost, on all the days of Easter Week, and on Ascension Day; and at other times as desired; but it is not used on the Sundays or ordinary weekdays of Advent or Lent.

• If there is no Communion, all that is appointed through the Prayers of the People may be said. (If it is desired to include a Confession of Sin, the service begins with the Penitential Order.) A hymn or anthem may then be sung, and the offerings of the people received. The service may then conclude with the Lord's Prayer; and with either the Grace or a blessing, or with the exchange of the Peace.

• The following anthem may be used at the Breaking of the Bread: Lamb of God, you take away the sins of the world: have mercy on us. Lamb of God, you take away the sins of the world: have mercy on us. Lamb of God, you take away the sins of the world: grant us peace.

• A hymn may be sung before or after the postcommunion prayer.

Music Rubrics in the Rites of Holy Eucharist and Daily Offices

In this section the outline of the services of Holy Eucharist, Rites One and Two; and the Daily Offices of Morning Prayer, Rites One and Two; Noonday Prayers; and Evening Prayer, Rites One and Two; and Compline are listed. All rubrics that regard the placement or selection of music within those services are included in *italics*. Become familiar with them to know more fully the options for music.

Holy Eucharist: Rite One (*BCP* 323)

THE WORD OF GOD

A hymn, psalm, or anthem may be sung.

Opening Sentences

Collect for Purity

Decalogue or Summary of the Law

Here is sung or said

Lord, have mercy upon us (*Kyrie eleison*) *or*

Holy God (*Trisagion*)

When appointed, the following hymn or some other song of praise is sung or said, in addition to, or in place of, the preceding, all standing

Glory be to God on high (*Gloria in excelsis*)

The Collect of the Day

The Lessons

A Psalm, hymn, or anthem may follow each Reading.

The Sermon

The Nicene Creed

The Prayers of the People

Confession of Sin and Absolution

The Peace

THE HOLY COMMUNION

During the Offertory, a hymn, psalm, or anthem may be sung.

Offertory

The people remain standing. The Celebrant, whether bishop or priest, faces them and sings or says

The Great Thanksgiving

Here a Proper Preface is sung or said on all Sundays, and on other occasions as appointed.

Holy, holy, holy, Lord God of Hosts (*Sanctus*)

The Breaking of the Bread

Then may be sung or said

[Alleluia.] Christ our Passover is sacrificed for us;

Therefore let us keep the feast. [Alleluia.]

The following or some other suitable anthem may be sung or said here

O Lamb of God (*Agnus Dei*)

Prayer of Humble Access (*BCP* 337)

During the ministration of Communion, hymns, psalms, or anthems may be sung.

The Communion

Postcommunion Prayer

Blessing

Dismissal

Holy Eucharist: Rite Two (*BCP* 355)

THE WORD OF GOD

A hymn, psalm, or anthem may be sung.

Opening Sentences

Collect for Purity (*BCP* 355)

When appointed, the following hymn or some other song of praise is sung or said, all standing

Glory to God in the highest (*Gloria in excelsis*)

On other occasions the following is used:

Lord, have mercy upon us (*Kyrie eleison*) *or* Holy God (*Trisagion*)

The Collect of the Day

The Lessons

A Psalm, hymn, or anthem may follow each Reading.

The Sermon

The Nicene Creed

The Prayers of the People

Confession of Sin and Absolution

The Peace

THE HOLY COMMUNION

During the Offertory, a hymn, psalm, or anthem may be sung.

Offertory

The people remain standing. The Celebrant, whether bishop or priest, faces them and sings or says

The Great Thanksgiving

Here a Proper Preface is sung or said on all Sundays, and on other occasions as appointed.

Holy, holy, holy, Lord God of Hosts (*Sanctus*)

The Breaking of the Bread

Then may be sung or said

[Alleluia.] Christ our Passover is sacrificed for us;

Therefore let us keep the feast. [Alleluia.]

In place of, or in addition to, the preceding, some other suitable anthem may be used.

During the ministration of Communion, hymns, psalms, or anthems may be sung.

The Communion

Postcommunion Prayer

Blessing

Dismissal

Daily Morning Prayer: Rite One (*BCP* 37)

Opening Sentence(s) of Scripture (optional)

Confession of Sin (optional)

The Invitatory and Psalter

Versicle and Response

One of the following Antiphons may be sung or said with the Invitatory Psalm.

Antiphon

Venite or *Jubilate* or

In Easter Week, in place of an Invitatory Psalm, the following is sung or said. It may also be used daily until the Day of Pentecost.

Christ our Passover

The Psalm or Psalms Appointed

At the end of the Psalms is sung or said

Glory to the Father, and to the Son and to the Holy Spirit; as it was in the beginning, is now and will be for ever. Amen.

The Lessons

Silence may be kept after each Reading. One of the following Canticles, or one of those on pages 85–95 (Canticles 8–21), is sung or said after each Reading. If three Lessons are used, the Lesson from the Gospel is read after the second Canticle.

1 A Song of Creation, *Benedicite, omnia opera Domini*

2 A Song of Praise, *Benedictus es, Domine*

3 The Song of Mary, *Magnificat*

4 The Song of Zechariah, *Benedictus Dominus Deus*

5 The Song of Simeon, *Nunc dimittis*

6 Glory be to God, *Gloria in excelsis*

7 We Praise Thee, *Te Deum laudamus*

The Apostles' Creed

The Prayers

Versicle and Response

The Lord's Prayer

The Suffrages (A or B)

The Collect of the Day

Collects

Prayer for Mission

Here may be sung a hymn or anthem.

General Thanksgiving and/or

A Prayer of St. Chrysostom

Dismissal

Grace

Daily Morning Prayer: Rite Two (*BCP* 75)

Opening Sentence(s) of Scripture (optional)

Confession of Sin (optional)

The Invitatory and Psalter

Versicle and Response

One of the following Antiphons may be sung or said with the Invitatory Psalm.

Antiphon

Venite or *Jubilate* or

In Easter Week, in place of an Invitatory Psalm, the following is sung or said. It may also be used daily until the Day of Pentecost.

Christ our Passover

The Psalm or Psalms Appointed

At the end of the Psalms is sung or said

Glory to the Father, and to the Son and to the Holy Spirit; as it was in the beginning, is now and will be for ever. Amen.

The Lessons

Silence may be kept after each Reading. One of the following Canticles, or one of those on pages 47–52 (Canticles 1–7), is sung or said after each Reading. If three Lessons are used, the Lesson from the Gospel is read after the second Canticle.

8 The Song of Moses, *Cantemus Domino*

9 The First Song of Isaiah, *Ecce, Deus*

10 The Second Song of Isaiah, *Quaerite Dominum*

11 The Third Song of Isaiah, *Surge, illuminare*

12 A Song of Creation, *Benedicite, omnia opera Domini*

13 A Song of Praise, *Benedictus es, Domine*

14 A Song of Penitence, *Kyrie Pantokrator*

15 The Song of Mary, *Magnificat*

16 The Song of Zechariah, *Benedictus Dominus Deus*

17 The Song of Simeon, *Nunc dimittis*

18 A Song to the Lamb, *Dignus es*

19 The Song of the Redeemed, *Magna et mirabilia*

20 Glory to God, *Gloria in excelsis*

21 You are God, *Te Deum laudamus*

The Apostles' Creed

The Prayers

    Versicle and Response

    The Lord's Prayer

    The Suffrages (A or B)

    The Collect of the Day

    Collects

    Prayer for Mission

    Here may be sung a hymn or anthem.

General Thanksgiving and/or

A Prayer of St. Chrysostom

Dismissal

Grace

An Order of Service for Noonday (*BCP* 103)

Versicle and Response with *Gloria*

    A suitable hymn may be sung.

    One or more of the following Psalms is sung or said.

Psalm 119:105–112 or Psalm 121 or Psalm 126

At the end of the Psalms is sung or said

Glory to the Father, and to the Son and to the Holy Spirit; as it was in the beginning, is now and will be for ever. Amen.

Scripture passage

A meditation, silent or spoken, may follow.

The Prayers

Kyrie

The Lord's Prayer

Versicle and Response

Collects

Intercessions

Dismissal

Daily Evening Prayer: Rite One (*BCP* 61) and Rite Two (*BCP* 115)

Sentence(s) of Scripture (optional)

Confession of Sin (optional)

The Invitatory and Psalter

Versicle and Response with *Gloria*

The following, or some other suitable hymn, or an Invitatory Psalm, may be sung or said.

O Gracious Light, *Phos hilaron*

The Psalm or Psalms Appointed

At the end of the Psalms is sung or said

Glory to the Father, and to the Son and to the Holy Spirit; as it was in the beginning, is now and will be for ever. Amen.

The Lessons

Silence may be kept after each Reading. One of the following Canticles, or one of those on pages 47–52, or 85–95, is sung or said after each Reading. If three Lessons are used, the Lesson from the Gospel is read after the second Canticle.

The Song of Mary, *Magnificat*

The Song of Simeon, *Nunc dimittis*

The Apostles' Creed

The Prayers

   Versicle and Response

   The Lord's Prayer

   The Suffrages (A or B)

   Collects

   Prayer for Mission

   Here may be sung a hymn or anthem.

General Thanksgiving and/or

A Prayer of St. Chrysostom

Dismissal

Grace

An Order for Compline (*BCP* 127)

Versicle and Response

Confession of Sin

Versicle and Response with *Gloria*

   One or more of the following Psalms are sung or said. Other suitable selections may be substituted.

   Psalm 4, Psalm 31:1–5, Psalm 91, or Psalm 134

   At the end of the Psalms is sung or said

Glory to the Father, and to the Son and to the Holy Spirit; as it was in the beginning, is now and will be for ever. Amen.

Scripture passage

   A hymn suitable for the evening may be sung.

Versicles and Responses

Kyrie

The Lord's Prayer

Versicle and Response

Collects

The service concludes with the Song of Simeon with this Antiphon, which is sung or said by all

Antiphon and Song of Simeon

Dismissal

Grace

Recommended
Resources FOR CHAPTER FOUR

• Stuhlman, Byron D. *Prayer Book Rubrics Expanded.* New York: Church Publishing, 2000.

CHAPTER FIVE

Music for the Daily Offices

Come, let us sing to the Lord:
let us shout for joy to the Rock of our salvation.
Let us come before his presence with thanksgiving
and raise a loud shout to him with psalms.
For the Lord is a great God,
and a great King above all gods. (Psalm 95:1–3)

Tradition and the Daily Offices

Marking the times of the day with daily prayers was traditional in Judaism long before Christianity took up the practice. Times of private prayers in Judaism were the third (9 am), sixth (noon), and ninth (3 pm) hours. The Christian monastic schedule of prayers at seven times in each day was based on the Jewish pattern of prayer.

In Christianity, the congregational and cathedral forms of office, *lauds* (Latin for "daybreak") and *vespers* (Latin for "evening" or "sunset"), developed under Constantine (late third to early fourth century) and were known and observed by the people.

The monastic forms of office developed at this same time, to include: *matins* (also known as *nocturnes*) and *lauds*, usually with a single hour and in the middle of the night; *prime*, at sunrise; *terce*, 9 am; *sext*, noon; *none*, 3 pm; *vespers* at sunset; and *compline* at bedtime.

Archbishop Thomas Cranmer (1489–1556) reduced the number of monastic offices to two, the services of Morning and Evening Prayer. He combined matins, lauds, and prime, called Matins in the 1549 Prayer Book; in the 1552 Prayer Book Matins become known as Morning Prayer. Cranmer combined vespers with other evening offices to become Evening Prayer. The services were printed in the vernacular English and intended for use by all members of the church. Participation in the Daily Offices was a tradition in the Anglican Church. [42]

Daily prayer is a centerpiece of spirituality for Episcopalians today. Saying or singing the Daily Offices is the form of daily corporate worship in the church with Holy Eucharist the central service for Sundays, feast days, and other special occasions.

The Daily Offices can be sung or said in the church, at times of meetings or rehearsals, workshops and conferences, or in the privacy of the home. Beauty of language, ancient connections, and the regularity of being tuned with God make the Daily Offices invaluable in the spiritual lives of the people of God.

In addition to Daily Morning Prayer and Daily Evening Prayer in traditional (Rite One) and contemporary (Rite Two) language, the Daily Office also includes forms for Noonday Prayer, Order of Worship for the Evening, Compline, and Daily Devotions for Individuals and Families. Prayers, selections from the Psalter, readings from the Scriptures, one or more canticles, the Lord's Prayer, and additional prayers and collects form each office.

A Daily Office Lectionary lists readings and psalm choices for Morning and Evening Prayer (*BCP*, 936–1001) and is arranged in a two-year cycle. Year One begins on the First Sunday of Advent preceding odd-numbered years, and Year Two begins on the First Sunday of Advent preceding even-numbered years. (Thus, Year One begins on the First Sunday of Advent preceding 2013 and Year Two begins on the First Sunday of Advent preceding 2014.)

The officiant in the Daily Office may be a member of the clergy or a lay person. A priest is not required in order to say the Daily Offices. If a lay person leads the office, read closely the rubrics regarding lay participation. For example, look at Morning Prayer, Rite Two, *BCP* 80: under the words of the absolution the rubrics say, "A deacon or lay person using the preceding form remains kneeling, and substitutes 'us' for 'you' and 'our' for 'your.'"

---

42. Armentrout and Slocum, eds., *An Episcopal Dictionary of the Church,* and J. G. Davies, ed., *The New Westminster Dictionary of Liturgy and Worship: Canonical Hours* (Philadelphia: The Westminster Press, 1986), 140–147.

Service Music and Canticles

The majority of service music for the Daily Offices of Morning Prayer, Noonday Prayer, Evening Prayer, and Compline is found throughout *The Hymnal 1982: Service Music, Accompaniment Edition Volume I*, and is sung or led by the officiant.

Canticles are texts, usually biblical although not from the Psalms (except for the *Venite* and *Jubilate*), that are sung or said after the lessons at the Daily Offices of Morning or Evening Prayer. The word *canticle* derives from the Latin *canticulum*, which means "little song."[43] In some churches the Daily Office of Morning Prayer is said or sung throughout the week; at those services a wide choice of canticles is likely, presuming the availability of keyboard accompaniment. The Invitatory Canticle is either the *Venite*, or *Jubilate*, or the *Christ our Passover*, the latter most appropriate for the Easter season. After each lesson, a canticle is sung or said. Morning Prayer (Rite One) offers canticles 1–7 in more traditional language; Morning Prayer (Rite Two) offers canticles 8–21 in more contemporary language.

There are different musical styles for the canticle settings. Some are based on a hymn tune or mode, verse/antiphon or song, but the majority of canticles are in plainsong (a single and unaccompanied melodic line with a free, non-metered rhythm); Anglican chant (a harmonized melody matching the rhythm of the text, as the words would be carefully spoken with single chant consisting of seven measures/ten chords and double chant with fourteen measures/twenty chords); or through-composed, a setting with a different melody for each stanza.

Choosing the Canticles

Enriching Our Music 1 contains eleven through-composed settings for the eucharist, three settings of the *Phos hilaron* for evening worship, single settings of *A Song to the Lamb* and *Te Deum laudamus*, two settings for each of the Canticles A-K from *Enriching Our Worship 1*.

Enriching Our Music 2 contains single settings of the ordinary texts of the eucharist; selections that may be used as the hymn of praise or during com-

---

43. The Rev. John N. Wall, Jr. A New Dictionary for Episcopalians, p. 37. (San Francisco: Harper & Row, Publishers, 1985). Armentrout and Slocum, eds., *An Episcopal Dictionary of the Church*.

munion; specific psalms for Morning and Evening Prayer, and two settings for each of Canticles L-S.

With so many different canticle choices for the Daily Offices, how and what does one choose? There are three good sources to assist you in planning:

1. *The Hymnal 1982, Service Music, Accompaniment Edition, Volume1*, S 355.

2. *Enriching Our Worship: Supplemental Liturgical Materials prepared by The Standing Liturgical Commission.* New York: Church Publishing, 1997, pp. 44–45.

3. *The Book of Canticles: Church Hymnal Series II.* New York: The Church Hymnal Corporation, 1979, pp. 10–11.

In addition, a chart of canticles and their suggested use in the Daily Offices may be found at *www.churchpublishing.org/AllThingsNecessary, A List of Canticles.*

Use of Canticles beyond the Daily Offices

Canticles are integral to the Daily Offices, yet they may also be used in services of Holy Eucharist, the principal order of Sunday worship in the Episcopal Church, in which singing canticles is not the norm. There are some churches that occasionally use Morning Prayer as their main service on Sunday morning and many others that use Morning Prayer as the liturgy of the word before Holy Eucharist, thus continuing the use of canticles in those liturgies.

In the service of Holy Eucharist rubrics preceding the *Gloria* ("Glory be to God on high" in Rite One/*BCP* 324 and "Glory to God in the highest" in Rite Two/356 and additional directions, 406) allow for the *Gloria* or some other song of praise to be sung or said. Canticle settings not only provide a great source of music for the selection of that song of praise, but they can be sung in place of a hymn after the readings, sung at the offertory by choir and/or congregation, selected as communion anthems, or used as a source of quality anthem material for children's and youth choirs.

If your congregation has forgotten or has never learned settings of the canticles, consider selecting one for each liturgical season or for a designated period of time, as appropriate, so that the repetitive singing allows the canticle to become part of the congregation's song and tradition.

This great body of texts and music may be lost to Episcopalians if we, the music leaders and liturgical planners in the church, do not make a conscious effort to teach and include canticles in worship services. Canticles are a part of our rich musical heritage and still vital today.

Canticles with Instruments

Some canticles in the Episcopal Church's hymnal and supplements have indications for handbells, solo instruments, and percussion, all of which add musical interest and a dimension of sound to the congregational singing of canticles and service music.

Your congregation may have adult instrumentalists who are willing to offer their talents. Encourage capable high school band and orchestra members, or their school friends, to contribute to the music-making and congregational song.

Here are some canticle selections that are scored for handbells:

H 82/S 46, Christ our Passover; Plainsong, Tone I; Introit Form; adapt. Norman Mealy; acc. David Hurd

WLP/896, Glory to God (*Gloria in excelsis*); Canticle 20 John Karl Hirten

EOM 1/20, Glory to God (*Gloria in Excelsis*); from *Music for the Holy Eucharist Rite II*; Peter Crisafulli

H 82/S 407, You are God (*Te Deum laudamus*); Plainsong, Te Deum tone (Simple form); adapt. *Hymnal 1982*; acc. Gerard Farrell

H 82/S 212, The Song of Moses; Daniel Pinkham; handbells, Mollie Nichols Shuler

EOM 2/174, Canticle P: A Song of the Spirit; Monte Mason; from the Orthodox Church

Recommended
Resources FOR CHAPTER FIVE

• Black, Vicki K. "Praying throughout the Day: The Daily Office." *Welcome to the Book of Common Prayer*, p. 61. Harrisburg, PA: Morehouse Publishing, 2005.

• Hatchett, Marion J. "The Daily Office." *Commentary on the American Prayer Book*, p. 89. New York: The Seabury Press, 1980.

• Mitchell, Leonel L. "The Daily Office." *The Hymnal 1982 Companion, Volume One,* p. 101. New York: The Church Hymnal Corporation, 1990.

• _____. *Pastoral and Occasional Liturgies: A Ceremonial Guide.* Boston, MA: Cowley Publications.

 —"The Offices as Daily Devotions," p. 5.

 —"Liturgical Celebration of the Office," p. 6.

 —"Celebrating Morning Prayer," p. 12.

 —"Celebrating Evensong," p. 20.

 —"Noonday Prayer and Compline," p. 27.

Music for the Daily Offices: A complete listing of music for preces, invitatory antiphons and canticles, salutations and suffrages, collect tones, morning and evening canticles, anthems at the candle lighting, and sung Scripture for the Daily Offices may be found at *www.churchpublishing.org/AllThingsNecessary.*

CHAPTER SIX

Psalms and Psalm Settings

Shout with joy to the Lord, all you lands;
lift up your voice, rejoice, and sing.
Sing to the Lord with the harp,
with the harp and the voice of song.
(Psalm 98:5–6)

Psalms

The word *psalm* is derived from the Greek *psalmos*, literally meaning "the twanging of a harp," and *psallein*, meaning "to pluck, play a stringed instrument"; eventually the word *psalm* came to mean "a song, a sacred song, or hymn."[44] References to stringed instruments such as the harp and lyre throughout the Psalter indicate that the psalms might have been intended to be accompanied by a stringed instrument.

A *psalm* is one of 150 Hebrew poems that constitute the Book of Psalms, also known as the *Psalter*. Information about the Psalter may be found in the *BCP* on pp. 582–584; the Psalter begins on p. 585 of the *BCP*.

A History of Psalms in the Church

Psalms are the hymns of the Hebrew people and were included in daily prayers. At Jerusalem, temple worship marked the day liturgically with morning and evening sacrifices and services of psalms and prayers at 9 am and 3 pm.[45] In Jewish tradition, psalms were often sung from the steps in front of the temple, a public performance intended to teach, encourage, and connect with the people. The Levites had the privilege of singing the psalms and playing instruments from the steps of King Solomon's temple.

---

44. *The Merriam-Webster Dictionary* (Springfield, MA: Merriam-Webster, 1998).
45. Hatchett, *Commentary on the American Prayer Book*, 36.

While many people believe that David wrote almost half of the psalms, there were other authors. The oldest psalms were written by Moses (ca. 1300 B.C.) and include the Song of Moses, a song of triumph after crossing the Red Sea (Exodus 15:1–15), and a song of exhortation in Deuteronomy, chapters 32–33. Moses is also the author of Psalm 90, a song of prayer and reflection. Psalm texts taught moral values, expressed praise and thanksgiving, suffering and lament, and even articulated the coming of the Messiah.

As early as the second century, Christians marked the day with morning and evening services. The morning service, imitating the Jewish tradition of psalms and prayers, consisted of psalmody, canticles, prayers, and reading of Scripture. The evening service also included psalmody and prayers, readings, and a blessing of the light, sometimes associated with an agapé meal.[46]

The Psalter has been included in every prayer book of the Anglican Communion from 1549 to the current books. Miles Coverdale translated the psalms not from the original Hebrew, but from the Latin translation of the Greek translation from the Hebrew for the Great Bible of 1539–1541.

The Psalter of *The Book of Common Prayer* is in the "spirit of Coverdale" and is a more complete revision of that begun in the 1928 American prayer book. A re-examination of the Hebrew text using more recent scholarship resulted in the removal of obsolete and archaic words and inaccurate texts, but kept the same rhythmic expression which characterized Coverdale's work.[47]

Psalms are included in almost every rite in *The Book of Common Prayer*, certainly in the Daily Offices. The entire Psalter is recited over a period of seven weeks in the Daily Offices, with the exceptions of time around Christmas Day, Holy Week, and the week following Easter. Psalms have been in use in the services of Holy Eucharist since the fourth century, particularly used at the entrance rite, after readings, offertory, and communion.[48] Note that verse divisions, translations, and numbering of the psalms differ among various editions of the Bible and in denominational prayer books.

Some psalms have become central to our worship lives, particularly:

---

46. Hatchett, *Commentary on the American Prayer Book*, 89.

47. James Litton, ed., *The Plainsong Psalter*, (New York: The Church Hymnal Corporation, 1988), vii.

48. Litton, *The Plainsong Psalter*,

- Psalm 51 on Ash Wednesday: "Have mercy on me, O God, according to your loving-kindness; in your great compassion blot out my offenses."

- Psalm 22 on Good Friday: "My God, my God, why have you forsaken me? and are so far from my cry and from the words of my distress?"

- Psalm 23, recited so often at funerals: "The Lord is my shepherd; I shall not be in want."

- Psalm 103: "Bless the Lord, O my soul, and all that is within me, bless his holy Name."

- Psalm 121: "I lift up my eyes to the hills; from where is my help to come?"

- Psalm 130: "Out of the depths have I called to you, O Lord; Lord, hear my voice; let your ears consider well the voice of my supplication."

- Psalm 139: "Lord, you have searched me out and known me; you know my sitting down and my rising up; you discern my thoughts from afar."

- Psalm 150: "Hallelujah! Praise God in his holy temple; praise him in the firmament of his power."

In the last few hours before my father-in-law slipped into a coma, he quietly spoke the first half of a psalm verse and I, sitting at his side, responded with the second half. Ah, this could have been a test of some kind, but fortunately the psalms he knew were also familiar to me. Given that he anticipated an antiphonal response between the two of us, I could not help but wonder if there was also a response on the other side, beyond the veil. Psalms were important to him all of his life in the church, and they surely gave him comfort on his way home.

Composers have been inspired by the psalms and created great works of music that bring the texts to new life. Consider the works of Leonard Bernstein (Chichester Psalms), cantatas of Johann Sebastian Bach based on Psalms 29, 50, 75, 103, 104, 149 and 150, the inclusion of psalms in the Requiem Masses of Johannes Brahms and John Rutter. Consider also the many individual choral settings by Orlando di Lasso, Heinrich Schütz, William Billings, Ralph Vaughan Williams, Gustav Holst, Charles Ives, Gerald Finzi, Alan Hovhaness, Benjamin Britten, Daniel Pinkham, Ned Rorem, Samuel Adler, William Mathias, John Corigliano, and so many more that are based on psalms.

Methods of Singing or Reading the Psalter

- Direct recitation—The psalm is read or sung in unison.

- Antiphonal recitation—The psalm is read or sung verse by verse (or half-verse by half-verse, divided at the asterisk) between congregation and choir or one side section of the congregation and the other. The antiphonal recitation may conclude with the *Gloria Patri* in the Daily Offices and with a refrain or antiphon sung or recited in unison at the end of the psalm in services of Holy Eucharist.

- Responsorial recitation—The verses of a psalm are sung by a cantor (solo voice) with choir and congregation singing a refrain after each verse or group of verses. Many modern settings of the psalms have the choir singing the verses with the congregation singing the refrain or antiphon as noted.

- Responsive recitation—In this method the officiant or lay person alternates whole verses with the congregation, usually read and not sung. (*BCP*, p. 582)

Styles of Singing the Psalms

Plainsong Chant

Plainsong chant is derived from the thirteenth-century Latin term *cantus planus*, meaning "plain song." Plainsong is also called plainchant and Gregorian chant and was the first singing form to develop, firmly established by the end of the fourth century. Plainsong refers to a text of unmeasured rhythm with a single line of melody. In the West, Ambrosian, Gallican, and Mozarabic chants also featured unmeasured rhythm with melody; in the East the chants were called Byzantine, Syrian, Coptic, Ethiopian, and Armenian, all with slightly different features but essentially the same principles.[49]

Good chanting is good singing. Word accents create the rhythm in chant and the text determines the shape of the chant's musical phrase.

Some notation symbols are peculiar to chant:

- A black notehead without a stem indicates pitch; the word accent determines duration.

---

49. Armentrout and Slocum, eds., *An Episcopal Dictionary of the Church.*

• An open or white notehead is usually found at the ends of phrases and is held approximately double the length of the black noteheads.

• Notes slurred together indicate one syllable is sung to two or more notes.

Each psalm tone has five parts:

• The *intonation* is sung to the first two syllables (or first two single-syllable words) of the first verse. The Intonation is indicated in the text by italics. Successive verses of the psalm begin on the first reciting tone. The intonation is always sung to the first two syllables of a verse following the singing of an antiphon.

• The *first reciting note*, marked by a lozenge (black rectangular symbol), is used for all words and syllables of the first half of the psalm verse not included in the Intonation or the subsequent mediant cadence.

• The *mediant cadence* occurs before the asterisk, the end of the first half of the verse. The mediant cadence consists of one or two accented syllables and one, two, or three preparatory syllables. Accent marks in the text are matched with accent marks in the psalm tone. Notes in parentheses are used only when needed.

• The *second reciting tone* is the same as the first reciting tone, only occurs in the second half of the psalm verse. All words are sung to the second reciting tone until the ending or final cadence.

The *final cadence* is the end of the psalm verse. The same markings as the mediant cadence apply. (See plainsong psalm tones at S 446 in *The Hymnal 1982, Accompaniment Edition, Volume 1* for Tones 1–8 and Tonus Peregrinus.)

In the case of collect tones and other chants sung by presider, officiant, or deacon in plainsong style, as well as plainsong chant, there are several other markings to understand:

• For chanting in the service a two-line staff is used, indicating plainsong with a limited range. The flat indicates that the interval from one line to another is a minor third (G–B flat); those pitches do not have to be chosen, but they remain an indication of the intervals implied.

• A jagged marking over a note, much like the music symbol for a mordent, is called a *quilisma*; a common practice is to lengthen slightly the note preceding the quilisma and then move quickly and lightly over the ornamented note to the next pitch.

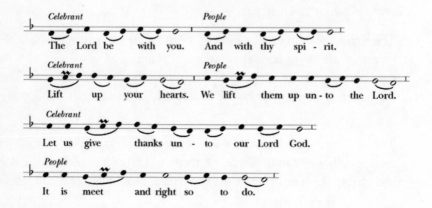

• Two dots over a syllable or single-syllable word indicates that syllable/word is sung over two notes.

• A short line before the beginning of a half verse indicates that the reciting tone is omitted.

Traditionally, plainsong has been sung without accompaniment. If support for the singing is required or if the acoustic is not favorable, then very light accompaniment may be provided. A simple and effective way to teach the psalm and support the congregation is to play the plainsong melody in octaves. If organ is used, refrain from using pedals and substantial registrations. Especially avoid using a 16' manual stop. Flute stops and/or very light diapasons would accompany plainsong lightly and well.

Handbells can provide a pleasant accompaniment to plainsong:

• An ostinato pattern may be rung throughout the chant, with no attempt to synchronize.

• Random ringing, using the tonic note, fourth, fifth, and octave as the primary notes, adding the second or sixth occasionally for musical interest is another option. In random ringing players try to avoid ringing their bells at the same time as others and abstain from ringing in a metered fashion. The ringing can precede the singing by about five to ten seconds prior to the plainsong melody being played on organ or flute;

the choir and congregation sing the Psalm and then the random ringing continues for another five to ten seconds after the singing has ceased.

- Chord clusters, using three or four bells, may be rung at the mediant and final cadences of each verse, adding interest and impetus for the next verse or half-verse.[50]

Sources for Psalms in Plainsong Chant

Ford, Bruce E. *Gradual Psalms with Alleluia Verses and Tracts, Years A, B, C.* New York: Church Publishing, 2007.

Plainsong settings of the gradual psalms without complicated pointing, as each verse is fully set to music (notation for each word or syllable) for choir or cantor, using the RCL. Congregational refrains are available in TIF and EPS file formats for use with service leaflets.

_____*Gradual Psalms for the Occasional Services.* New York: Church Publishing, 2000. Contains psalms for the eucharistic lectionary and other liturgical occasions in plainsong with congregational antiphons.

Crocker, Richard. *Gradual Psalms: Holy Days and Various Occasions.* New York: The Church Hymnal Corporation, 1981.

Compiled by Richard Crocker for the Standing Commission on Church Music. Contains Gradual Psalms, Alleluia Verses and Tracts for Holy Days, Various Occasions, Pastoral Offices and Episcopal Services in plainsong settings with congregational refrain, in a reproducible format.

Litton, James, ed. *The Plainsong Psalter.* New York: The Church Hymnal Corporation, 1988, pp. xi–xii.

The Hymnal 1982: Service Music, Accompaniment Edition, Volume 1: "Music for Plainsong Psalm Tones 1–7: Appendix, S#446." New York: The Church Hymnal Corporation, 1985.

Anglican Chant

Anglican chant is a way of singing prose translations of the psalms, non-metrical texts, to a short piece of music. Anglican chant was developed from harmonized plainsong psalm tones (fauxbourdons) and festal psalm settings

---

50. *The Plainsong Psalter*, James Litton, ed., xi–xiv. *The Hymnal 1982: Service Music, Accompaniment Edition, Volume 1*, p. 12. New York: The Church Hymnal Corporation, 1985.

by English composers of the late sixteenth century and early seventeenth century. Like the plainsong chants, Anglican chants were also non-metrical, intended to be settings for prose translations of the earlier Greek, Aramaic, and Hebrew originals.

Some of the earliest examples of Anglican chant were written by Thomas Tallis (ca. 1505–1585) and other musicians of the time, indicating they may have composed the chants to provide musical settings of Coverdale's English translation of the Psalter. The earliest double chants are from around 1700 and Anglican chant was well established by the eighteenth century.

Parish churches, collegiate chapels, and Anglican cathedrals have a long history of singing psalms in Anglican chant. In Episcopal churches the custom is less strong, yet Anglican chant is sung in many churches with a strong choral tradition and where a congregation is not defeated by the challenge of singing psalms in four-part harmony according to a series of markings.

A single Anglican chant is made up of ten chords: a reciting chord followed by a mediant cadence of three chords, ending at the asterisk; then a second reciting chord followed by five chords which make up the final cadence or ending. The first half of each psalm verse is sung through to the mediant cadence, ending at the interior double bar line; the second half is sung to the end of the verse. A double Anglican chant is made up of twenty chords, two complete sets of a single chant.

Because of the fixed meter of the music of the Anglican chant, the text must be pointed or marked in such a way that the choir and congregation can sing together successfully. Five marks indicate the pointing:

• A short vertical line corresponds to the bar lines of the chant

• A brace connects two or three syllables to be sung on one chord

• Two dots over a syllable indicate the syllable is to be sung over two chords

• A short horizontal line before a half verse indicates the reciting chord is to be omitted

• A cross (†), indicates that the second half of a double chant is to be sung to the indicated verse[51]

---

51. *The Anglican Chant Psalter,* Alec Wyton, editor. Performance Notes, pp. viii–x. New York: The Church Hymnal Corporation, 1987. The Hymnal 1982: Service Music, Accompaniment Edition Volume 1: *Harmonized (Anglican) Chant,* p. 14. New York: The Church Hymnal Corporation, 1985.

1 My heart is stirring with a noble song;
  let me recite what I have ¦ fashioned for the ¦ king; *
  my tongue shall be the ¦ pen of a ¦ skilled ¦ writer,

2 You are the ¦ fairest of ¦ men; *
  grace flows from your lips,
  because ¦ God has ¦ blessed you for ¦ ever.

3 Strap your sword upon your thigh, O ¦ mighty ¦ warrior, *
  in your ¦ pride and ¦ in your ¦ majesty.

4 Ride out and conquer in the ¦ cause of ¦ truth *
  — ¦ and for the ¦ sake of ¦ justice.

Whether plainsong or Anglican, good chanting is good singing. The singing should neither be rushed nor held too long on any one chord. Syllable emphasis is given by slightly elongating the vowel.

The organ is the main instrument used for accompanying Anglican chant. The organist would be well-served to have the chant memorized so that proper attention can be given to following the text. For particularly long psalms set to Anglican chant, I recommend doing a cut-and-paste of the music and text so that the music appears before every four verses or so. Just about every organist who has led Anglican chant could tell a horror story about looking at the music on one page and text on another, going back and forth until the eyes, and therefore the hands, catch a verse the congregation is not singing. Organ registrations should be supportive but not dominant. Some organists color the verses of the psalm by diminishing or swelling the sound, choosing a trumpet or reed or low pedal stop to more greatly emphasize specific words or phrases of the text.

Sources for Psalms in Anglican Chant

• *The Anglican Chant Psalter*, Alec Wyton, editor. New York: The Church Hymnal Corporation, 1987.

• *The Hymnal 1982, Accompaniment Edition, Volume 1.* New York: The Church Hymnal Corporation.

    Single chant settings: Appendix—S 417–S 427

    Double chant settings: Appendix—S 428–S 445

Simplified Anglican Chant

For many congregations, singing psalms to simplified Anglican chant was their first introduction to psalm singing, and I would venture a guess that most started off with S 415 in the Appendix of the *The Hymnal 1982, Accompaniment Edition, Volume 1.*

Simplified Anglican chant is intended for unison singing by the congregation, although choirs could sing in parts. Each half verse of the psalm is sung on the reciting note (the first open chord in each measure) up to the last accented syllable, which is sung on the pitches of the filled noteheads at the end of each measure.[52] Avoid a race on the reciting note to a slow finish at the filled noteheads.

Two verses of the psalm are sung in the four measures of simplified Anglican chant. The first half of the first verse is complete at the end of the first measure, the second half is complete at the double bar line. The next verse begins at the third measure, and the second half of that verse is sung during the last measure of the four-measure simplified Anglican chant. If there is an extra verse, then the last half of the chant setting is usually used, unless this repetition makes more sense within the psalm text. Again, good chanting is good singing; place musical accents on the vowels of syllables or words that you would accent if you were reading the text aloud.

Organ accompaniment supports congregational singing very well for simplified Anglican chant. One suggestion for the organist: move to the next chord a split second before the congregation and the congregation will follow.

Sources for Simplified Anglican Chant Settings

• S 408–S 416, Appendix, *The Hymnal 1982, Accompaniment Edition, Volume 1.*

• Roberts, William Bradley. Simplified Anglican Chant/Anglican Chant. St. James Music Press, 2011.

> Moderately easy, very accessible settings based on familiar hymn tunes; there are twenty-four Simplified Anglican Chants, five Anglican Chants, and an Anglican Chant in jazz style with gospel Hallelujah.

---

52. *The Hymnal 1982 Accompaniment Edition: Service Music Volume 1*, performance notes about S#408–S#416.

Metrical Psalms

After the Reformation, psalms began to be translated into metrical texts, sometimes paraphrased, and eventually matched with metrical hymn tunes. When the Episcopal Church was established in this country, metrical psalmody was the basis of the hymnody.[53] While singing psalms in Anglican chant or plainsong chant may be desired in many Episcopal churches, singing psalms in metrical form, as a hymn, enables congregations to sing that portion of the liturgy with confidence.

Sources for Metrical Psalms

• *The Hymnal 1982, Accompaniment Edition, Volume 1*: p. 679.

A listing of metrical psalms and hymns based on psalms.

• Webber, Christopher L. *A New Metrical Psalter*. New York: Church Publishing, 2008.

A pay-and-download edition of psalm paraphrases for the RCL, with suggested tunes in short, common, and long meters, easily singable for congregations. Also includes a Metrical Index for ecumenical use and a Liturgical Index useful in worship planning.

Gradual Psalms in Responsorial Form

A *gradual* is a psalm, hymn or anthem, usually based on the appointed psalm, that is sung between the Old Testament reading and the New Testament, even though a psalm is optional in services of Holy Eucharist. The psalm may be sung in plainsong chant, simplified Anglican chant, Anglican chant, as a metrical psalm (hymn), or an elaborate setting sung by the choir.

In the early church a cantor sang the verses of the psalm from a lectern or ambo, and the seated congregation responded with a sung refrain after individual or groups of verses. The sung refrain is called an *antiphon* and is usually taken from Scripture, especially the psalms, and is chosen specifically for the liturgical season or occasion.[54]

---

53. Alec Wyton. *A New Metrical Psalter* by Christopher L. Webber, pp. ix–x. (New York: Church Publishing, 2008).

54. Glossary definitions from Armentrout and Slocum, eds., *An Episcopal Dictionary of the Church.*

Sources for Gradual Psalms in Responsorial Form

• Daw, Carl P., Jr. and Kevin R. Hackett. *A Hymn Tune Psalter. Book One— Gradual Psalms: Advent through the Day of Pentecost*, Revised Common Lectionary Edition. New York: Church Publishing, 2007.

• _____. *A Hymn Tune Psalter. Book Two—Gradual Psalms: The Season after Pentecost*, Revised Common Lectionary Edition. New York: Church Publishing, 2008.

These gradual psalms are responsorial in form, with verses in many different settings of simplified Anglican chant and antiphons based on phrases of familiar hymn tunes. Verses and antiphons may be sung by the choir and congregation together or by the choir singing verses and congregation singing each antiphon as indicated in the text. The antiphons or the entire music setting may be reproduced in service leaflets, either copied from the collection or downloaded in EPS or TIF format, with the inclusion of copyright permission.

• Ford, Bruce *Gradual Psalms*, New York: Church Publishing.

Gradual psalms for the RCL, a complete revision of the 1980 edition. Verses are fully set to music rather than pointed; alleluia verse or tracts are included; congregational refrains are accessible and in a format for easy inclusion in service leaflets.

• Hawthorne, Robert A. *The Portland Psalter Book One: Liturgical Years ABC*. New York: Church Publishing, 2002.

• _____. *The Portland Psalter Book Two: Responsorial Psalms for Congregation, Cantor & Choir*. New York: Church Publishing, 2003.

Books One and Two contain the psalms for liturgical years A,B, and C for both the *BCP* lectionary and the Revised Common Lectionary. Psalm settings are also included for other *BCP* liturgical occasions. Psalms are listed in numerical order and indications for *BCP* and RCL propers are indicated on each page. Verses are set to simplified Anglican chant. Refrain texts are set to original music by Robert Hawthorne. Performance notes, ideas, and permission for copying and congregational use are included.

• Pavlechko, Thomas, arr. *St. Martin's Psalter: The Revised Common Lectionary, Years A, B, and C, Based on Hymn Tunes and Other Familiar Melodies*. Tryon, NC: St. James Music Press.

Available on CD-ROM, the *St. Martin's Psalter* contains more than 550 psalm settings, based on the RCL, with files for service leaflets. The settings may be sung by cantor, choir, congregation, or a combination thereof. A new pointing system, tested in Lutheran and Episcopal parishes for ten years, provides easy singing for all. Antiphons are matched with hymn-based psalm tones.

• Pulkingham, Betty and Kevin Hackett. *The Celebration Psalter, The Lectionary, Years A, B, and C.* Pacific, MO: Cathedral Music Press, 1992 and 1991.

This three-volume set comes from the Community of Celebration, a religious order in the Episcopal Church with members residing in Aliquippa, Pennsylvania, and England. They live out a modified Benedictine Rule with worship being the center of their life and mission. *The Celebration Psalter* is based on the prayer book lectionary, not the RCL. For those who enjoy and appreciate this style of psalm singing, this is a fine resource. Psalms for each year are in numerical order, so can be found for usage with the RCL. Verses could be sung by cantor or choir with the congregation singing the antiphon. Accompaniments for piano or organ are provided, as well as chords for use with guitar and autoharp, and solo instrumental parts. Antiphons may be reproduced for congregational use. Before using these psalms, check the number of verses in the psalm setting with those listed in the RCL to be sure they match. www.communityofcelebration.com

• Shafer, Keith, ed. *Psalms Made Singable: The Psalms of David set to Anglican and Plainchants with text and music aligned.* Church Music Services, 2011.

Available in hard copy and CD-ROM and with permission to copy, these psalm settings are easily accessible even to the smallest volunteer choir. There are no symbols to interpret because the words and notes are completely aligned. As of this publication, editions available include: Anglican Chant Psalms, Year A; Anglican Chant Psalms, Year B; Anglican Chant Psalms, Year C; Plainchant Psalms: Advent and Lent.

Additional Styles and Sources of Psalms

• Everett, Isaac. *The Emergent Psalter.* New York: Church Publishing, 2009.

For those people exploring alternative and church communities *The Emergent Psalter* provides antiphons, which may be accompanied by keyboard or guitar, chords included, to all 150 psalms. Verses are spoken by the assembly, wherever gathered. The "Overview" (Part I, p. 1) and "An In-depth Analysis of Four Psalms and Their Antiphons" (Part II, p.11) are most helpful in understanding the emerging church and their Psalter.

• Lift Every Voice and Sing II

Refrains in gospel style with pianistic accompaniments are sung by the congregation and the choir sings verses in simplified Anglican chant.

273 Psalm 126 with refrain *His Love Is Everlasting,* Leon C. Roberts (1950–1999); Simplified Anglican Chant: Carl Haywood (b. 1949); from *Mass for Grace.*

274 Psalm 145: 8–13 with refrain *I Will Praise Your Name,* Leon C. Roberts; Simplified Anglican Chant: Robert Knox Kennedy.

275 Psalm 104: 25–26,28–32,35 with refrain *Lord, Send Out Your Spirit,* Rawn Harbor (b. 1947); Simplified Anglican Chant: Jerome Webster Meachen.

276 Psalm 22:1–2,7–8,14–21 with refrain: *My God, Why have You Abandoned Me?*Rawn Harbor (b. 1947); Simplified Anglican Chant: Carl Haywood.

277 Psalm 27:1–9 with refrain *The Lord Is My Light and My Salvation,* Leon C. Roberts; Anglican Chant: Clarence Witeman.

278 Psalm 100:1–4 with refrain *Serve the Lord With Gladness, Alleluia,* David Hurd (b. 1950); Anglican Chant: Henry Walford Davies.

279 Psalm 23 with refrain *The Lord Is My Shepherd,* Leon C. Roberts; Simplified Anglican Chant: Robert Knox Kennedy.

280 Psalm 24:1–10 with refrain To You, O Lord, Rawn Harbor; Simplified Anglican Chant: Curtis Sisco (1958–1992).

• *My Heart Sings Out* contains songs based on Psalms 19, 23, 34, 62, 96, 136, 139, and verses of other songs. Consult the Scriptural Index, p. 283 of the Teacher's Guide.

• *Psalm Settings for the Church Year: Revised Common Lectionary.* Minneapolis: Augsburg Fortress, 2008.

New settings of all the psalms in the RCL in a variety of styles, including responsorial, Anglican chant, hymnic, and through-composed by Lorraine S. Brugh, Donald Busarow, David Cherwien, Robert Buckley Farlee, Marty Haugen, Thomas Pavlechko, William Bradley Roberts, Mark Sedio, Wayne L. Wold and more. Includes CD-ROM with congregational parts.

• *Voices Found*

148   Psalm 43 with antiphon *Send out your light*, melody adapted from Hildegard of Bingen; setting by Lisa Neufeld Thomas.

151   Psalm 95:1–7 *Come, let us sing to the Lord!* Music by Dorothy J. Papadakos.

150   para. Psalm 96 with refrain *Declare his glory*, Native American chant style; words and music by Carol Gallagher and Michael Plunkett.

97   Psalm 130 *In deepest night*. Words by Susan Palo Cherwien; Music by Emily Maxson Porter.

• *Wonder, Love, and Praise*

764   para. Psalm 34 *Taste and See*. Words and Music by James E. Moore, Jr.

727   para. Psalm 42 *As panting deer desire the waterbrooks*. Words by Carl P. Daw, Jr. Music by John Carter. 810Psalm 91 *You who dwell in the shelter of the Lord*. Words and Music by Michael Joncas.

825   from Psalm 103 *Bless the Lord my soul*. Music by Jacques Berthier.

829   Psalm 117 *Laudate Dominum*. Music by Jacques Berthier. Portions of psalms are found in other hymns and songs; see p. 251 of the Leader's Guide.

Recommended
Resources FOR CHAPTER SIX

In addition to the resources mentioned above, these articles are suggested for your increased knowledge and understanding of psalms and psalm singing.

• The Book of Common Prayer

—"Concerning the Psalter," p. 582.

• *The Hymnal 1982: Accompaniment Edition, Volume 1*: New York: The Church Hymnal Corporation, 1985.

—"Singing the Chant," p. 12.

—"Plainsong and other Unison Chant," p. 13.

—"Harmonized (Anglican) Chant," p. 14.

• *Enriching Our Music 1: Canticles and Settings for the Eucharist.* New York: Church Publishing, 2003.

  —"Notes on the Pointing of the Canticles" (with information about chant).

• *Enriching Our Music 2: More Canticles and Settings for the Eucharist.* New York: Church Publishing, 2004.

  —"Notes on the Pointing of the Canticles" (with information about chant).

• Ford, Bruce E. "Charles Winfred Douglas and Adaptation of Plainsong to English Words in the United States." *The Hymnal 1982 Companion, Volume One,* p. 194. New York: The Church Hymnal Corporation, 1990.

• Gallagher, Robert. *Leading the Church's Song:* "Chant," p. 26. Augsburg Fortress, 1998.

• Litton, James, editor. *The Plainsong Psalter.* New York: The Church Hymnal Corporation, 1988.

  —"Introduction," pp. vii–viii.

  —"Concerning the Psalter," pp. ix–x.

  —"Performance Notes," pp. xi–xiv.

• Wyton, Alec, editor. *The Anglican Chant Psalter.* New York: The Church Hymnal Corporation, 1987.

  —"Introduction," pp. vi–vii.

  —"Performance Notes," pp. viii–x.

  —"Concerning the Psalter," pp. xi–xii.

CHAPTER SEVEN

Music for the Holy Eucharist / Music for the Sacraments

I will give thanks to you, O Lord, with my whole heart;
before the gods I will sing your praise.
I will bow down toward your holy temple and praise your Name,
because of your love and faithfulness;
For you have glorified your Name
and your word above all things. (Psalm 138:1–3)

Music for the Ordinary

In planning music for the service of Holy Eucharist there are many options for the ordinary of the mass (*Kyrie eleison, Gloria, Credo, Sanctus*, and *Agnus Dei*), those texts that are generally invariable, and those musical portions that are almost always sung by the congregation.[55]

Some music leaders and liturgy planners in Episcopal churches select music by one composer for all parts of the ordinary of the mass and others choose music by different composers for each part of the ordinary. Both ways are quite acceptable.

Some congregations know and sing a wide repertoire of music for services of Holy Eucharist and others may know one or two settings. Some congregations experience a change of music settings at the beginning of each liturgical season and other congregations sing the same setting(s) throughout the year. The traditions of your parish and the opportunities and desire to teach and learn new music always need to be considered carefully.

---

55. *A History of Western Music*, pp. 35–38. Donald Jay Grout. New York: W. W. Norton & Company, Inc. 1960.

As you plan, keep in mind that the priest and deacon, and occasionally the cantor, have additional music to sing in the service (some of which also includes the assembly): Opening Acclamation, Gospel Acclamations, Prayers of the People, the Peace, *Sursum Corda*, all or portions of Fraction Anthems, Blessings and Dismissals, beyond the ordinary.

There are settings of the ordinary for eucharist in both *Enriching Our Music 1* and *Enriching Our Music 2*.

An extensive list of options, Music Selections for the Holy Eucharist, may be found at *www.churchpublishing.org/AllThingsNecessary* and includes all settings from H 82, EOM 1, EOM 2, AB, WLP, MHSO, and LEVAS. They are provided for you to make the task of worship planning just a bit less daunting. Use them as a guide as you work with the priests, deacons, cantors, liturgists, and others on your staff in planning worship for your parish.

Service Music with Instruments

Some service music selections in the Episcopal Church's hymnal and supplements have indications for handbells, solo instruments, and percussion, which add musical interest and an additional dimension of sound to the congregational singing.

Your congregation may have adult instrumentalists who are willing to offer their talents. Encourage capable high school band and orchestra members, or their school friends, to contribute to the music-making and congregational song.

A list of suggested service music appropriate for a variety of musical accompaniment, Service Music with Instruments, may be found at *www.churchpublishing.org/AllThingsNecessary*.

Music for the Sacraments

The Sacrament of Holy Baptism (*BCP*, p. 299), and the sacramental rites of Confirmation (*BCP*, p. 413) and Ordination (*BCP*, Bishop/p. 513; Priest/p. 525; Deacon/p. 537) are celebrated with the service of Holy Eucharist. Each liturgy is unique and specially selected music is appropriate. Read and understand the rubrics regarding music for each of these liturgies.

Note: See the Abbreviations list on page xxi of this book for full names of resources.

Holy Baptism

S 71—Opening Acclamation; Ambrosian chant; adapt. Mason Martens

S 72—Opening Acclamation in Easter Season; Ambrosian chant; adapt. Mason Martens

S 73—Opening Acclamation in Lent; Ambrosian chant; adapt. Mason Martens

S 74—Versicles; Ambrosian chant; adapt. *The Hymnal 1982*

AB 373—Versicles at Baptism and Confirmation

S 75—Litany and Thanksgiving over the Water

H82—Hymns 294–299

MHSO—Hymns 119–122

LEVAS II—Hymns 121–145

VF—Hymns 51–52, 58, 67–70, 77, 96

WLP—Hymns 765–769

Hymn suggestions in *A Liturgical Index to The Hymnal 1982*, p. 282

Hymn suggestions in *The Episcopal Musician's Handbook*, 56th Edition, 2012–2013, p. 212

Holy Eucharist

EOM 2—Hymns 149–157

H82—Hymns 300–347

LEVAS II—Hymns 146–155

MHSO—Hymns 46–52

VF—Hymns 71–89

WLP—Hymns 760–764

Confirmation

AB 373—Versicles at Baptism and Confirmation

H82—Hymns 348–349

MHSO—Hymns 123–127

Hymn suggestions in *A Liturgical Index to The Hymnal 1982*, p. 283

Hymn suggestions in *The Episcopal Musician's Handbook*, 56th Edition, 2012–2013, p. 214

Marriage

Hymn suggestions have been listed for The Celebration and Blessing of a Marriage (*BCP*, p. 423). One can always hope that those planning weddings will understand them as sacred occasions and that a choice of a hymn or two will unite their family and friends in witnessing and affirming the blessing with song. These hymns may also be sung as solos; the texts and music are appropriate for the occasion, far better than the secular music chosen by the bride and groom as *our song* and desired to be sung at the service.

> *H82*—Hymns 350–353
>
> *VF*—Hymns 140–143, 145
>
> Hymn suggestions in *A Liturgical Index to The Hymnal 1982*, p. 289
>
> Hymn suggestions in *The Episcopal Musician's Handbook*, 56th Edition, 2012–2013, p. 216

Healing and Reconciliation

There are some excellent hymns available for use at services of healing, which are becoming more prevalent in churches who seek a more intentional prayer for those who are in need of healing, whether physical, spiritual, or emotional.

> *MHSO*—Hymns 143–149
>
> *VF*—Hymns 90–97
>
> *WLP*—Hymns 770–774

Burial of the Dead

At funerals and memorial services, hymns provide comfort and strength to those singing and those who can only listen with their hearts. The services for The Burial of the Dead: Rite One (*BCP*, p. 469) and Rite Two (*BCP*, p. 491) provide several places in the liturgy for the use of hymns. Note that the word *anthem* appears throughout both rites, not indicating that a choir must sing these parts, but that they may be sung.

I played a funeral service at which a paid choir of eight voices was present and prepared to sing anthems at the lessons, communion, and before the committal. A service leaflet had been prepared and listed the familiar words at the entrance to the liturgy (*BCP*, p. 469) as Opening Anthems, which they are. The service began with the officiant walking up the aisle saying these words, then sitting once he was finished. We should have remained standing for the Collect, but the congregation copied his stance by sitting. After a few seconds he looked at me, nodded his head, and I had the sinking suspicion he was expecting the choir to sing an anthem. I held up the leaflet, from my semi-hidden position, and pointed to the leaflet, hoping he would note that he should say the Collect. He looked at the choir and back at me, then gave an abrupt physical gesture for me to conduct the choir. I held up the prayer book, which he had open on his lap, and pointed to the place he should be. At that he got up, walked over to the organ console, and demanded that the choir sing an anthem. When I whispered that he had already said the anthems and that we should move on to the Collect, he yelled, most audibly, that he knew what an anthem was and that I ought to do one. He returned to his seat and I improvised quietly on the organ until he calmed down, understood that the choir was not going to sing, and decided it was time to move on and do the Collect. That was a horrible embarrassment for the vested participants, the grieving family and congregation, and was something that never would have happened if he had understood the word *anthem* at this liturgy or if we had had a discussion about this before the service. Enough said. Be prepared.

The Burial of the Dead, Rite One

S 375–378—Entrance Anthems

S 379—Anthem at the Committal; John Merbecke; adapt. Elizabeth Morris Downie

S 384—Anthem: *Christ is risen*; Plainsong, Mode 8; adapt. Bruce E. Ford

S 385—Anthem: *The Sun of Righteousness*; Plainsong, Mode 1; adapt. Bruce E. Ford

S 386—Anthem: *The Lord will guide our feet*; Plainsong, Mode 4; adapt. Bruce E. Ford

S 387—Anthem: *Christ will open the kingdom*; Plainsong, Mode 2; adapt. Bruce E. Ford

S 388—Anthem: *Into paradise*; Plainsong, Mode 7; adapt. Bruce E. Ford

H82—Hymns 354–358; Hymn suggestions in *A Liturgical Index to The Hymnal 1982*, p. 291; Hymn suggestions in *The Episcopal Musician's Handbook*, 54th Edition, 2010–2011, p. 232

VF—Hymn 97

WLP—Hymns 775–777

The Burial of the Dead, Rite Two

S 380–382—Entrance Anthems

S 383—Anthem at the Commendation; Plainsong, Mode 1; adapt. Bruce E. Ford

S 384—Anthem: *Christ is risen*; Plainsong, Mode 8; adapt. Bruce E. Ford

S 385—Anthem: *The Sun of Righteousness*; Plainsong, Mode 1; adapt. Bruce E. Ford

S 386—Anthem: *The Lord will guide our feet*; Plainsong, Mode 4; adapt. Bruce E. Ford

S 387—Anthem: *Christ will open the kingdom*; Plainsong, Mode 2; adapt. Bruce E. Ford

S 388—Anthem: *Into paradise*; Plainsong, Mode 7; adapt. Bruce E. Ford

S 389—Anthem at the Committal; Mode 1 melody; adapt. Bruce E. Ford

H82—Hymns 354–358; Hymn suggestions in *A Liturgical Index to The Hymnal 1982*, p. 291; Hymn suggestions in *The Episcopal Musician's Handbook*, 56th Edition, 2012–2013, p. 220

VF—Hymn 97

WLP—Hymns 775–777

Ordination

Hymns are suggested for the ordination of a bishop, priest, or deacon. Others will be recommended for use, based on texts chosen and other considerations, by those being ordained. I served on a committee planning the music for the ordination of a bishop-elect and was delighted to receive his hymn requests at the first meeting. As I looked through the list I noticed that some of the greatest hymns of the church had been selected, songs that would evoke joy, praise, adoration, and thanksgivings, fitting for the occasion. H82 474, *When I survey the wondrous cross,* had also been selected and I knew there had to be a story behind this choice. When asked, the bishop-elect responded: "This hymn was sung at my baptism, my confirmation, my graduation from high school, my ordination to the diaconate, my ordination to the priesthood, and it will be sung at my consecration." And it was so. Every time I play that hymn, I think of him and how important stanza 4 is to all of us in service to God in the church: *Were the whole realm of nature mine, that were an offering far too small; love so amazing, so divine, de-mands my soul, my life, my all.*

H82—Hymn 359

VF—Hymns 13, 16, 51–52, 98–100

Hymn suggestions in *A Liturgical Index to The Hymnal 1982*, p. 292

Hymn suggestions in *The Episcopal Musician's Handbook*, 56th Edition, 2012–2013, p. 218

AB—389, Blessing at the Ordination of a Priest

Recommended
Resources FOR CHAPTER SEVEN

• Black, Vicki K. *Welcome to the Book of Common Prayer*. Harrisburg, PA: Morehouse Publishing, 2005.

—"Sharing a Common Meal: The Holy Eucharist," p. 37.

—"Becoming Christian: Holy Baptism," p. 23.

—"Making Vows: Confirmation, Marriage, and Ordination," p. 93

• Hatchett, Marion J. *Commentary on the American Prayer Book*. New York: The Seabury Press, 1980.

—Holy Baptism, p. 251.

—The Holy Eucharist, p. 289.

—Pastoral Offices, p. 423.

—Episcopal Services, p. 501.

• Mitchell, Leonel L. *Pastoral and Occasional Liturgies: A Ceremonial Guide.* Boston, MA: Cowley Publications, 1998.

—Rites Related to Christian Initiation, p. 48.

—Marriage Rites, p. 55.

—Reconciliation of a Penitent, p. 66

—Ministry to the Sick and Dying, p. 76

—The Burial of the Dead, p. 88.

—Ordination Rites, p. 119.

CHAPTER EIGHT

Muʃic and Liturgical Planning

*I will bless the Lord at all times; his praise shall ever be
in my mouth. I will glory in the Lord; let the humble hear and
rejoice. Proclaim with me the greatness of the Lord; let us exalt
his Name together. (Psalm 34:1–3)*

Liturgy

In the Greek city-states of a time five hundred years before Christ, every adult citizen was required to serve the state for one month of each year, whether by giving a professional service, providing manual labor, serving in the military, or in a more general way. As the Christian church emerged, the word *litourgia,* a civic responsibility, was adopted to designate the worship, also considered to be the work of the people for a common good.[56]

Leonel L. Mitchell described liturgy as an expression of congregational unity and ultimately the concern of the whole people of God.

> The full, active, intelligent participation of all the people of God in the liturgy is the right and duty of every baptized man, woman, and child, by reason of their baptism, because worship is a part of the priestly activity of Jesus Christ in which the priestly people of God participate as members of the Body of which he is the Head. Worship is not a performance by skilled professionals for a passive audience. It is the common work of a group of brothers and sisters.[57]

In the Episcopal Church, a liturgy is a planned service using texts from *The Book of Common Prayer,* some of which date to the middle of the six-

56. Edward Kryder. *Essentials of Good Liturgy.* Syllabus for the Leadership Program for Musicians Serving Small Congregations, 1995, p 8.

57. Leonel L. Mitchell. *Planning the Church Year.* Morehouse Publishing, 1985, pp. 2–3.

teenth century. Liturgical worship has specific elements of order, ritual, and ceremony that are part of every worship service. Roman Catholic and Lutheran services are also liturgical, as they follow a prescribed order in their prayer books or missals, using specific texts for rites and observing ceremonial customs. Orthodox Christians use the word *liturgy* to refer to the Eucharistic portion of the service. Other denominations may be considered non-liturgical, as they may not have a prayer book or a set of texts used repeatedly or celebrate with communion on a regular basis, yet they may have a printed bulletin with an order of worship that could be considered a liturgy. In whatever denomination, liturgy is the work of the people, performed as a community by the people and for the people, an active celebration.

Purposes of Liturgy

The primary purpose of liturgy is to worship God with the full participation of the gathered assembly, including the structure and words that *The Book of Common Prayer* provides and the manner of performing the liturgy as may be customary for the Episcopal Church and/or within the local setting.

First, the liturgy must bring worshipers into an awareness of the sacred if even for a moment in time, into the mystery which may be experienced but not fully understood. Some aspects of our faith go beyond our human ability to comprehend. For example, what words would you use, beyond the texts in the Bible or the *BCP*, to describe the meaning of bread and wine becoming body and blood?

For a few years in the early 1970s I served as organist and choir director in a Presbyterian church in suburban Washington, D.C. Communion was offered every three months and was served to people in the pews. One time, the deacons and elders observed that the parents of a five-year-young girl offered the bread and grape juice to her when the plates were passed. The officials of the church discussed among themselves, albeit within earshot of others, that this was improper, that she had not yet received instruction regarding communion, that she was too young to know the meaning, and that her parents should not allow her to take communion. Three months later they saw the young girl again receive communion. Agitated, deacons and elders approached the parents after the service and demanded to know why they let their child receive. The parents looked at their daughter and said to the gathered assembly, "Why don't you ask her?" One of the elders squatted down to face the child and said, "We have noticed that you take the bread and juice with your parents. Yet you have not yet learned about communion in Sunday School. So, why do you take communion?" The girl looked up at them, smiled broadly, and said, "Because I love Jesus!"

Like the disciple Thomas, some of us need an explanation for the inexplicable. Mystery becomes miracle and miracle becomes mystery and God is present and acting boldly. That we, as a community, may enter such a state of awareness in our liturgy is a gift beyond measure.

The next purpose of liturgy is to change and transform us. This does not mean that we will not recognize ourselves when we leave the building. But hopefully, a lesson read well, or a rich silence, an appropriate hymn sung with strength and conviction, or dignified movement, voluntaries that bring us in and send us out, a community united in holy love and mission, or an impressive sermon that causes us to squirm in our seats, will cause us to think differently, open our hearts, make us more conscious of all the children of God, or amend our lives in some way. That is change. That is transformation.

The final purpose of liturgy is to send us into the world to serve and witness to the inestimable love of our Creator, Redeemer, and Companion. In the liturgy we are inspired and fed. We offer prayers for the entire church, our country and those who rule at all levels, the concerns of the world as well as the concerns of the community around us, those who suffer in any way, and those who feast at the heavenly banquet table in another realm. We give thanks for what we have received, the bounty in our lives, and the love that sustains us. Strengthened, at the end of the service the dismissal sends us forth in the name of Christ, in peace and love, to serve. Just attending church and putting a check in the box for you and your family is not enough. Participating in the fullness of the liturgy is wonderful, but not enough. We must take what we have received and go into the world and use our lives for God.[58]

Elements of Liturgy

Liturgical worship is distinguished by the presence of three main elements: order, rite, and ceremony.

Order is the overall shape and design, the framework upon which the liturgy rests. People want and need to know what to expect so they can fully

---

58. Three purposes of liturgy from lecture notes, the Rev. Dr. Edward Kryder, Virginia Theological Seminary, 1991.

participate. Using *The Book of Common Prayer*'s service of Holy Eucharist, they know that the Collect of the Day precedes the Lessons, the Sermon follows the Gospel, the Nicene Creed will be recited on Sundays and other major feasts, the exchange of the Peace precedes the Offertory, the Lord's Prayer will be said at the conclusion of the Eucharistic Prayer, there will be a blessing and dismissal. Rubrics that tell us when to sit or stand or kneel, cue our responses, and keep the liturgy flowing contribute to that sense of order.

Rite indicates the words that are said or sung. Rite One uses sixteenth-century wording. Contemporary English wording is found in Rite Two texts. Each rite follows the same order, and the words within each rite are invariable.

Ceremony is the manner of doing the liturgy, a variable opportunity at best. Some individuals will genuflect, cross themselves, kneel rather than stand when the option is given. Others will not. Some churches will have a formal procession, use incense and sanctus bells in appropriate places in the liturgy, sing all that can be sung by celebrant and people. Others will not. There is great diversity in the manner of ceremony throughout the land by people using the same order in the *BCP* and with the same ritual.[59]

I attended a Methodist church as a child, the only church in a village of fewer than two hundred people in upstate New York. At a tender age I became organist in a Methodist church in the next town, and, after a few years, served as organist at a Baptist church during high school. At college I was asked to be the assistant organist at the downtown Episcopal Church, where I became simply enthralled with the beauty of the liturgy, the history and traditions of the Episcopal Church, so far removed from my Protestant roots. The rector had been a choir boy at St. John the Divine in New York City, knew liturgy well, and celebrated with dignity and reverence, with an underlying tone of grandeur and joy. I learned all that I could from him, like the proverbial sponge in water, and was confirmed the next year. Most of the members of the Episcopal Church are not *cradle Episcopalians*, Episcopal since birth, but people who were drawn to the church by a common and acceptable ground, by the beliefs and mission, or, like me, were simply overwhelmed by something I could not live without, the liturgy of the Episcopal Church.

---

59. Elements of liturgy from *Essentials of Good Liturgy*. The Rev. Dr. Edward Kryder. *Syllabus for the Leadership Program for Musicians Serving Small Congregations*, 1995, p. 10.

Liturgical Planners

Title II, Canon 5, Of the Music of the Church, from the Constitution and Canons of the Episcopal Church, 2009 General Convention:

> It shall be the duty of every Member of the Clergy to see that music is used as an offering for the glory of God and as a help to the people in their worship in accordance with the Book of Common Prayer and as authorized by the rubrics or by the General Convention of this Church. To this end the Member of the Clergy shall have final authority in the administration of matters pertaining to music. In fulfilling this responsibility the Member of the Clergy shall seek assistance from persons skilled in music. Together they shall see that music is appropriate to the context in which it is used.

The rector or vicar is canonically responsible for worship in the congregation. The clergy studied liturgics in seminary, experienced a range of worship styles, and developed preferences of liturgical ritual and ceremony. While liturgy planned by clergy alone may have all the elements of a prayer book rite, include appropriate and known hymns, and be executed with dignity and good drama, the perceived needs of the people may or may not have been met. When clergy plan alone, part of the work of the people becomes, more or less, the work of one.

In the best of situations, the music leader and clergy sit down together, read the appointed lessons, consider and select hymns, service music, and psalm settings for a three- to six-month period or a liturgical season ahead. They talk about liturgical detail, how and when to introduce new music, and other important worship needs for the good of the community. In smaller congregations the musician may be a volunteer or employed part-time, unable to attend weekly meetings that interfere with a paid position outside the church. Then the selection of music may either be done by the rector or the church musician, or the church musician makes hymn and service music suggestions based on the assigned lessons for the rector's final decision-making.

Another example of liturgical planning brings together the rector or vicar, other clergy on the staff, deacon or seminarian, if available, and music director each week to finalize in detail the next Sunday's service and plan several weeks beyond. Meeting early in the week gives the group a time to evaluate the previous Sunday's services to determine what worked and what did not, information that is important to remember for future services.

A worship committee provides an opportunity for clergy, musicians, director of Christian education, other staff members involved in seasonal and weekly activities, interested congregational representatives, and lay leaders who oversee altar guild, acolytes, ushers, lectors, and eucharistic ministers to meet several times a year to consider the seasons, how they could or should be observed, and any changes that would affect the worship life of the congregation. To plan the details of an individual liturgy by a large group of people might be a source of frustration, as every person has individual requests and desires. But to look at a larger picture, an overview of the seasons, and to consider the worship and mission life of the congregation could offer a time of great creativity, conversation, and interest in serving. Lay people represent the congregation, listen to the people, make evaluations, and provide an important communication link with the clergy. When significant changes are made, the lay people on the worship committee can help support the decisions within the congregation.

Long-range planning is most desirable, especially for the music leader. When the liturgy for the next Sunday is planned only during the preceding week, then opportunities for teaching, adequately preparing the choir and other participants, or preparing an organ voluntary based on one of the selected hymns, simply disappear. Ideally, planning for Advent, Christmas, and Epiphany would be complete by the end of September, planning for Lent and Easter through Pentecost complete by the end of January, and planning for Trinity Sunday through Christ the King Day complete by the end of May.

Whether planning is done by a worship committee or staff or rector and music leader, there should be more than one person involved. Success will be achievable if the rector and music leader and/or those on the worship committee have a basic knowledge of:

- the liturgy, its purposes and elements
- the nature of the congregation
- the liturgical year
- hymns and service music and the resources available to assist in planning
- the multiple ways of singing psalms and resources for that singing

The Nature of the Congregation

If you are new to your position, then the congregation has already experienced change in the style of hymn playing, music selections, and the presence of a different personality. In getting to know *The Hymnal 1982* and hymnal supplements you may find hymns you really like and want to share with the congregation, but the people may not be open to your desire to do so. There may be issues of contention in the church that have nothing to do with music, but misplaced anger may rear its ugly head over the choice of hymns. Church people are often passionate about what they know and sometimes fearful of change or what they do not know. This is not unusual. To build a relationship of trust and respect takes time, thoughtful listening, openness, and constant teaching. Understanding your congregation and their communal worship life is a big step toward that goal.

Reflect on the answers to the following questions by yourself, with clergy, or with a group of people supportive of music in the church. Consider how the answers have an effect on worship in your community.

Worship

- Does the congregation regularly use Rite One at one service and Rite Two at another, Rite Two or Rite One only, or a combination of the two rites throughout the year? What is the normal schedule of services?
- Is Holy Eucharist offered every Sunday? Are there occasional services of Morning Prayer on a Sunday morning? Is Morning Prayer ever offered as the Liturgy of the Word before Holy Communion?
- Is the worship informal or formal?
- How are All Saints' Day, the church's patronal feast, Ascension, and Pentecost observed?
- How are the services of Holy Week observed?

Music and Liturgy

- Does the congregation enjoy a variety of music styles in the services?
- Have there been significant, or even subtle, changes in the liturgy and/ or style of music in the last five years? Ten years? What changes have taken place?
- How does the congregation respond to new hymns, psalm settings, or service music?
- Is the music program welcoming and accessible to all who desire to participate? Or is it limited by singing ability, space, funding, or heritage?
- Over what issues in worship and music has there been conflict in years past?

The Congregation

- How many people are considered members of the church?

- What is the average Sunday attendance at each service?

- What is the average age of the congregation?

- Are there children and young people involved in the life of the church?

- Is there much turnover in the congregation or has the congregation remained mostly unchanged for the past five years? Ten years? Longer? What is the reason for the turnover?

- Is there multicultural diversity within the congregation? Is this encouraged?

- Does your church have mission, pastoral, education, or building goals?

- How does your church practice hospitality to members, to newcomers, to the community? How are newcomers incorporated into the life of the parish?

Other questions will arise and be addressed and the ideas expressed may help you in your planning efforts. Take time to get to know the people before suggesting any significant change in the style of music and worship. Be assured of the support of clergy and lay leaders on the worship committee before going forward with change. The decisions that are made by music and liturgical leaders will have a profound effect on the people who sit in the pews, the children of God who gather in community to worship.

I am often amused when I overhear seminarians or less-experienced clergy begin a sentence with "When I get my church, I'm going to. . . " I would really like to say to them: "This is not your church. This is God's church. We are entrusted to be faithful, to build up and strengthen, to minister, to turn the hearts of the people to the love of God for the span of time we serve together, not do just what we want to do." Unless a parish is broken, a really wise clergy person will walk through the church's cycle of a year, seeing what the parish values, before making major changes. My children attended a preschool for four-year-olds in the church where I served. The director was often heard saying to distraught mothers, "You're doing just fine. Remember that these children belong to God and that they are just entrusted to our care for awhile." That is good advice for those of us working in the church, too.

The Liturgical Year

The structure of the liturgical year has evolved over the centuries to what we know and observe today. Each season has distinctive themes, liturgical colors and symbols, music, and possibilities for creative traditions. Understanding the rhythm and meaning of each season or day ensures that beauty and significance will be a part of each liturgy.

For the selection of hymns, consult:

- *Liturgical Music for the Revised Common Lectionary, Years A, B, or C*
- The current edition of *The Episcopal Musician's Handbook*
- The Liturgical and Subject Index (p. 684) of *The Hymnal 1982, Accompaniment Edition, Volume 1*, and *Wonder, Love, and Praise* (p. 251)
- For services in which collects, salutations, litanies are sung, refer to the Altar Book.
- Hymns for each liturgical season are found in *H82, WLP, LEVAS II, VF*, and *MHSO*.

Advent

Calendar

The four Sundays before Christmas; the first season of the liturgical year

Themes

- The word *advent* derives from the Latin word for *coming*. Advent is a time of preparation for the coming of Christ at Christmas, anticipating Christ's second coming, and God's continual birth in us.
- The First Sunday of Advent is eschatological in nature, that is, having to do with endings, things final. Gospel selections for Advent Two and Three focus on John the Baptist. Advent Four features Mary: the angel's appearance to Joseph, Gabriel's appearance to Mary and the Annunciation, or Mary's visit to Elizabeth and the *Magnificat*.

Colors

Purple or Blue (often called Sarum Blue)

- In ancient times, purple dye was difficult to make and therefore very expensive. In medieval Roman custom the color purple came to signify royalty and its accompanying wealth and power. Purple also came to be interpreted as a penitential color, as the seasons of Advent and Lent called for reflection and repentance in preparation for the coming of the King.

• The use of blue was an ancient English custom; blue was interpreted to represent the robes of Mary and the color of the sky, thus heaven. At Christmas, heaven came to earth in the form of the Christ child.

Symbols

• *Advent wreath*: four candles in a setting of greens; the candles may be white, but are usually purple or blue; one candle may be rose and is lighted on Advent Three, *Gaudete* (Rejoice) Sunday, so named for the first word of the introit ("Rejoice in the Lord always. Again I say, rejoice") of the ancient mass on Advent Three. The first candle of the Advent wreath is lighted each day of the first week, two candles are lighted each day of the second week, three and four candles lighted in the third and fourth weeks. Some add a fifth candle, white, placed in the center of the wreath, to be lighted on Christmas Eve and Day and throughout the twelve days of Christmas. Rubrics concerning the Advent wreath are found in *The Book of Occasional Services* 2003, p. 30.

• *Jesse Tree*: a symbol based on Isaiah 11:1 ("A shoot shall come out from the stump of Jesse, and a branch shall grow out of his roots"), representing the royal lineage of Jesus from his ancestor Jesse, father of King David. An Advent symbol, the Jesse Tree signifies the faithfulness of God through almost four thousand years before the birth of Jesus. One of the oldest stained glass windows of the Jesse Tree (ca. 1145) is in Chartres Cathedral, France, and depicts a reclining Jesse at the bottom of the center panel, with King David, King Solomon above him, followed by two crowned monarchs, then the Virgin Mary, and finally Christ in Majesty surrounded by doves bearing the gifts of the Spirit. The side panels depict prophets and the vines of the tree are interwoven throughout the glass. Many other symbols may be included in Jesse Tree art, such as the dove (creation), tree with fruit (Adam and Eve), rainbow (flood), ram (offering of Isaac), shepherd's crook or harp (David), crown (kings). While the Jesse Tree does not have the popularity of the Advent wreath, the symbol can be effectively used in educational opportunities with the congregation, especially the children.

• *The Great "O" Antiphons:* short anthems that begin with "O" and invite the Christ to come in different manifestations (Emmanuel, Wisdom, Lord of might, Branch of Jesse's tree, Key of David, Dayspring on high, Desire of nations). See Hymn 56, "O come, O come, Emmanuel" for the complete text. The antiphons were sung in church in the days before Christmas; note the dates listed by Hymn 56.

Music

- Hymns for Advent are located in *H82, WLP, LEVAS II, VF*, and *MHSO.*
- Canticles 6 and 20 (*Gloria in excelsis*) and any other setting of the *Gloria in excelsis* are omitted during Advent.
- Canticles 7 and 21 (*Te Deum laudamus*) and any other setting of the *Te Deum* are omitted during Advent.
- *Kyrie eleison* (in Greek or English) and *Trisagion* may be sung in place of the *Gloria in excelsis.*
- Canticles 3 and 15 (*A Song of Mary/Magnificat*), canticles 4 and 16 (*The Song of Zechariah*), canticles 5 and 17 (*The Song of Simeon/Nunc dimittis*), canticles 11 (*The Third Song of Isaiah*) and 19 (*The Song of the Redeemed*) and D (*A Song of the Wilderness*) and R (*A Song of True Motherhood*) are appropriate for Advent.

Liturgies

- Advent Festival of Lessons and Music, modeled after the traditional Festival of Lessons and Carols held at Kings College Cambridge on Christmas Eve
  - —Format found in *BOS* 2003, p. 31
  - —Information, lesson and hymn suggestions are given in *The Episcopal Musician's Handbook.*
  - —Lessons and hymn suggestions are found in *A Liturgical Index to The Hymnal 1982*, pp. 297–299.
- An Order of Worship for the Evening (*BCP* p.109) celebrated on one or all four Sundays of Advent would emphasize the theme of darkness and the coming light.
  - —Suitable hymns are 61/62 ("Sleepers, wake!"), 68 ("Rejoice! Rejoice, believers"), 60 ("Creator of the stars of night"), 63/64 ("O heavenly Word, eternal Light"), and 73 ("The King shall come when morning dawns").
- The Great Litany (*BCP* p. 148), may be sung in procession on the First Sunday of Advent to mark the beginning of the season.

Tradition

Episcopalians observe Advent. Although difficult for some, we sing Advent hymns throughout the four weeks of Advent, not Christmas carols. Our culture is bombarded with Christmas carols, secular and sacred, beginning at Thanksgiving or even before. Our hymnal and supplements have extraordinary texts and music for Advent and these hymns should be sung and known for the fullest observance of the liturgical season. The Season of Advent, its lessons and music, provide a great teaching opportunity for liturgical leaders in the church.

Christmas

Calendar

December 25 is Christmas Day; historians have many ideas how this date came to be, most associated with the pagan calendar and celebrations around the winter solstice. The Christmas Season lasts until Twelfth Night, the Eve of the Epiphany.

Theme

The birth of Jesus, the incarnation of God. The word *Christmas* is short for *Christ's mass*.

Color

White. The color white was used to describe angels, who announced Jesus' birth to the shepherds, and the risen Lord in the New Testament.

Symbols

- Candles, representing Christ, the Light of the World
- Evergreens, holly and ivy, and Christmas trees representing life in the bleak winter
- Poinsettias, thought by Mexicans to be symbolic of the Star of Bethlehem, brought to America in 1828
- Christmas trees, originated in Germany in the sixteenth century and were brought to America by Pennsylvania Germans in the 1820s
- Crèches are often set up after Advent Four is over; figures depicting Mary, Joseph, the infant Jesus, shepherds, and animals in the stable in Bethle-

hem, a source of contemplation and rejoicing for Christmas. The Wise Men may be seen at a distance, but make their appearance on January 6.

- "Greening of the church," so called by many Episcopal churches. As soon as the last service is finished on Advent Four, churches are decorated for Christmas. Poinsettias and other flowers adorn the church and greens are hung.

Music

- Appropriate canticles are 6 and 20 (*Gloria in excelsis*) or any other setting of the *Gloria in excelsis*, 9 (The First Song of Isaiah), 3 and 15 (*The Song of Mary/Magnificat*), C (*A Song of Hannah*), N (*A Song of God's Love*), R (*A Song of True Motherhood*).

- Consider these hymns not found in the Christmas section of *H82*: 496/497 ("How bright appears the Morning Star"), 421 ("All glory be to God on high"), 491 ("Where is this stupendous stranger?"), 468, verses 1–2 ("It was poor little Jesus").

- An abundance of anthems and solos, instrumental and organ music tell the story.

Liturgies

The main celebrations of Christmas take place on Christmas Eve and Day. Other seasonal options include:

- Vigil for Christmas Eve, rite located in the *BOS* 2003, p. 35.

- Station at a Christmas Crèche, rite located in the *BOS* 2003, p. 36.

- Christmas Festival of Lessons and Music, *BOS* 2003, p. 38.
  —Information, lesson and hymn suggestions are given in *The Episcopal Musician's Handbook*.
  —Lessons and hymn suggestions are found in *A Liturgical Index to The Hymnal 1982*, p. 299.
  —For inspiration, see the service leaflets and hear the music at the Kings College website: www.kings.cam.ac.uk. (Go to Events, then Chapel Services, to find A Festival of Nine Lessons and Carols.)

- Service for New Year's Eve, *BOS* 2003, p. 42.

- Lessons and hymn suggestions are found in *A Liturgical Index to The Hymnal 1982*, p. 302.

Traditions

- The white Christmas candle in the Advent wreath continues to be lighted through the twelve days of Christmas.

- Nativity plays, pageants, and caroling can involve all generations within the congregation and throughout the community.

- Some churches try to downplay the secular themes of Christmas, particularly Santa Claus, and invite a person in the congregation to dress up and play the role of St. Nicholas, answering questions asked by children and older children. A tutorial may be needed prior to the event. (St. Nicholas' day is December 6.)

The Epiphany and the Epiphany Season

Calendar

- The Epiphany is observed on January 6.

- The Season of Epiphany ends at Ash Wednesday and can last as many as nine or as few as four Sundays, depending on the date of Easter.

Themes

From the Greek, the word *Epiphany* means *appearance* or *manifestation*.

- Epiphany commemorates the visit of the wise men (Magi), who traveled to Bethlehem, guided by a star. They represent the Gentiles, or all non-Jewish people. Their honoring of the Christ child symbolizes the truth that God became human in the being of Jesus Christ, God the Son, and that all the nations came together to worship the child. The Magi brought gifts of gold (a symbol of wealth and kingship on earth, and a reminder that all we have comes from God), frankincense (a gum resin burned in temple worship, the smoke represents prayers rising heavenward, a symbol of the priestship of Jesus), and myrrh (also a gum resin, used to make an embalming oil, symbol of Jesus' death for us.) The date was chosen before the mid-fourth century. The legend of the Magi and their gifts came from the Middle Ages, when the wise men were given the names Melchior, Caspar, and Balthazar and eventually became "kings." The text in Matthew only tells of wise men, no number given, who came to the Christ Child bearing gifts.

- The baptism of Jesus in the Jordan River, observed on the First Sunday after the Epiphany every year, is another epiphany, or manifestation, of

Christ, revealed to all as God's chosen one. The focus on baptism in *The Book of Common Prayer* brings increased prominence to this event.

- On the Second Sunday after the Epiphany in Year C, the story of the first miracle is heard, when Jesus changed water into wine at the wedding feast in Cana of Galilee, signifying the beginning of a ministry of miracles and teachings. This story is considered the third epiphany.

- On the Last Sunday after the Epiphany, the story of the Transfiguration is heard in all three years of the RCL.

- During the Epiphany season we acknowledge the light of Christ in the world and hear stories of the ministry and mission of Jesus. This is an excellent time for the church to focus on mission at home and throughout the world.

Colors

- White, for the Epiphany and the First Sunday after the Epiphany
- Green, for the rest of the Sundays in the Epiphany season

Symbols

- Star(s), lights/candles, and crowns
- Gifts of gold, frankincense, myrrh
- Scallop shell with water, drops of water for baptism, dove

Music

- Canticles for the Epiphany season include 5 or 17 (*The Song of Simeon*), 9 (*The First Song of Isaiah*), 11 (*The Third Song of Isaiah*), 19 (*The Song of the Redeemed*).

- Hymns especially appropriate for the Last Sunday after the Epiphany are 122/123 ("Alleluia, song of gladness"), 129/130 ("Christ upon the mountain peak"), and 135 ("Songs of thankfulness and praise").

Liturgies

- If the Feast of Epiphany is not celebrated on January 6, the Revised Common Lectionary offers an optional Gospel lesson focusing on the Epiphany for the Second Sunday after Christmas Day.

- An evening celebration of the Epiphany might begin with An Order of Worship for the Evening (*BCP*, p. 109) with candlelighting, continuing with a service of Holy Eucharist. The singing of *H82* 128 ("We three kings") while three costumed singers process with gifts of gold, frankincense, and myrrh would be appropriate and a delight for all. A reception after the service could include an Epiphany cake with three almonds buried in the cake before frosting; the finders could wear gold crowns. Ornaments on the Christmas tree could be replaced with stars. The outside of the church could be decorated with luminaria and white lights on trees and bushes.

• On the First Sunday after the Epiphany, the Baptism of Our Lord, baptism(s) should precede the Holy Eucharist; if there are no baptismal candidates, then the renewal of The Baptismal Covenant (*BCP*, p. 304) should be part of the service.

• Vigil for the Eve of the Baptism of Our Lord, *BOS* 2003, p. 51.

• Blessing in Homes at Epiphany, rite located in *BOS* 2003, p. 47.

• Candlemas Procession (February 2, Presentation of Our Lord in the Temple), *BOS* 2003, p. 53. Mary and Joseph took Jesus to the Temple in Jerusalem forty days after the birth to complete Mary's ritual purification from childbirth and to perform the redemption of the firstborn, according to the law of Moses. At the Temple they encountered Simeon, who had been promised that he would not see death before he saw the Messiah. Simeon's words became known as the *Nunc dimittis* (*The Song of Simeon*), a canticle sung at Evensong and this season of the liturgical year: "Lord, you now have set your servant free to go in peace as you have promised; for these eyes of mine have seen the Savior, whom you have prepared for all the world to see; a Light to enlighten the nations, and the glory of your people Israel." (Canticle 17, adapted from Luke 2:29–32)

• The lessons for the Sixth, Seventh, and Eighth Sundays after the Epiphany are the same as Propers 1, 2, and 3, sometimes heard in May of the calendar year, depending on the date of Easter.

Traditions

Customs abound regarding the celebration of Epiphany. In some parts of the world, gifts are exchanged on Epiphany rather than Christmas. In some places the baptism of Jesus far outweighs the observance of the visit of the Magi.

- Twelfth Night, an occasion for celebration, may take place on the eve of the Epiphany, marking the end of the twelve day Christmas season. Caroling and feasting can reach out to the community and involve all ages in the congregation.

- The wise men take their place of adoration before the Christ Child in the crèche.

- All Christmas decorations are removed from the church before the First Sunday after the Epiphany, when the celebration focuses on the Baptism of our Lord, not Christmas.

- On the Last Sunday after the Epiphany the words *Alleluia* and *Hallelujah* or abbreviations thereof are heard for the last time, so that their absence during the next liturgical season, Lent, is noticed, and their return at the Great Vigil of Easter and Easter Day adds greater glory. For teaching purposes, create a bulletin cover with the words and their shortenings (*Alle, Halle, Allelu, Hallelu*) printed in many fonts and sizes. Include *Alleluia* and *Hallelujah* through the selection of hymns and anthems and as appropriate in the liturgy. Invite the children to count the number of Alleluias heard in text and song and offer a prize for those who come closest to the correct number. Then "bury" the Alleluia until it can be "dug up" and used again on Easter Day.

Ash Wednesday

Calendar

Wednesday, forty-six days before Easter Day

Themes

- Repentance of sins, awareness of our mortality
- Beginning of Lent

Colors

Purple or neutral color, such as unbleached linen or muslin

Symbols

- Ashes
- Cross (metal or wood, veiled or not)
- Simplicity in visual symbols; absence of ornate church decorations

Music

- There is no prelude or procession with music, no rubric for a hymn, anthem, or instrumental music at the beginning of the service or through to the conclusion of the Ash Wednesday liturgy.

- Psalm 51 may be said or sung, in unison or antiphonally by choir or cantor and congregation.

- Music selections during the communion should not undo the penitential solemnity and dignity created by silence in the Ash Wednesday liturgy.

- Options for the postcommunion hymn include a hymn reflecting the lessons or the beginning of the Lenten season: *H82*: 142 ("Lord, who throughout these forty days"), 143 ("The glory of these forty days"), 150 ("Forty days and forty nights").

- Many organists omit a postlude at the end of this liturgy, ending as the service began.

- Silence is the music for the liturgy.

Liturgy

- The Ash Wednesday liturgy begins on p. 264 of the *BCP*. The service opens with the Salutation and the Collect of the Day, then continues with the lessons, psalm, Gospel, Sermon, Imposition of Ashes, Psalm 51, the Litany of Penitence, Absolution, and the exchange of the Peace. At the conclusion of the Ash Wednesday liturgy, the service continues with Holy Communion and the regular options for music in the liturgy of Holy Communion apply.

Traditions

- The ashes for Ash Wednesday are made from leftover palms from the previous Palm Sunday; they are burned and made into a paste, and placed in a sign of the cross on the foreheads of the faithful and penitent. During that action the words offered are: "Remember that you are dust, and to dust you shall return." The word *Alleluia* is omitted on this day and throughout Lent.

- Some churches replace purple vestments, paraments, and frontals with unbleached muslin, or leave the altar completely uncovered. Some churches do not have arrangements of flowers through the entire season, but may have arrangements of dried branches instead. Some will use a wood cross in place of silver, brass, or gold crosses for the processions. Some will drape the processional cross with a veil; larger crosses may also be veiled. Pottery vessels may be used for chalice, paten, and cruets in place of metal ones. Baskets or wood bowls may be used instead of brass collection plates.

• One tradition that occurs in many churches on the night before Ash Wednesday is the Shrove Tuesday pancake supper. *Shrove* comes from the word *shriving*, meaning confession and absolution; traditionally, Christians would confess their sins before Lent began. At one time in the history of the church, oil, eggs, and butter were forbidden foods during Lent; making pancakes was a good way to use them up and not waste them before Lent started. Shrove Tuesday is also called Fat Tuesday, the translation of *Mardi Gras*, and is the last time to party until after Easter.

Lent

Calendar

• Forty days before Easter

• Sundays are *in* Lent but not *of* Lent. There are actually forty-six days from Ash Wednesday to Easter and six of those are Sundays. The weekly celebration of Holy Eucharist, which recalls the story of the Last Supper, the death, resurrection, and ascension of Christ, makes each Sunday service a "little Easter." That is why, when you were younger and gave up candy or chocolate or broccoli as a Lenten discipline, you may have been allowed to consume those foods on Sunday. Sundays are *of* Advent, *after* Christmas, *after* the Epiphany, *of* Easter, *after* Pentecost, and *in* Lent.

Themes

• Penitence and fasting, a recalling of the forty days Jesus spent in the wilderness

• Preparation for Easter; a time of renewing and strengthening our spiritual lives

• The word *Lent* comes from the Anglo-Saxon word *lencten* meaning the "lengthening of days" or "spring."

Colors

Purple or natural cloth (beige to white), such as unbleached muslin or linen, with accents in purple, red, or black.

Symbols

- Cross, sometimes a crucifix, although that may be reserved for Good Friday.

- The cross may be draped with a cloth (black, purple, or unbleached muslin) during Lent.

Music

- Music in the penitential Season of Lent should reflect the lessons, like every other liturgy during the year. In some churches a more somber tone is reflected in all the music choices and worshipers lament the Season of Lent, saying the music is too funereal. Surely a balance can be achieved.

- Canticles 6 and 20 (*Gloria in excelsis*) and any other setting of the *Gloria in excelsis* are omitted during Lent.

- Canticles 7 and 21 (*Te Deum laudamus*) are omitted during Lent.

- *Kyrie eleison* (in Greek or English) and *Trisagion* may be sung in place of the *Gloria in excelsis* as a song of praise.

- Canticles 4 or 16 (*The Song of Zechariah*), 10 (*The Second Song of Isaiah*), 14 (*A Song of Penitence*), 19 (*The Song of the Redeemed*) are appropriate, as are canticles F (*A Song of Lamentation*), H (*A Song of Hosea*), L (*A Song of Christ's Humility*), S (*A Song of Our True Nature*).

- Quiet, reflective preludes are suitable, especially those based on Lenten chorales or hymn tunes.

- Lent may be a time to omit descants, hymn reharmonizations, and improvisations and save them for the glorious Easter Day that will come.

- Some organists omit the postlude in favor of the congregation leaving in silence, if such a thing is possible.

Liturgies

Several possibilities exist for keeping the Season of Lent.

- The Great Litany (*BCP*, p. 148) is appropriate to mark Lent, at the beginning or part way through Lent.

- The Litany of Penitence (*BCP*, p. 267) may be used, preceded by an appropriate invitation and a penitential Psalm.

- An Exhortation and The Decalogue (Traditional) (*BCP*, p. 316 and 317) for Rite One may be used.

• A Penitential Order: Rite One (*BCP*, p 319) and A Penitential Order: Rite Two (*BCP*, p 351) may be used at the beginning of each liturgy of Holy Eucharist. The Decalogue (*BCP*, p. 317 and p. 350) may be included in the Penitential Order.

• A rite for The Way of the Cross, the offering of prayers at a series of locations associated with the passion and death of Jesus, also known as Stations of the Cross, is located in the *BOS* 2003, p. 57.

• The rite is appropriate in a public service, particularly Fridays during Lent, but should not replace the Good Friday liturgy. The fourteen stations may be marked by icons, banners, or works of art attached to the wall seasonally or permanently.

• In the *BOS*, p. 57 form, the text of the *Trisagion* appears at the end of each station; some music settings to consider are: S#99–S#102 and S#360 in *H82*; *WLP* 843–946; 8, 22, 34, and 55 in *EOM 1*; 116–118 in *EOM 2*; 16–17 in *MHSO*.

• The Way of the Cross may also be a private devotion, away from the church or in the church, as made available during the day or evening. Leaflets with the service should be placed near the First Station.

Traditions

• The word *Alleluia* is omitted throughout Lent; choose hymns and settings of the Fraction Anthem carefully.

• See notes about church decoration in Traditions, Ash Wednesday, above.

Palm Sunday

Calendar

• The sixth Sunday in Lent, the Sunday before Easter

• The beginning of Holy Week

Theme

Recalls the day Jesus entered into Jerusalem with triumphal shouts of "Hosanna" before the events that led to his crucifixion and resurrection

Color

Red

Symbol

Palm fronds or branches, a symbol of triumph and victory in Jewish tradition

Music

- The liturgy for Palm Sunday is the only distinctive two-part liturgy in the *BCP*. The service starts out with excitement and anticipation of the arrival of the King of Kings and ends firmly entrenched in the passion of Holy Week.

- The opening anthem (*BCP*, p. 270—"Blessed is the King who comes in the name of the Lord: Peace in heaven and glory in the highest") may be sung by priest/deacon/cantor and choir or congregation (*H82* 153) or another suitable anthem may be sung by the choir.

- After the blessing of the palms, the anthem before the procession may be sung antiphonally as noted above (*H82* 153), or the choir may offer an anthem based on the text "Hosanna in the highest," of which there are many.

- The hymn(s) or music for the procession (or parade) should be festive and triumphant. If the congregation parades from an outside location or some distance from the nave but within the church, a trumpet player, brass ensemble, or handbells would assist the congregation in singing while walking.

- After the reading of the Passion Gospel, all hymns and anthems, organ, or instrumental music should be devoted to the crucifixion. Triumphal hymns about the entry into Jerusalem are no longer appropriate, even at the end of the service.

- The word *Alleluia* is omitted throughout Lent and on this day; choose hymns and settings of the Fraction Anthem carefully.

- Consider using *H82* 164 ("Alone, thou goest forth, O Lord") or the first three verses of *H82* 168 ("O sacred head, sore wounded") or another hymn of similar character as the postcommunion hymn. Then depart in silence.

- No postlude may be the best option at the end of the service.

Liturgy and Traditions

The possibilities for creativity and meaning on this day are numerous.

- The liturgy for The Sunday of the Passion: Palm Sunday begins on p. 270 of the *BCP*.

- Plan a parade of parishioners, or, if you are close to other churches, have a larger, more inclusive, triumphal parade. Use palm fronds and branches that can be waved high during the parade.
- Create palm crosses after the service, when they would seem more appropriate.
- Adorn the processional cross with a red veil and/or palm fronds for the beginning of the liturgy. Ask the crucifer to change vestments to a black cassock and carry a wood cross with a crown of thorns at the procession out.
- Use one of the "readers' theater" versions of the Passion Gospel, assigning parishioners well ahead of the day to allow time for rehearsal.
- The Nicene Creed and Confession of Sin may be omitted.

Holy Week

Calendar

The days following Palm Sunday in the week before Easter through Holy Saturday

Theme

The last days of Jesus; the events leading to the crucifixion

Color

Red, the continuing color through Holy Week

Symbols

In general, the cross

Music

- Hymn suggestions are found in *Liturgical Music for the Revised Common Lectionary, Years A, B, and C.*
- Hymns may be chosen from *H82, WLP, LEVAS II, VF,* and *MHSO.*

Liturgies

- Propers for the services of Holy Eucharist on Monday, Tuesday, and Wednesday are found in the Revised Common Lectionary, pp.70–74.
- *Tenebrae* (from the Latin, meaning darkness or shadows) is derived from the ancient monastic Matins and Lauds (night and early morning) ser-

vices of the last three days of Holy Week, observed on the preceding evening. One of the characteristics of the service is the gradual darkening of the church by extinguishing candles until only one candle remains, signifying the light of Christ. Near the end of the service the candle is hidden from sight, a symbol of the apparent victory of evil. A loud noise is heard, then the candle is returned in the sight of all. The congregation departs in silence. The order of service for Tenebrae is found in the *BOS* 2003, p. 75. This service is intended for Wednesday of Holy Week only, so that the services prescribed for Maundy Thursday and Good Friday may be observed.

Maundy Thursday

Calendar

Thursday of Holy Week

Themes

- The Institution of the Eucharist (the Last Supper)
- The Footwashing
- Reserving the Sacrament
- Stripping of the Altar

Color

Red

Symbols

- Bread and wine
- Chalice and paten
- Basin and towel
- Cross

Music

- During the washing of the feet the choir or cantor may sing quietly or the congregation may sing music that is easily memorized and invites participation, not requiring focus on hymnal or service leaflet.
- The ancient text *Ubi caritas* is found at *H82* 576/577 ("God is love, and where true love is"), 606 ("Where true charity and love dwell"), and 831 (*Ubi caritas*) in *WLP* and is exceptionally appropriate for this service.

• *H82* 602 ("Jesu, Jesu, fill us with your love") is a particularly good choice for the foot-washing.

Liturgy

The liturgy for Maundy Thursday begins on p. 274 of the *BCP.*

Traditions

• The name *Maundy* comes from the Latin words *mandatum novum,* meaning "new commandment." Jesus said to his disciples: "I give you a new commandment: Love one another as I have loved you." (adapted, John 13:34)

• The optional ceremony of the washing of feet follows the Gospel and homily. Rubrics and an address regarding the ceremony of foot-washing are found in the *BOS* 2003, p. 93.

• In some traditions, after the Maundy Thursday liturgy the Sacrament is reserved in a place where people keep vigil, in a Garden of Repose outside or created inside the church or just in a quiet, darkened church, remembering Jesus' agony in the Garden of Gethsemane.

• At the end of the Maundy Thursday liturgy the altar is stripped to prepare for Good Friday. Candles are extinguished, altar hangings and other moveable ornaments are taken to the sacristy. In some churches the chairs, prayer desks, and all things not fixed to the floor are removed. The drama of this action is far more meaningful when a team (clergy, acolytes, altar guild, whoever is engaged for this task) knows specifically what to do so that there is not a traffic jam going in and out of the sacristy or people hanging around waiting for instructions or wondering what to do next. The wearing of black cassocks or black street clothes helps to keep the attention focused on the action and not on the people; also helpful in keeping the mood is the wearing of black "quiet" shoes. The singing or recitation of Psalm 22 and silence conclude the Maundy Thursday service. There is no other hymn or closing voluntary.

• The *BOS* 2003, p. 95, contains a rite for an Agapé Meal, a "love feast," for Maundy Thursday, a simple and usually meatless meal offered in a plain setting, following the Eucharist service.

• In some traditions an all-night vigil in the church takes place from the end of the Maundy Thursday service to the time of the Good Friday service, usually noon. Parishioners sign up for half-hour or hour time periods to pray in a dimly-lit church, keeping in mind the words of Jesus to Peter in the Garden of Gethsemane: "So, could you not stay awake with me one hour? Stay awake and pray that you may not come into the time of trial; the spirit indeed is willing, but the flesh is weak." (adapted, Matthew 26:40–41)

• The *Triduum* (Three Days) begins on the evening of Maundy Thursday Day and continues through Good Friday, Holy Saturday, and the Great Vigil of Easter.

Good Friday

Calendar

The Friday of Holy Week

Theme

The crucifixion of Jesus Christ

Color

Red, although some churches use black

Symbol

• Cross

• Crucifix

• Crown of thorns

Music

• There is no music before the Good Friday liturgy, *BCP*, p. 276. The ministers enter in silence, then kneel for silent prayer before beginning the liturgy with the Collect of the Day.

• A hymn may follow the sermon.

• The music for the Solemn Collects is found in the *AB*, pp. 332–338.

• The music for the three anthems in the *BCP*, p. 281, is found in *The Hymnal 1982, Accompaniment Edition, Volume 1*, S 349–S 351.

• After the anthems the rubric suggests *Sing, my tongue, the glorious battle* (*H82*: 165 or 166; S 352 in *The Hymnal 1982, Accompaniment Edition, Vol-*

ume 1) or some other hymn extolling the glory of the cross is then sung. (S352 is the same as *H82* 165 with the exception of an added verse).

• There is no more music after the hymn. All leave in silence.

Liturgy

• The liturgy for Good Friday begins on p. 276 of the *BCP*.

• The three anthems in the rite begin on p. 281. These may be recited with the congregation reading the parts in italics or may be sung. (*H82, Accompaniment Edition Volume I*, S 349–S 351)

• The rubric allows one or all three anthems.

Traditions

• *The Book of Common Prayer* offers a Good Friday liturgy in which the ministers enter in silence, begin with a collect and the readings, and continue with the Passion Gospel. The Solemn Collects are a noteworthy part of this liturgy. They are an old Roman form of the Prayers of the People, in which the officiant first bids the people to silent prayer, then the people pray, and the officiant concludes the silent prayer with a collect.[60] After The Solemn Collects the service may conclude with a hymn or anthem, the Lord's Prayer, and the final prayer on p. 282.

• If the service continues, then, if desired, a cross may be brought into the view of the congregation and spoken or sung anthems of veneration follow. The first anthem begins: "We glory in your cross, O Lord, and praise and glorify your holy resurrection; for by virtue of your cross joy has come to the whole world." The Good Friday liturgy is not a funeral for Jesus, but a remembering that his death destroyed death for the salvation of all.

• If the reserved Sacrament is to be consumed, it is preceded by a Confession of Sin and the Lord's Prayer. A concluding prayer ends the liturgy. There is no blessing or dismissal on Good Friday.

• A wooden cross is ideal for Good Friday.

• Some congregations observe the time between noon and 3 p.m. with meditations, hymns, prayers, and silence.

---

60. Marion J. Hatchett Commentary on the American Prayer Book, p. 235.

Holy Saturday

Calendar

The day after Good Friday and the day before Easter

Themes

The body of Jesus is in the tomb

Color

Red

Symbols

Cross

Music

- There is no music before the service. The entrance of the clergy should be in silence.

- Even though there is no rubric designating music at the lessons, a Tract or a Sequence would work well between the Epistle and Gospel. Hymn suggestions from *H82* include 173 ("O sorrow deep!"), 172 ("Were you there when they crucified my Lord?"), or 458 ("My song is love unknown"). [61] "In deepest night," p. 97 in *VF* would also be fitting.

- After the Gospel and homily, in place of the Prayers of the People, the only music of the Holy Saturday liturgy suggested is the anthem "In the midst of life," which may be sung or said. The text is from the Committal portion of the Burial of the Dead: Rite One (p. 484) and as an opening anthem in Rite Two (p. 492). The Rite Two setting has italicized responses for the congregation. Musical settings of this anthem are found in *H82 Accompaniment Edition Volume 1* at S 379 (Rite One) and S 382 (Rite Two).

Liturgy

The rite for Holy Saturday is on p. 283, *BCP*. The rite begins with the Collect of the Day and includes an Old Testament lesson, Psalm, Epistle, and Gospel. A homily may be given, then the Anthem "In the midst of life" is sung or said. The service concludes with the Lord's Prayer and Grace.

---

61. Hatchett, A *Guide to the Practice of Church Music*, 77.

Traditions

This service is not nearly as well known as others. Consider gathering the forces preparing the church for Easter and take a few moments to observe this liturgy at the beginning or end of their work. Holy Saturday lasts until dusk, after which the Easter Vigil is celebrated.

The Great Vigil of Easter

Calendar

Between sunset on Holy Saturday and sunrise on Easter Day morning

Themes

- First service of Easter
- Resurrection
- Baptism
- Holy Eucharist

Color

White

Symbols

- Cross
- Paschal candle
- Symbols of baptism

Music

- There is no music at the beginning of this service, no opening voluntary or hymn. The congregation gathers in silence.
- If nothing in the rest of the liturgy is sung, other than hymns and service music, the *Exsultet* should be sung. It is the privilege of the deacon to carry the Paschal candle and chant the *Exsultet*. If no deacon is present, or if the deacon is unable to sing, then the priest or cantor sings.
- During the Liturgy of the Word (lessons after the *Exsultet*), a psalm or canticle is sung after each lesson. Those options are in the *BCP*, pp. 288–291.
- The choice of canticle at the Easter proclamation (*Pascha nostrum, Te Deum laudamus,* or *Gloria in excelsis*) should be festive, in contrast to the canticles during the Liturgy of the Word.

• At the Easter proclamation, sound the state trumpet on the organ, play a fanfare with or without brass instruments, ring handbells, dinner bells, or jingle bells. Make a joyful sound to proclaim that Christ is indeed risen from the dead.

• Music for the priest or deacon or cantor:
  —AB 348—Procession of the Paschal Candle
  —S 68—Versicle and Response: The Light of Christ
  —AB 351—The *Exsultet*
  —S 69—The *Exsultet*: Responses for the congregation
  —AB 361—Prayers for the Candidates at Baptism
  —AB 362—Thanksgiving over the Water
  —AB 365—Consecration of the Chrism
  —S 70, AB 369—Great *Alleluia*

Liturgy

The rite for the Great Vigil of Easter is found in the *BCP*, p. 285. Rubrics concerning the service are on p. 284. There are four distinct parts to this historic and significant service:

• *Lighting of the Paschal Candle, Acclamation,* and *Exsultet.* The Paschal candle is lighted from a newly-kindled fire, carried by the deacon or another appointed person into the darkness, pausing three times to sing or say, "The light of Christ" followed by the congregational response, "Thanks be to God." Candles of the worshipers are lighted from the Paschal Candle and assisting candles. The *Exsultet* is then sung. The first part of this ancient chant is a song of victory and rejoicing; the second part contains the themes of the Passover, deliverance from bondage in Egypt, and resurrection triumph.

• *Liturgy of the Word.* The story of Creation and lessons about God's saving acts in history and continuing presence in our lives are heard; the rubric requires that at least two of the nine lessons be read. Psalms, canticles, and hymns are sung in response to those lessons.

• *Holy Baptism.* The Great Vigil intends that baptism or the renewal of baptismal vows be an integral part of the service. In the early church, catechumens spent all of Lent preparing for their baptism or initiation into the church at the Great Vigil. If baptismal candidates are not present, the renewal of baptismal vows continues. The congregation may be asperged (sprinkled) with holy water.

• *The Holy Eucharist.* After the baptism, the Easter greeting "Alleluia. Christ is risen. The Lord is risen indeed. Alleluia!" is proclaimed. The room is fully lighted, a fanfare may be heard, bells are rung, and the faithful prepare for the first Eucharist of Easter.

Traditions

This is the first celebration of the Easter season, observed in the darkness of Saturday night or early Sunday morning, Easter Day. The Christian tradition considers feasts and other days of observance where Eucharist is celebrated (like Christmas) to begin at sunset of the previous day, adopting the ancient Jewish custom that the day begins and ends with sunset.

• Although inappropriate for this liturgical season, the call of John the Baptist needs to be heard here: prepare, prepare, prepare! This is a complicated service and requires that all participants plan well in advance of the service and know their parts. A rehearsal is well-advised. If your church has never done an Easter Vigil before, gather a group of people and attend one in another parish so that you can experience the service first before planning for the next year.

• As much as possible, include all the congregational music as well as the rite in the service leaflet. If there are baptisms, there will be relatives of the baptismal candidates who may or may not be familiar with the Episcopal Church or this service. Juggling the *BCP* and the *H82* in the dark and in a service that will last approximately two hours is difficult at best; a service leaflet containing the entire service with music is an act of hospitality.

• The Paschal candle is lit at all liturgies through the Day of Pentecost. The flame should be present when the first worshipers arrive and extinguished after the last one has left the building. The Paschal candle symbolizes the light that God made at the beginning of Creation, the presence of the risen Christ, and the flame of the Holy Spirit. The Paschal candle is used at funeral and memorial services and often at services of Holy Baptism throughout the year.

• The word *Alleluia* is restored in all its fullness.

Easter Day and Season
Calendar

- Easter Day is always the Sunday after the full moon that occurs on or after the spring equinox on March 21.

- This full moon may happen on any date from March 21 to April 18 inclusive. If the full moon falls on a Sunday, Easter Day is the Sunday following. But Easter Day cannot be earlier than March 22 or later than April 25. The rules for finding the date of Easter Day and a table to find Easter Day up to the year 2089 are found in the *BCP*, pp. 880 and 882.

- The Easter Season begins at sundown the evening before Easter Day and goes until the Day of Pentecost. The season, also known as Eastertide or the Great Fifty Days, includes the six Sundays after Easter, within the seven weeks. Note that the Sunday after Easter Day is called the Second Sunday of Easter, as Easter Day is the first Sunday of Easter.

Themes

- Resurrection
- Appearances of Jesus to the disciples

Color

White

Symbols

- Cross
- Paschal candle
- Kneeling lamb (Paschal lamb, the *Agnus Dei* or Lamb of God)
- Flowers (new life), Easter lily (white, symbolizing purity and trumpet shape, announcing the resurrection)

Music

- There are many hymns appropriate for Easter Day and the Easter Season. The choices for Easter Day will most likely be partially determined by tradition, familiarity, and whether or not instrumental arrangements are available, if instrumentalists are to participate. The music is festive, in great contrast to the season of Lent.

- As brass players are not always available for Easter Day, either because there are not enough players for all the churches that want brass music or their performance fees for the day are beyond the budget, consider engaging flute, violin, cello, oboe, or other instrument for the service(s). The music on Easter Day does not have to be loud, louder, and "Oh, my God!"

- The Sunday after Easter, the Second Sunday of Easter, is too often called "Low Sunday," usually because the energy of the clergy and church musicians has been spent from all the services in Holy Week. This is a day in which the deacons and seminarians are often invited to preach, the choir gets a day off to recover, and the organist may take a Sunday off. Frankly, I believe this Sunday is a great day to pull out all the stops, hire a trumpet player or a brass quartet, and continue to celebrate the resurrection. There should never be a low Sunday in the praise and worship of God.

- One canticle unique to the Easter season is "Christ our Passover" (*Pascha nostrum*) found in the *H82* (S 11–S 20) and *WLP* (879, 880). To sing this canticle throughout the Easter Season would emphasize that Easter is not just a day but a season.

- Other appropriate canticles are: 7 or 21 (*Te Deum laudamus*), 8 (*The Song of Moses*), 18 (*A Song to the Lamb*), A (*A Song of Wisdom*), G (*A Song of Ezekiel*), K (*A Song of Our Adoption*), and M (*A Song of Faith*).

- Another hymn often used as a song of praise during the Easter season is "This is the feast of victory for our God," *H82* 417, 418.

- Services for Easter Day and the Easter Season follow the rites of Holy Eucharist with great festivity.

- Blessings Over Food at Easter, rite in *BOS* 2003, p. 97.

- Rogation Procession rite in *BOS* 2003, p. 103. Rogation Days are usually observed on the Monday, Tuesday, and Wednesday before Ascension Day, but may be observed on other days.

Traditions

The journey through Holy Week culminates in the glorious celebration of the resurrection of our Lord and Savior, Jesus Christ, on Easter Day. Many call this day Easter Sunday, but Easter Day is more appropriate. Every Sunday, when we gather together to worship and celebrate the Eucharist, we hear the story of the Last Supper, the Crucifixion and Resurrection of Christ in the Eucharistic Prayer. Every Sunday, therefore, is an "Easter Sunday." But there is only one Easter Day in the liturgical year.

Ascension Day

Calendar

Thursday, forty days after Easter

Theme

The ascension of Jesus into heaven

Color

White

Symbols

- Cross with banner, empty tomb
- A lion (Jesus) conquering a dragon (Satan)
- A broken chain, open gates

Music

There are great hymns for Ascension Day in *H82* and hymnal supplements. See *The Episcopal Musician's Handbook*, 56th Edition, Lectionary Year C, 2012–2013, p. 108 for suggestions.

Liturgy

- The story of the Ascension is found in Acts 1:1–11.
- The service of Holy Eucharist is the rite for Ascension Day.

Traditions

The Ascension is an important feast that completes the Paschal story, beginning with the passion of Jesus, his crucifixion, death, burial, descent into hell, resurrection and now ascension. The ascension proves yet again the divinity of Jesus, who is God, the Messiah, and who ascends to God his Father with a promise to return. With the ascension, Jesus is present to the whole world, not just those living in Palestine. Jesus is Christ, the King.

- By the time Ascension Day arrives, so has spring in some geographic locations and the escape of the congregation to weekend retreats. Education about Ascension Day, clergy encouragement, and the participation of choir and/or school children could help the attendance at a service.
- The release of helium balloons outside the building, signifying the rise of Jesus, used to be popular but now is known to be ecologically un-

sound. However, balloons inside the building create a similar effect and symbol in the service.

- The *BCP* permits the observance on the Sunday after the Ascension, the Seventh Sunday of Easter, if a celebration on Ascension Day is not possible.

Day of Pentecost

Calendar

- The fiftieth day of Easter, ending the Easter Season
- The seventh Sunday after Easter Day

Themes

- The day the Holy Spirit descended on the disciples, empowering them for ministry
- The birthday of the church

Color

Red

Symbols

- Flames (tongues of fire), representing the flames above the disciples' heads
- Dove (symbol of the Holy Spirit), baptismal font (our baptism into the body of the church), droplets of water and scallop shell (baptism)
- Seven lamps representing the seven gifts of the spirit: wisdom, understanding, counsel (right judgment), inward strength (courage), knowledge, reverence (piety), fear of the Lord (wonder and awe), a sailing ship (symbol of the church)
- Pomegranate (many seeds in one fruit resemble the many people in the church)

Music

- The singing of Pentecost hymns is central to this celebration.
- Given the theme, this would be a good occasion to go beyond the *H82* and look at music from other cultures and expressions of faith, in *WLP* and *LEVAS II, VF,* and *MHSO.*

- Canticles 7 or 21 (*Te Deum laudamus*), 1 or 12 (*A Song of Creation*), 19 (*The Song of the Redeemed*) are appropriate for the Day of Pentecost.

- *Veni Sancte Spiritus, WLP* 832, from the Taizé Community has gained a wider use on the Day of Pentecost.

- Singing in a variety of languages would emphasize the lesson from Acts.

- Invite brass or other instrumentalists to assist the celebration of this day.

Liturgies

- Acts 2:1–6 is the essence of the Pentecost story.

- The sacrament of Holy Baptism or the renewal of baptismal vows is an important element of this service.

- A Vigil of Pentecost may be observed. See rubrics on p. 175 (Rite One) or p. 227 (Rite Two) of *BCP*.

Traditions

- The Day of Pentecost is a joyous service and can involve the entire congregation, including all children, in celebrating the birth of the church.

- Reading the Scripture in a variety of languages is most effective. One model would be to have a lector read the lesson (Acts 2:1–21) in English, after which other voices read the same lesson in other languages, from within the congregation, spacing out their starting times. Another option is to experience the chaos of having all languages heard at the same time.

- If your church has a high ceiling, consider using kites (long slender, flexible poles with artificial doves or long streamers in red, orange, yellow, gold) in the procession. The kites are swirled around in a looping pattern, side to side.

- Invite the congregation to wear red (ties, shirts, dresses, shoes, socks, hats, jewelry, accessories) on the Day of Pentecost.

- You may see other names for the Day of Pentecost and the Pentecost Season: Whitsun, Whitsunday, or Whitsuntide. These words were used in the 1928 *Book of Common Prayer* and are still in use today in parts of the Anglican Communion.

- A birthday party reception/coffee hour, complete with red balloons, would be a festive way to celebrate the day.

Trinity Sunday

Calendar

The first Sunday after the Day of Pentecost

Theme

Celebrates the Christian doctrine of the Trinity, the three persons of God: Father, Son, and Holy Spirit

Color

White

Symbols

- Trefoil, circle within a triangle, interwoven circles, equilateral triangle, a triangular shape formed by three overlapping rings
- Symbols of the Father: crown, all-seeing eye, hand of God
- Symbols of the Son: lamb, lamb with banner of victory, phoenix (symbol of resurrection), fish (with first letters of *rebus*, based on the Greek word for fish, stands for "Jesus Christ, Son of God, Savior")
- Symbols of Holy Spirit: dove, descending dove, sevenfold flame, seven lamps

Music

In addition to Trinity hymns in the *H82* and supplements, canticles highly appropriate for Trinity Sunday are 7 or 21 (*Te Deum laudamus*), 2 or 13 (*A Song of Praise*).

Liturgy

The Holy Eucharist

Traditions

- This is the only major festival that celebrates a doctrine and not an event in the sacred story.
- In some churches the Creed of Saint Athanasius (*BCP*, p. 864) is recited. The Athanasian Creed has been in use since the sixth century and is the first creed to state with detail the equality of the three persons of the Trinity.

Season after Pentecost

Calendar

- All Sundays after the Day of Pentecost and before the first Sunday of Advent
- This season is framed by Trinity Sunday at the beginning and ends with the Last Sunday after Pentecost, also known as *Christ the King* or *Reign of Christ*.

Theme

There is not a specific theme except for the fairly consecutive reading in the RCL of the Gospel of Matthew during Year A, Mark during Year B, and Luke during Year C, with selections from the Gospel of John interspersed. Two tracks of readings are available for this time: one, a semi-continuous track, offers in-course readings of the salvation history stories in the Hebrew Scriptures; the other, a Gospel-related track, offers the most similarity to the *BCP* lectionary no longer in use.

Color

Green

Music

- Hymns are selected, as always, to support the lessons assigned.
- Service music could be planned for two months at a time (June–July, August–September, October–November) so that more settings could be taught and sung, avoiding singing the same settings for almost a quarter of the year.
- The choir commitment may end on Trinity Sunday and resume in August or September, allowing a break for them and an opportunity for chosen singers, ensembles, and instrumentalists to provide special music during the summer.
- Consider having the congregation, instead of choir or soloists, sing a hymn as an offertory anthem, dividing the verses for men and women or other options, adding youth instrumentalists.

Liturgies

- The service of Holy Eucharist is offered every Sunday in the custom of the church.

- In a congregation that has numerous baptisms during the year, more than can be easily accommodated on All Saints' Day, First Sunday after the Epiphany, Easter Vigil, and the Day of Pentecost (the regularly scheduled baptismal occasions), two or more Sundays for baptisms could be offered.

- In addition to saints' days which could be honored within this season, special liturgies could be planned for The Transfiguration of Our Lord Jesus Christ (August 6), Holy Cross Day (September 14), Blessing of the Animals (on or around October 4/St. Francis of Assisi), Service for All Hallows' Eve (*BOS*, p. 108), Vigil for the Eve of All Saints' Day (*BOS*, p. 106), and Christ the King Day (Last Sunday after Pentecost).

Traditions

- The Season of Pentecost is often referred to as *ordinary time.*

- Some parishes consolidate their worship into a single Sunday service during the summer, making allowances for vacationing parishioners and hotter weather. This shift can involve combining those accustomed to worshiping without music and those that regularly sing. Sensitivity to worship planning is necessary.

- If children and young people do not participate regularly in the worship life of the church, engage them to serve as acolytes, lectors, ushers, and readers, especially during the summer.

- Plan a liturgy to be held outdoors and use a theme of creation or steward-ship of our earth or an agricultural emphasis. Considerations will need to be made for seating, amplification, music and music leadership, and a service leaflet that includes the liturgical texts and all music.

Patronal Feast

Calendar

Dates for many patron saints may be found in the Holy Days section of the *BCP*, pp. 921–925, or in *Lesser Feasts and Fasts* (2003) or *Holy Women, Holy Men* (2010).

Theme

The life and works of the saint

Color

Red

Symbols

- Each saint has a unique symbol, that of a particular accomplishment, how a life was lived or the symbol of the saint's martyrdom.
- Symbols could be incorporated into the service leaflet, made into a processional banner, and used in teaching opportunities.

Music

- Hymn suggestions for saints are found in *A Liturgical Index to The Hymnal 1982*, Holy Days section, beginning on p. 260, and throughout each annual edition of *The Episcopal Musician's Handbook*.
- Where possible, plan and prepare music attributed to the saint or patron and select organ, instrumental, and choral music from the time period in which that person lived.

Liturgy

- Service of Holy Eucharist with lessons selected from *Lesser Feasts and Fasts* or *Holy Women, Holy Men*, with information from *Brightest and Best: A Companion to the Lesser Feasts and Fasts*

Traditions

- Include a history of why that saint was chosen for your parish.
- Consider having a member of the congregation learn about the saint or patron, dress as that person, mingle with the congregation during coffee hour, and answer questions about the life and times of the saint and his/ her contribution to the church and Christianity.

Resources Needed for Music and Liturgical Planning

The bibliography contains a listing of excellent books that will assist all those in planning liturgy and music in the church. Especially for the sake of those music leaders who are new to the Episcopal Church, the following resources are listed in three sections, starting with those most needed to do your work.

In the *Requisite Resources* section below, only the Carl P. Daw, Jr. and Thomas Pavlechko psalm settings are listed. If a congregation has not experienced singing psalms, this style is very accessible. Other resources for singing psalms are located in Chapter Six: Psalms and Psalm Settings.

Only titles and authors are listed; full publishing information is found in the bibliography.

Requisite Resources

These books are critical as you begin to plan hymns and service music for Sundays and special liturgies.

The Bible—Your favorite edition of the New Revised Standard Version with the Apocrypha

The Book of Common Prayer 1979

The Revised Common Lectionary—Years A, B, C, and Holy Days—According to the Use of The Episcopal Church

The Hymnal 1982, Accompaniment Editions, Volume 1 (Service Music) and *Volume 2* (Hymns)

Daw, Carl P., Jr. and Thomas Pavlechko. *Liturgical Music for the Revised Common Lectionary, Year A*

_____. *Liturgical Music for the Revised Common Lectionary, Year B*

_____. *Liturgical Music for the Revised Common Lectionary, Year C*
Note: For each Sunday of Years A, B, and C suggested hymns for the lessons assigned are found on the right hand page. Their placement as entrance, sequence, offertory, communion, and postcommunion hymns are noted under the columns of *H82* and other hymn sources used. Descants for voice or instrument are also indicated. On the left hand page are anthem titles and composers, solo and duet suggestions for the same set of propers. These are extraordinary resources which will assist you for years to come.

Daw, Carl P., Jr. and Kevin R. Hackett. *A HymnTune Psalter for the RCL, Book One: Gradual Psalms: Advent through the Day of Pentecost*

_____. *A HymnTune Psalter, Book Two: Gradual Psalms: The Season after Pentecost*
Note: These collections of psalm settings feature an antiphon based on a familiar hymn tune and simplified Anglican chant for psalm verses. The choir or cantor introduces the antiphon, the congregation imitates then sings the antiphon after every two or three verses. Choir or congregation sings the verses.

Hatchett, Marion J. *Hymnal Studies Five: A Liturgical Index to The Hymnal 1982*

Note: Propers for the Holy Eucharist, Sundays of Years A, B, and C in this resource are not based on the RCL and therefore should no longer be used for the selection of hymns for services of Holy Eucharist. However, music selections for the lessons assigned for Holy Days, Common of Saints, Various Occasions, Pastoral Offices, Episcopal Services, liturgies from *The Book of Occasional Services* and *Lesser Feasts and Fasts*, as well as the Two-Year Lectionary for the Daily Office, are included and well known to be very fine choices.

Kucharski, Joseph A., ed. *The Episcopal Musician's Handbook: Lectionary Year C, 2012–2013*

Note: The *Episcopal Musician's Handbook* is published annually and contains hymn suggestions for the assigned lessons on the left page, a liturgy checklist sheet on the right page, and a hymn use checklist in the back. The handbook includes suggestions for musicians, information on service music, choral services, sung offices, table of canticles in *H82*, metrical or paraphrased psalms, pastoral rites, Advent and Christmas Festivals of Lessons and Carols, and other resources.

Essential Resources

These books are very important to have and should become part of your working library as soon as possible. If your congregation is already singing from *LEVAS II, WLP, VF, MHSO*, or *El Himnario*, those hymnals should be included in the first category of *Requisite Resources*.

Although it is lovely to have all these books in your personal library, acquiring all of them is costly indeed. Ask for a book allowance in your church's music budget, or borrow the rector's resources, or, with permission, ask for special donations to place these books in the music library at church.

Enriching Our Music 1: Canticles and Settings for the Eucharist

Enriching Our Music 2: More Canticles and Settings for the Eucharist

Note: EOW I contains supplemental liturgical materials, including seventeen additional canticles and a third Eucharistic Prayer. *EOM 1* contains additional service music, eleven settings for the Eucharist, two settings each of Canticles A–K. *EOM 2* contains settings of Canticles L–S and more settings of the Eucharist.

Enriching Our Worship I: Morning and Evening Prayer, the Great Litany, The Holy Eucharist

Lift Every Voice and Sing II: An African American Hymnal

The Book of Occasional Services, 2003
A valuable resource for liturgies beyond Sunday and special days, *BOS* contains numerous rites for the church year, pastoral and episcopal services, including Spanish rites.

Haskel, Marilyn L. and Lisa Neufeld Thomas. *Voices Found: Leader's Guide*

Hooker, John L. *Wonder, Love, and Praise. A Supplement to The Hymnal 1982*: *Leader's Guide*

Glover, Raymond F., ed. *The Hymnal 1982 Companion,* Vols.1–3B
Note: Volume One contains essays on congregational song, popular religious song, cultural diversity, *The Hymnal 1982* and *The Book of Common Prayer*, service music, hymn forms, and a historical survey of hymnody in the U.S. and Britain. Volume Two contains text and music information for all service music selections in H82 and biographies of authors and composers of hymns and service music. Volumes Three A (hymns 1–384) and B (hymns 385–720) contain music and text information on all the hymns in *H82*. While Volumes Two and Three A–B can be purchased individually, I cannot imagine not having all four volumes at my fingertips. Yes, the set is expensive. Give up dining out and movies for a couple months and the set is yours.

Vidal-White, Fiona. *My Heart Sings Out, Teacher's Guide*

Other Important Resources

These treasures should also be in your library, perhaps on your birthday and Christmas lists for friends and family.

Holy Women, Holy Men: Celebrating the Saints

*Lesser Feasts and Fasts,—*2003

Black, Vicki K. *Welcome to the Book of Common Prayer*

Haskel, Marilyn L. *As We Gather to Prayer: An Episcopal Guide to Worship*

Morris, Clayton L. *Holy Hospitality: Worship and the Baptismal Covenant*

Portaro, Sam. *Brightest and Best: A Companion to the Lesser Feasts and Fasts*

Webber, Christopher L. *Welcome to Sunday: An Introduction to Worship in the Episcopal Church*

Plan the Liturgy and the Music

You are ready. You have read and inwardly digested books and articles and previous chapters in this resource. You have explored *The Book of Common Prayer* and *The Hymnal 1982*, resources for planning, and have a foundational understanding of what is necessary to choose hymns, service music, psalm settings, and canticles for the congregation. Meet with those planning liturgy and begin.

1. First, pray. Pray for divine presence, wisdom, and clarity. Pray for awareness and openness, patience and guidance. Pray for each other.

2. Look up the assigned lessons in the *BCP*/RCL or Bible and read aloud the passages, looking and listening for themes or words or phrases that remind you of a hymn text.

3. Using planning resources, consider hymns that are familiar to the congregation and those less so. Which hymns most closely match the lessons or Gospel or season? Which hymns will be best suited for the entrance or sequence, offertory, communion, or the leaving?

4. Choose settings of the ordinary that work best for a particular Sunday or season. Does the music of the *Kyrie, Gloria, Sanctus,* and Fraction Anthem need to be by a single composer or can the choice be eclectic? What settings does the congregation know already and what new music could successfully be added to the repertoire of the congregational song? Should settings be selected by season to help define a season or has that not been done before? Is there a particular hymn or canticle that could be sung as a song of praise in place of the *Kyrie, Gloria,* or *Trisagion*?

5. Choose the setting for the psalm. Is the music accessible for the congregation? Will a cantor be needed? Will the choir sufficiently support the music? In what ways have the psalms been sung in the past? Will the selection of psalm settings help define a season?

6. If the Daily Office of Morning Prayer is used as the Liturgy of the Word in a service of Holy Eucharist, what canticles will best serve the lessons?

7. What other portions of the liturgy will be sung? What settings will be used?

8. For the music leader, what anthems reflect the assigned lessons? What organ or instrumental voluntaries are based on the hymn tunes se-

lected? What music will bring the people in to the sacred, inspire and transform them, then enable them to depart with strength to do the work of God?

9. End with a prayer of thanks for what has been done and strength to follow through. Say *Amen* with conviction and understanding.

Keep a Customary

Keep records of hymns, service music, psalm settings, canticles, anthems, organ or instrumental voluntaries for each Sunday and special service in a customary, the musical and liturgical customs of your parish. Save Sunday and special service leaflets, articles written about music, hymns, composers and authors, and liturgical detail, choir schedules, and diocesan or community events. Reminiscing alone cannot always recall the details of a particular service from last year or years before. A customary maintains the memory.

When a worship committee contemplates the details of Christmas Eve services, for example, questions will arise. How many ushers did we have last year? How many acolytes are needed for each service? What are the extra supplies the altar guild needs to have on hand? When does the church get decorated and who did the job last year? Who read lessons last year so we make sure to include others this year? What anthems did the choir sing? What Christmas carols were selected? How many eucharistic ministers are needed for the services? If these details are recorded in a worship/music customary, then there will be less anxiety for all worship leaders.

A customary can include details for Palm Sunday, Maundy Thursday, the Great Vigil of Easter, Christmas Eve, weddings, and funerals. A diagram of the nave and sanctuary with table, pulpit, lectern, baptismal font, bishop's chair, and seating is useful for weddings and funerals, confirmation, and occasional services. Orders of procession in and out, seating assignments, placement of banners, cross, and torches can also be included in the customary. This document serves well only when maintained by the music leader or a clergy person or a volunteer who is detail-oriented and willing to devote time to the task.

Since leaving full-time music ministry in 1999 I have served as an interim musician in several parishes, at times for only three months during sabbatical or maternity leaves, at other times from six months to fourteen months, even two years while the church engaged in a search process for the next musician.

In places where the previous musician had a long tenure or left unhappily, healing of the choir(s) and congregation was needed. Maintaining or refining the quality of the previous music program, engaging the people, working with and supporting the clergy were high on my list of goals and time allotments. Frustrating, though, was the lack of information that would help me in effective and efficient planning. Records of music selections for choir and congregation, which would inform choices for the future, were not recorded. Choral and instrumental libraries needed organization, recording on the computer, removal and destruction of illegally reproduced music.

In one church, some members of the church were so unhappy about the untimely departure of the previous musician that they sabotaged the choral library, leaving music in more than several hiding places and destroying the only hard copy record of anthems in the library. Knowing the frustration of not knowing what exists in a church's choral library compels me to leave a choral library in the best shape possible.

In some of the interim positions I developed a customary for the next musician, including specifics of the budget, annual report, choir rosters, concert series, instruments and maintenance information, funeral and wedding customs and information, area instrumentalists and substitute organists, details for special services, to mention some of the categories.

I did this work, frankly, because I would greatly appreciate entering a new relationship with a congregation, knowing that a collected history, a clean choir room and office, a recorded and organized music library, and welcoming and happy people were there to greet me. The customary is a tremendously helpful tool, not only for music and liturgical planning now and in the future, but eventually for a new music leader.

Recommended
Resources FOR CHAPTER EIGHT

- Black, Vicki K. *Welcome to the Book of Common Prayer.* Chapter 5, "Marking the Seasons: The Church Year," p. 79–92. Harrisburg, PA: Morehouse Publishing, 2005.

- _____. *Welcome to the Church Year: An Introduction to the Seasons of the Episcopal Church.* Harrisburg, PA: Morehouse Publishing, 2004.

- Giles, Richard. *Times and Seasons: Creating Transformative Worship throughout the Year.* New York: Church Publishing, 2008.

- Haskel, Marilyn L. and Clayton L. Morris. *As We Gather to Pray: An Episcopal Guide to Worship.* New York: The Church Hymnal Corporation, 1996.

"How to Form a Parish Worship Committee," p. 103, Juan Oliver.

"How to Review and Evaluate a Congregation's Worship Program," p. 109, Joseph Robinson.

"How to Plan Worship," p. 117, Juan Oliver.

"How to Design Service Leaflets Which Are Helpful to the Newcomer," p. 128, Marilyn L. Haskel.

- McCollister, John C. *The Christian Book of Why*. New York: Jonathan David Publishers, Inc., 1983.

- Mitchell, Leonel L. *Lent, Holy Week, Easter and the Great Fifty Days*. Boston, MA: Cowley Publications, 1996.

- _____. *Planning the Church Year*. Harrisburg, PA: Morehouse Publishing, 1985.

- Porter, H. Boone, Jr *Keeping the Church Year*. New York: The Seabury Press, 1977.

- Post, W. Ellwood. Saints, Signs, and Symbols. Wilton, Connecticut: Morehouse-Barlow Company, 1974.

- Webber, Christopher L. *Welcome to Sunday: An Introduction to Worship in the Episcopal Church*. "The Christian Year," p. 41. Harrisburg, PA: Morehouse Publishing, 2003.

Three Appendices for use with this chapter may be found online at *www.churchpublishing.org/AllThingsNecessary*.

- *Church Websites*. A sampling of church websites from Regions 1-8 of the Episcopal Church that offer information about anthem selections, descriptions of the choirs, concert ideas, recordings, guidelines for wedding and funeral music and more.

- *Composers of Choral Music for the Church*. A partial list of composers of choral music from the sixteenth to twentieth centuries and a list of present-day composers.

- *Seek and You Will Find*. An extensive listing of topics with sources and information on choral music, alternate and emergent worship, contemporary music, liturgy and planning, organ and instruments, publishers and distributors of church music.

CHAPTER NINE

Coda

Bless the Lord, you angels of his,
you mighty ones who do his bidding,
and hearken to the voice of his word.
Bless the Lord, all you his hosts,
you ministers of his who do his will.
Bless the Lord, all you works of his,
in all places of his dominion;
bless the Lord, O my soul.
(Psalm 103:20–22)

I have had the privilege of serving in Methodist, Presbyterian, Baptist, Christian Science, Congregational/UCC churches with occasional stints in Lutheran, Roman Catholic, Unitarian, and Disciples of Christ congregations. I have worshiped with the Taizé Community in France and the Iona Community in Scotland, attended Greek Orthodox, Russian Orthodox, and Jewish services, and experienced emerging church and charismatic renewal services. I have attended services at St. Gregory of Nyssa in San Francisco, an extraordinary and eclectic worship experience that is way beyond the norm in an Episcopal Church and, for me, positively energizing. From every service, every experience, and from every denomination I learned much.

My extreme privilege, though, has been serving in the Episcopal Church most of my life and career, where I applied some of those observations and learnings and added to them a host of others through the most present, humbling, and honest teacher of all: on-the-job training.

This chapter is a miscellany of topics that simply do not fall into the categories of the previous chapters but that are worthy of note for those serving in Episcopal churches. They come from mistakes made and lessons learned. Without a doubt, more than music skills are needed to serve the church.

Questions to Ask Before a Service

Every parish has a manner of conducting the liturgy that may differ slightly from another. Clergy know the specific customs of their church and the organist needs to know those customs and accompanying cues to provide the best music leadership possible. Without understanding what is expected, there may be moments of awkward silence or the clash of a chord at the same time words are spoken. The musician should have a conversation with the clergy person well in advance of the service, not two minutes before the prelude begins when people are centering and preparing for worship.

- For a presider singing the service, what pitches need to be given on the organ or will the presider self-select his/her own pitches without organ?

- Is there anything extra happening in the service that indicates a change from the printed bulletin and for which a cue for the musician may be needed?

- Which clock is used for the official time? The clock on the organ console, a wall clock in the office or sacristy or vesting room, the secretary's computer clock, your cell phone, or the rector's watch, all of which could differ by seconds, if not minutes?

- Does the prelude end at the hour of the service, or is the prelude considered a part of the service and thus begins on the hour?

- What signal is used to indicate clergy and lay participants are ready for the procession? Signal light on the organ console, crucifer in place in the center aisle, hand wave from appointed person, or should the organist start the service on time, ready or not?

- If the hymns are not printed in the service leaflet, only numbers given, will they be announced or not? Often at large gatherings of people who are not all members of the church (primarily for weddings and funerals), hymn numbers may be announced to assist the people in the worship. In some parishes the hymn numbers are announced anyway, for those who get their information from listening rather than reading.

- In a Rite One service will the Ten Commandments (*BCP* 317) or the Summary of the Law (*BCP* 324), both optional, be used?

- In a Rite Two service will the optional Collect for Purity (*BCP* 355) be said?

• At the Lessons there is a "may" rubric regarding silence (*BCP* 326, 357). Is this observed? If so, for how long? In most parishes the reader finishes the text, immediately says, "The Word of the Lord" and the people respond by saying, "Thanks be to God." For many, when the congregational response is finished, that is the cue for the organist to begin the psalm or canticle or hymn or anthem. If the organist allows some space the congregation wonders if the organist has lost her/his place or is having a health crisis. Personally, I like the idea of the reader finishing, waiting a few seconds before looking at the congregation and saying "The Word of the Lord." In that way, the words of the text are still swirling in our heads, a good silence is held, and, as soon as the congregation has responded, the organist can continue the service.

• There is a rubric for mandatory silence at the Breaking of the Bread (*BCP* 337, 364). How much silence is desired? What is the cue for the fraction anthem—a count of seconds, the celebrant placing the elements on the table, after a genuflection?

• At the distribution of the elements at communion, does the choir receive first or last? Is the music to begin right away or after the clergy and lay people at the altar have received?

• Is communion music to come to an end as soon as the communion is finished, even if there are a couple verses left of the hymn?

• Is improvisational music to cover a specific action expected? In the Episcopal Church, improvisations are more likely to be heard when there are not enough hymn verses to complete the procession in or out, if communion music has ended and there is more time before the distribution is finished, if the offertory music has ended before the action, and if there is a hymn for the procession of the gifts. Ask, to be sure.

Job Interview and Audition

A book that should be required reading for clergy and church musicians is *Music and Vital Congregations: A Practical Guide for Clergy* by William Bradley Roberts. In "Hiring a Musician" (chapter eight, p. 101) you will read useful information for the rector and search committee, particularly regarding references, site visits, and the audition.

As a church musician, always remember that, in the Episcopal Church, the rector is ultimately responsible for choosing staff members, recommended and supported but not totally determined by committee as in some other denominations. In most parishes the rector invites people to serve on a search committee, usually comprised of a choir member or two, people knowledge-able and interested in music, a vestry person, someone who has been in the church a long time, someone who represents younger families, perhaps even a young person who served as a chorister in the church's choirs.

Consider the ways in which you can prepare yourself for a job interview and audition, especially in the Episcopal Church. Arrange your *curriculum vitae* carefully, so that a rector/search committee can clearly see where you studied, what churches you served, and what you have accomplished. Do check for spelling errors. I once saw a CV where the candidate spelled his own name incorrectly.

- You might consider including your philosophy of church music, which may be a sentence, or paragraph, or no more than a page in length. If you have never written such a philosophy, see if you can express your call to this ministry and your beliefs regarding the integral presence of music in the liturgy, for a start.

- Ask for church documents before arriving at the church for an interview. Service leaflets, the church's annual report, budget information, history of the music program and choir(s), outreach, educational opportunities for adults and children, mission statement, youth activities, and newslet-ter tell much about a church and provide questions for you.

- Consider what you might be asked in an interview long before that time begins:
  —Why are you leaving your present situation?
  —What interests you most in our church and music program?
  —If you have not served in an Episcopal Church before, what attracts you now?
  —What strengths would you bring to our church?
  —What accomplishments have brought you the most satisfaction so far?
  —As a church musician, what challenges have you overcome? What challenges do you struggle with now? Before responding, consider how your answers will affect the minds of the search committee.
  —Can you explain why you have held six positions in the past nine years? Actually, if you have to answer that one you may not have made the final cut.
  —What do you do for fun? What hobbies or sports do you enjoy? What music do you listen to when away from church?

- An interview is a two-way conversation. People are on their best behavior. Consider questions you might ask in your interview time alone with the rector and those reserved for the search committee.
  - —Listen carefully to the questions and respond. If you like to talk, go off on tangents, and take twenty minutes out of an hour-long interview to answer one question, then other important questions will not be asked nor critical answers given.
  - —Listen between the lines for not only what is said but what is not said. Follow body language and choice of words to hear what topics might not be on the table.
- Some questions you might ask the rector:
  - —Does the staff work well together? How many staff members have left in the past three years? What attracts them to stay? Why do they leave?
  - —Why did the previous musician leave? What kinds of things did your previous church musician do particularly well?
  - —How is liturgy planned here?
  - —Why am I of particular interest to you? What kinds of skills are you seeking for music leadership here? What do you see in me that makes you think we would be a good team in planning and leading liturgy and music here?
  - —If the rector has been at the church for five to eight years and has one or two positions left in him/her before retirement, ask how long the rector intends to stay. That may seem like a ridiculous question to ask, but often, when a new rector arrives, there are significant changes in the staff. You would not want to accept a position and then have to seek another one within a year or two.
  - —Does the musician have a liaison on the vestry to support music?
  - —Does the musician have a contract or letter of agreement? See a sample copy.
  - —Have you ever studied a musical instrument or sung in a choir?
  - —Express the need to keep your name and your application in strictest confidence with the rector and the search committee.
- Some questions for the search committee:
  - —Break the ice by asking each member of the search committee to tell you her/his favorite hymn and explain why in a sentence or two.
  - —What is the most recent new hymn, psalm, or service music setting the congregation has learned?

—What have been the strengths of past music programs and musicians?

—What has been the most upsetting event in the life of this congregation in the past five years? Ten years? How did the congregation cope? Did music provide support to the congregation at the time? How so?

—What areas of concern need to be addressed by this congregation?

• Tune up your personality. If you are painfully shy in front of a group of people, then psych yourself up to be a bit of an extrovert, albeit an honest one. If you have a cynical personality and express yourself with sarcasm or negativity, that will show; but then one wonders how well that type of personality would work with volunteer choir members.

• Mind your manners. If you are invited to the home of a search committee member for a meal with the committee, take a bottle of wine or flowers to the host/hostess and send a thank-you note afterwards. Look people in the eyes when you talk to them or shake hands. If you have trouble remembering names, repeat the name right after you are introduced. Meet everybody on the committee, not just those who surround you and want to tell you about their experiences in music. After the interview, thank the rector and follow through with a written letter of thanks. Thank the search committee for their time. Thank the choir for their responsiveness and singing in the rehearsal.

• Give careful consideration to the audition.

—You will be asked to perform at the organ, if that is the position for which you are applying. Make sure the church has planned for you to have at least three to four hours of uninterrupted practice time in the schedule for your audition/interview. Get to know the instrument and plan your repertoire accordingly. Show off the instrument as well as your skill. I have heard organists play one or two lengthy and technically impressive pieces on basically the same registrations, which left the search committee wondering if the candidate explored fully the colors of the instrument. One of the most impressive auditions I heard was a journey through the church year, performing a short chorale setting or selection on Advent, Christmas, Epiphany, Lent, Holy Week, Easter Day, Ascension, Pentecost, and All Saints' Day, all of which allowed for a great variety of styles, technical expertise, registration colors, and full range of sound on the organ. The candidate had written program notes and talked briefly at the beginning and midway through the program; the committee appreciated hearing the candidate's comments and the interplay at a time of concentration and performance.

—You should be asked and prepared to play hymns, a psalm setting, or a selection of service music with the search committee functioning as the congregation; you might be asked to sight-read a choral anthem.

—If you are auditioning as director of the choir, you should be asked to work with the choir for an hour or so. Choose a couple anthems from their music library and bring at least one they might not know. The committee will be looking at how you warm-up the voices, teach the anthems, produce the desired sound, and how the choir responds to your direction and your personality. Choir members may actually have an opportunity to complete a simple survey for consideration by the committee.

A Team: Musicians and Clergy

A service can include acolytes, lectors, ushers, eucharistic ministers, assisting clergy, deacons, seminarians, and choir in public view of the congregation. But the two people who have invested the majority of planning time and energy and contribute most to the flow of the liturgy are the rector and the music leader. If there are negative vibes in the air, the congregation will know and react. If there is an atmosphere of trust and respect, and joy in serving, then the congregation will sense that and respond in kind.

There are musicians who could tell stories of distress, distrust, and dismal interactions with clergy. The clergy could probably equal those tales. The rapport between rector and church musician does not have to fail. "There is every reason for relationships between clergy and musicians to be healthy, productive, and enjoyable. Intentionality, clarity, trust, honesty, humor, and, above all, God's good grace will make it so."[62]

Too often a congregation expects the rector to be a superb preacher, compassionate pastor, skillful administrator, trustworthy leader, terrific with people of all ages, outstanding at fund-raising, and a true visionary. Too often a congregation expects the musician to be an awe-inspiring organist or pianist, accomplished choir director, proficient at improvisation, exceptional

---

62. Source: *Music and Vital Congregations: A Practical Guide for Clergy.* Chapter 3: "Clergy-Musician Relationships," p. 43. William Bradley Roberts. New York: Church Publishing, 2009.

at teaching children, fabulous with people, incredibly pastoral, and highly organized. Pedestals are made of glass and simply not of this earth.

The truth is that we cannot possibly meet the unrealistic expectations of a congregation for us, nor those a rector and church musician might have for one another. Perfection is beyond us. We are human beings and we make mistakes. We have feelings that we allow to be hurt. And we have a tendency to blame others instead of accepting responsibility for our actions or inactions. If we can put aside our egos and personal needs, take the blinders of our professions off and be open to one another and to the call that brought us together, then there is hope that we—clergy and musicians—can truly work as a team, invest in the congregation, and serve as beacons of light for the God we all love.

- Pray for each other and have compassion.

- Talk to each other, not about each other.

- Listen with your heart, not with a mind ready to interject.

- Laugh often, just not at each other.

- Take a walk, share dreams and expectations.

- Be honest and maintain your integrity.

- Be flexible, willing to compromise.

- Stay positive, even in adversity.

- Try not to over-interpret or misinterpret, resulting in assumptions.

- Respond rather than react.

- Feel free to say: "I'd like to think about that. May I get back to you in a little while?"

- Find church music or liturgical events you can attend together.

- Praise when praise is due.

- Say *thank you* when you can.

Spiritual Attentiveness

When I was in high school I played in a Baptist church about fifteen miles from my home. My father drove me there and back for rehearsals and services each week. One Sunday we got home and found several men from the Methodist church in the village, the one I grew up in, waiting to ask my father, not me, if I would leave the Baptist church and be the organist in their church. Seems the organist had decided to retire. And, in their minds after all, as my membership was in the church, therefore I belonged to them. "Well," my father started. "How much are you willing to pay her?" "Well, God gave her talent and we gave her a start, so she should play the organ for free." My father replied: "Well, God doesn't pay for her organ lessons or the music she has to buy or the gas money she pays me to take her back and forth or even the amount of time she practices. So until He does, she's staying with the Baptists."

That was my first taste of the hypocrisy that can exist in the church. Another lesson was that the more you give, the more the church will ask of you. And the more you give, the more easily you will become exhausted, consumed by the details of your job, feel the pressure of deadlines and weekly performance goals, lose the balance of what needs to be done and what has to be done, and enter a state of burnout. You may not recover. You may even want to change jobs to start over. But if you do not make changes in yourself and how you respond to others, you will achieve the same state, again and again.

How can we prevent the slide into long-term exhaustion, which results in disinterest, depression, inappropriate anger, feelings of being out of control, and mental, spiritual, and possibly physical pain?

An unknown author, although attributed to Buddhism, said: "Religion is for those who are afraid of going to hell. Spirituality is for those who have already been there."

In the realm of religion and faith, music leaders and clergy make worship happen for other people on a Sunday morning and often are unable to have a deep and nourishing experience themselves. If that is the case for you, then find some source outside of your workplace that will feed you where you most need to be fed.

Spiritual attentiveness is a powerful balm for the weary soul.

• Honor yourself. You are worthy.

• See the extraordinary in the ordinary.

• Breathe. Inhale deeply, exhale long. Think about nothing except breathing.

• Set boundaries—how much time you are willing to work; what tasks you are willing to do; what day you will take off and how you will honor doing so.

- Consult your inner being for those things in your life that are life-giving and those that are life-draining; wake up and do something about what you have discovered.

- Meditate or find a yoga class.

- Let go of those things over which you have no control.

- Go on a retreat; spend a day in the mountains or by a body of water. Be quiet and go deep within yourself.

- Find a spiritual director or companion, one who will give you a verbal kick in the pants when you need one.

- Be creative outside of music—paint, quilt, write, photograph, dance wildly with no one around and to only the music in your heart.

- Pray without prayer book texts. If no words come, be assured that God knows the words in your heart.

- Give thanks for the sights, sounds, happenings, and people God puts in your path. Find friends and your primary relationships outside your workplace.

Recommended
Resources FOR CHAPTER NINE

- Roberts, William Bradley. *Music and Vital Congregations: A Practical Guide for Clergy.* New York: Church Publishing, 2009.

    —"Clergy-Musician Relationships," Chapter Three, p. 31.
    —"Music for Funerals and Weddings," Chapter Six, p. 75.
    —"Music and Money," Chapter Seven, p. 87.
    —"Hiring a Musician," Chapter Eight, p. 101.

Gracious God,
Source of our being, Creator of our song:
You are present in word and sacrament, people and place;
inspire us to lead
with melody and rhythm, harmony and praise.
You endow us with talents;
empower us to use them.
You direct all our ways;
challenge us to a life of service in your name.
Let the light of your love and grace pour through us
that you may be glorified by all your children.
Sanctify our works;
make us more holy for you.

Amen.

Terms and Definitions —
An Episcopal Perspective

Church Structure and Government

815—A reference to the Episcopal Church Center, offices of the Episcopal Church located at 815 Second Avenue, New York City, NY 10017.

ACNA—The Anglican Church in North America; a Christian denomination in the Anglican tradition formed by jurisdictions opposed to the election and consecration of an openly gay bishop in the Episcopal Church; developed out of a group of conservative Anglican churches founded in 2004; the ACNA is distinct from the Episcopal Church and the Anglican Church of Canada and is in full communion with the Anglican churches of Nigeria and Uganda.

Anglican—Refers to the English roots of the Episcopal Church; represents a body of Christians distinct from Roman Catholic, Protestant, or Orthodox traditions with historical connections to the beliefs and worship practices of the Church of England.

Anglican Communion—A world-wide assembly of 44 regional and national churches, including the Episcopal Church, in over 160 countries, 34 provinces, 4 United Churches, 6 other churches, consisting of an estimated 80 million Christians.

Apostolic Succession—Doctrine that the authority and mission given by Jesus to the apostles have descended in a direct and unbroken line of bishops to the bishops of today.

Archbishop of Canterbury—The leader of the Church of England and the Anglican Communion.

Canon—Written rules that guide the governing of the church; canons are adopted by Convention, Diocesan or General.

Church—From the Latin word *ecclesia*, which means "a gathering"; church is the place where the people worship, as well as the people themselves.

Church of England—The historically established Christian church in England.

Convention, Diocesan—A gathering of the bishop(s), clergy, and lay delegates of the diocese to worship together and conduct the business of the diocese.

Convention, General—A gathering of the national Episcopal Church, held every three years, attended by appointed or elected deputies from each diocese (House of Deputies) and all the bishops of the church (House of Bishops), at which decisions and rules are made for the governing of the church.

Diocese—A geographical area that includes churches and missions, a unity of administrative authority under the spiritual direction of a bishop.

ECUSA—The Episcopal Church in the United States of America.

Episcopal—Pertaining to a bishop; from Greek word *episcopos*, meaning *bishop* or *overseer*; church organization or government with bishops as overseers. We are Episcopalians because we have bishops.

Episcopate—Office of a bishop; period of time during which a bishop holds the office.

Full Communion—A relationship between distinct churches in which each recognizes the other as a catholic and apostolic church holding the essentials of Christian faith. The Episcopal Church became full communion partners with the Evangelical Lutheran Church in 2000, the Moravian Church in 2009.

House of Bishops—A legislative and judiciary body made up of all the bishops of the Episcopal Church.

House of Deputies—A legislative body of lay members and clergy, elected or appointed to the General Convention.

Lambeth Conference—A meeting of the bishops of all churches within the Anglican Communion, held every ten years, usually at Lambeth Palace in London, chaired by the Archbishop of Canterbury.

Mission Church—A congregation, usually small, sponsored by a parish or diocese until they reach self-supporting status.

Province—A geographical unit of several dioceses. **Province I**: Connecticut, Maine, Massachusetts, New Hampshire, Rhode Island, Vermont, Western Massachusetts. **Province II**: Albany, Churches in Europe, Central New York, Haiti, Long Island, New Jersey, New York, Newark, Rochester, Virgin Islands, Western New York. **Province III**: Bethlehem, Central Pennsylvania, Delaware, Easton, Maryland, Pennsylvania, Pittsburgh, Southern Virginia, Southwestern Virginia, Virginia, Washington, West Virginia. **Province IV**: Alabama, Atlanta, Central Florida, Central Gulf Coast, East Carolina, East Tennessee, Florida, Georgia, Kentucky, Lexington, Louisiana, Mississippi, North Carolina, South Carolina, Southeast Florida, Southwest Florida, Tennessee, Upper South Carolina, West Tennessee, Western North Carolina. **Province V**: Chicago, Eastern Michigan, Eau Claire, Fond Du Lac, Indianapolis, Michigan, Milwaukee, Missouri, Northern Indiana, Northern Michigan, Ohio, Quincy, Southern Ohio, Springfield, Western Michigan. **Province VI**: Colorado, Iowa, Minnesota, Montana, Nebraska, North Dakota, South Dakota, Wyoming. **Province VII**: Arkansas, Dallas, Fort Worth, Kansas, Northwest Oklahoma, Rio Grande, Texas, West Missouri, West Texas, Western Kansas, Western Louisiana. **Province VIII**: Alaska, Arizona, California, Eastern Oregon, El Camino Real, Hawaii, Idaho, Los Angeles, Navajo Land Area, Nevada, Northern California, Olympia, Oregon, San Diego, San Joaquin, Spokane, Taiwan, Utah. **Province IX**: Colombia, Dominican Republic, Ecuador Central, Ecuador Litoral, Honduras, Puerto Rico, Venezuela.

Seminary—Institution of higher learning that offers instruction leading to the Master of Divinity (M. Div.) degree necessary for ordination. Eleven seminaries are affiliated with the Episcopal Church: Berkeley Divinity School at Yale (New Haven, CT), Bexley Hall (Columbus, OH), The Church Divinity School of the Pacific (Berkeley, CA), Episcopal Theological Seminary of the Southwest (Austin, TX), The General Theological Seminary (New York City, NY), Nashotah House (Nashotah, WI), Seabury-Western Theological Seminary (Chicago IL), School of Theology at The University of the South (Sewanee, TN), Trinity Episcopal School for Ministry (Ambridge, PA), Virginia Theological Seminary (Alexandria, VA).

Standing Committee—A group of elected people, ordained and lay, who serve the bishop in an advisory role.

Clergy and Lay Participants

Acolyte—Lay person who performs ceremonial duties in the liturgy, such as light candles, carry a torch or candle, cross or crucifix in procession, hold the Gospel Book, assist during the setting up and cleaning up of the altar before and after communion, hand alms basins to ushers, receive gifts of alms, bread, and wine at the offertory, carry or swing incense.

Archbishop—Title given to bishops in the Anglican Communion who oversee a specific national church or cluster of dioceses; this title is not used in the Episcopal Church.

Assisting Ministers—Priests, deacons, and lay people who assist the presider at Holy Eucharist.

Bishop—One of the three orders of ordained ministers in the church, the others being priest and deacon; bishops are given authority over leading and uniting the church, administrative matters, and the spiritual leadership of the diocese. Bishops are addressed as The Right Reverend (abbreviated in writing as Rt. Rev.)

Bishop Coadjutor—A bishop elected to succeed the diocesan bishop when the diocesan bishop resigns or retires; at that time the word coadjutor is omitted from the title.

Bishop, Diocesan—The bishop of the diocese; the Ordinary of the diocese.

Bishop, Suffragan—An assistant bishop, elected to serve under the direction of the diocesan bishop, not permitted to succeed the diocesan bishop without an election.

Canon—A member of the clergy who serves on the staff of a bishop or a cathedral.

Canon Precentor—A clergy person in a cathedral or collegiate chapel, primarily responsible for preparing worship services.

Canon to the Ordinary—A canon or staff officer who is assigned tasks by the diocesan bishop, also known as the Ordinary.

Cantor—A person who leads congregational song with a singing voice; occasionally a title given to the leader of liturgical music in the church.

Catechumen—One receiving instruction in the principles of the religion in preparation for baptism.

Celebrant—The priest or bishop who officiates at the eucharist and other sacraments; see *Presider*.

Chalice Bearer—A lay person, licensed by the diocese, who administers the chalice/serves the wine at the Eucharist.

Choir—A group of singers who rehearse, support congregational singing, offer special music, and participate musically in the liturgies and sacraments of the church.

Choir Director—Conductor of the choir; the one who teaches music fundamentals, develops choral sound, prepares the choir for worship services, and encourages the choir to strive for goodness in singing and commitment to serve God through music.

Clergy—The ordained ministers of the church, as distinguished from lay people.

Communicant—Indicates a baptized or confirmed member, one who attends church regularly and receives communion, is on the church membership roster, contributes financially to the support of the church.

Concelebrant—A priest or bishop who celebrates the eucharist with the celebrant.

Congregation—The people of a parish or mission who worship together.

Crucifer—A person who carries the cross in procession.

Deacon—One of the three offices to which people can be ordained; deacons are called to a ministry of service under the direction of the bishop; a deacon reads the Gospel, leads prayers in some churches, sets the table at the offertory, assists in the distribution of communion, performs the ablutions, and dismisses the people; addressed as The Reverend.

Deacon, Transitional—A deacon who is on track to be ordained to the priesthood.

Deacon, Vocational—A permanent deacon; called to care for the needy outside the church and to bring this need to the attention of the congregation.

Dean—1) The principal clergy person in a cathedral; 2) the leader of a seminary; 3) the designated clergy person appointed or elected to lead the clergy of a region within the diocese; a dean is addressed as The Very Reverend.

Diaconate—A ministry of ordained servanthood as a permanent deacon in the church.

Domestic and Foreign Missionary Society of the Protestant Episcopal Church in the United States of America—full and legal name of the national Episcopal Church.

Episcopal Church Women (ECW)—A national organization for the ministry of women in the Episcopal Church with chapters in parishes and dioceses and a triennial convention.

Episcopalian—A member of or one who worships in the Episcopal Church.

Epistoler—Lay person who reads the Epistle in the worship service.

Gospeller—The deacon or priest who reads the Gospel in the worship service.

Interim Priest/Pastor—A priest who serves a congregation during a search for the next rector.

Laity—Non-ordained members of the church.

Lay—The people, from the Greek *laos* meaning "people of God."

Lay Ministers—Those who serve the church in specific areas of leadership and responsibility; all people, ordained to ministry at baptism, called to serve God and each other in Christ.

Lay Person—A non-ordained person.

Lay Reader—A non-ordained person who reads a lesson or part of a church service; a lay reader may lead the Daily Offices of the church, the Holy Eucharist liturgy through the Prayers of the People, the Burial Office, and portions of the Holy Week liturgies, all with some modifications in the services.

Lector—A person, lay or ordained, who reads a lesson from the lectionary, usually at a lectern.

Marshal—A designated person who organizes processions and seatings for special services.

Master of Ceremonies—A designated person, lay or ordained, who directs the ceremonial aspects of the liturgy, prompting acolytes, servers, readers, ushers, clergy to do their jobs at the appropriate times.

Ministers—All the people of the church: lay persons, bishops, priests, and deacons.

Officiant—A lay or ordained leader in the Daily Offices and other rites.

Ordinary of a Diocese—A diocesan bishop; the term is derived from the understanding of ordinary jurisdiction, which under canon law is determined to be the authority permanently and irremovably annexed to the office of bishop.

Organist—One who leads congregational song from the organ, accompanies the liturgy and the choir, offers opening and closing voluntaries.

Parish—A local gathering of worshipers within the diocese, self-supporting and governed by a vestry of elected lay members; synonymous with *congregation*.

Parishioner—A member of the parish or church.

Postulant—A person who has received support from the rector, vestry, and committee of the home parish, successfully completed physical and psychological exams, met with the diocesan commission on ministry, and been approved by the bishop to continue educational training toward ordination to the diaconate or priesthood

Preacher—One who gives the sermon or homily during the liturgy of the word in a service of Holy Eucharist and other sacramental services.

Precentor—From the Latin, "the one who sings before"; a person who helps facilitate worship planning and services, often the director of music in a cathedral or collegiate church.

Presider—The priest or bishop who officiates at the Eucharist and other sacraments; see *Celebrant*.

Presiding Bishop—The elected spiritual and administrative leader of the Episcopal Church in the United States of America.

Priest—Ordained minister in the church; addressed as The Rev.

Primate—The principal bishop in an Anglican province; in the Episcopal Church, the presiding bishop serves as chief pastor and primate.

Reader—One who reads a lesson (except for the Gospel), psalm, or prayer in the liturgy.

Rector—The chief priest of a parish, elected by the vestry after a search process and approved by the bishop.

Sacristan—A person in charge of altar vessels, linens, supplies, and actions that take place in the sacristy.

Seminarian—A student in a seminary or school of theology.

Server—One who assists at the altar, an acolyte.

Thurifer—The acolyte or server who carries and swings the thurible with incense.

Verger—A lay person who assists with the organizing and leading of processions and ceremonial duties; often carries a mace or wand or ceremonial staff in procession.

Vestry—The rector and elected members of the congregation, the governing group of a parish, responsible for hiring the rector, managing finances, deciding policy, and maintaining the buildings and grounds.

Vicar—A priest in charge of a mission, appointed by the bishop; becomes rector when the mission achieves parish status; has same responsibilities as a rector but not tenure.

Warden, Senior and Junior—Vestry members, elected by the vestry or appointed by the rector to positions of leadership, speaking for the parish, assisting the rector, providing care for buildings and property; in some churches they are known as the rector's warden (senior) and the people's warden (junior).

The Book of Common Prayer and Liturgical Terms

1928 Book of Common Prayer—The Episcopal prayer book used from 1928 to 1979; some services from the 1928 prayer book were retained as Rite One in *The Book of Common Prayer* (1979).

Aaronic Blessing—A prayer of blessing at the committal in the Burial of the Dead (*BCP*, p. 485 and p. 501) and optional blessing at the close of

An Order of Worship for the Evening (*BCP*, p. 114). The text is based on Numbers 6:24–26: "The Lord bless you and keep you; the Lord make his face to shine upon you, and be gracious to you; the Lord lift up his countenance upon you, and give you peace."

Ablutions—Ritual cleaning of the paten (or bread tray) and chalice after all have received the elements during the Eucharist; may take place at the altar, credence table, or in sacristy, before the postcommunion prayer or after the dismissal.

Absolution—Pronouncement of God's forgiveness after the Confession of Sin (*BCP*, pp. 332, 353, and 360), Daily Offices (*BCP*, pp. 42, 63, 80, 117, and 128), at Reconciliation of a Penitent (*BCP*, p. 448).

Acclamation—Versicle and response at the beginning of the service of Holy Eucharist (*BCP*, pp. 323 and 355).

Agnus Dei—"Lamb of God" in Latin; anthem sung or said after the breaking of the bread (*BCP*, p. 337).

Alleluia—"Praise God" in Hebrew; used before and after the words "Christ our Passover is sacrificed for us; Therefore let us keep the feast." (*BCP*, pp. 337 and 364). *Alleluia* is completely omitted during Lent, then included in Easter Acclamation (*BCP*, pp. 323 and 355) and after the dismissal from Easter Vigil through the Day of Pentecost.

Alleluia Verse—A Biblical text including the *Alleluia*, sung or said before the reading of the Gospel, except in Lent.

Alms—Money offering of the people for the work of the church; other offerings may be made.

Amen—"It is so" or "I agree" or "So be it" from the Hebrew, said or sung by the people after prayers that have been offered for them.

Antecommunion—Liturgy of the Word, first half of the service of Holy Eucharist, that which comes before the communion.

Anthems at the Burial Office—The words that are sung or said at the beginning of The Burial of the Dead (*BCP*, pp. 469 and 491).

Anthem at the Fraction—The words that are sung or said at the breaking of the bread (*BCP*, pp. 337 and 364).

Antiphon—Scriptural or traditional text sung or said before and after the Psalms in the Daily Offices (*BCP*, pp. 43–44, 80–81).

Apostles' Creed—Ancient summary of the faith, used in Daily Offices of Morning Prayer and Evening Prayer (*BCP*, pp. 53–54, 66, 96, 120), Renewal of Baptism Vows in the Easter Vigil (*BCP*, p. 293) and Baptismal Covenant of Holy Baptism (*BCP*, p. 304).

Baptismal Covenant—Part of the service of Holy Baptism in which the congregation renews their own baptismal vows through the words of the Apostles' Creed and a series of questions and responses (see *BCP*, pp. 304–305).

Book of Common Prayer, The (1979)—The official prayer book of the Episcopal Church, referred to as *BCP*.

Burial of the Dead, The—A service to commemorate the deceased person(s); Rite One is found in *BCP*, pp. 469–489 and Rite Two is found in *BCP*, pp. 491–505.

Catechism—An outline of the faith, found in *BCP*, pp. 845–862.

Choral Eucharist—A service of Holy Eucharist in which the ordinary (*Kyrie eleison, Gloria, Credo, Sanctus, Agnus Dei*) and the propers (collect, lessons, variable proper preface) are sung.

Choral Matins—A service of Morning Prayer in which the preces, versicles and responses, invitatory, canticles, psalm, collects, and prayers are sung.

Collect—A short prayer offered by the presider or officiant; contains an invocation, a petition, and an intercessory conclusion. Traditional (Rite One) Collects are found in *BCP*, pp. 159–210; Contemporary (Rite Two) Collects are found in *BCP*, pp. 211–261.

Collect for Purity—Prayer that dates from the 1549 Book of Common Prayer, mandatory in Rite One and optional in Rite Two; suggestive of lines from Psalm 51; known as but not titled "Collect for Purity" in *BCP*; title inspired by text "Cleanse the thoughts of our hearts . . ." in *BCP*, p. 323.

Comfortable Words—One or more of four sentences of Scripture said by the minister after the confession and absolution in Holy Eucharist Rite One, *BCP*, p. 332.

Commendation—Concluding rite between the service of the Burial of the Dead in the church and the committal at the grave site; *BCP*, pp. 482 and 499.

Communion—Receiving the bread and wine during the service of Holy Eucharist.

Compline—Last of the daily monastic offices, said or sung just before bedtime; *BCP*, p. 127.

Confession of Sin—Prayer of penitence at the Daily Offices (*BCP*, pp. 41, 62, 79, 116, 331, 352, 360), at the Reconciliation of a Penitent (*BCP*, p. 447), Ministration to the Sick (*BCP*, p. 454).

Consecration—Solemn dedication to a holy purpose; action by which the bread and wine become for us the body and blood of Jesus Christ; rite in which church buildings and appointments are dedicated for the service of God; liturgy in which a priest becomes a bishop.

Creed, Apostles'—Affirmation of the faith of the church, historically used for baptismal instruction, outlining the faith of the apostles; *BCP*, pp. 53, 66, 96, 120.

Creed, Athanasian—First creed in which the equality of the Trinity is clearly stated, *BCP*, p. 864, Historical Documents.

Creed, Nicene—Statement of Christian faith dating from the fourth century; *BCP*, pp. 326–327, 358.

Daily Offices—From the eight daily monastic services established by Archbishop Cranmer; Morning Prayer (*BCP*, pp. 37–60, 75–102), An Order of Service for Noonday (*BCP*, pp. 103–107), An Order of Worship for the Evening (*BCP*, pp. 109–114), Daily Evening Prayer (*BCP*, pp. 61–73, 115–126), An Order for Compline (*BCP*, pp. 127–135).

Daily Office Lectionary—A two-year cycle of readings (*BCP*, pp. 934–1001), not RCL, which takes the reader through most of the Bible, repeating the Psalms every seven weeks; instructions for determining Year One or Year Two are found in *BCP*, p. 934.

Decalogue—The Ten Commandments with congregational responses; optional in Rite One in place of summary of the law (*BCP*, pp. 317–318, 324) or as part of A Penitential Order: Rite Two preceding the Eucharist (*BCP*, pp. 350–353).

Dismissal—Words sung or said by the deacon or presider at the end of service of Holy Eucharist, sending people out into the world. The congregation responds *Thanks be to God*; *BCP*, pp. 339–340, 366.

Distribution—The giving or sharing of bread and wine during the communion.

Divine Liturgy—See *Eucharist*.

Doxology—Praise to the Holy Trinity, found at the end of eucharistic prayers (*BCP*, pp. 336, 343, 363, 369, 375), after Psalms in the Daily Office, final verses of some hymns.

Elements—Bread and wine.

Entrance Rite—The first part of the Eucharist, at the beginning of the Liturgy of the Word; includes a hymn, psalm or anthem, opening acclamation, (Collect for Purity), the *Kyrie, Trisagion, Gloria* or other song of praise, and the Collect of the Day.

Epistle—One of the letters of the New Testament, the Acts of the Apostles, or the Book of Revelation; precedes the Gospel in the service of Holy Eucharist.

Eucharist—"Thanksgiving" in Greek; principal act of worship on Sundays and other feasts; refers to the Lord's Supper; also called Holy Communion, Communion, Holy Eucharist, Mass, Divine Liturgy.

Eucharistic Prayer—The Great Thanksgiving; the prayer beginning with the salutation (*Sursum Corda*), Proper Preface, and *Sanctus,* and concluding with the doxology and Amen. Rite One: Prayer I (pp.333–336), Rite One: Prayer II (pp. 340–343), Rite Two: Prayer A (pp. 361–363), Rite Two: Prayer B (pp. 367–369), Rite Two: Prayer C (369–372), Rite Two: Prayer D (pp. 372–375), An Order for Celebrating the Holy Eucharist: Form I (pp. 402–403) and Form II (pp. 404–405); EOW: Prayer 1 (pp. 57–59), Prayer 2 (pp. 60–62), Prayer 3 (pp. 62–65), Form A (pp. 65–67), Form B (pp. 67–68).

Eulogy—Homily or remembrances of the deceased, brief remarks spoken at a funeral service.

Evening Prayer—Second of two Daily Offices (*BCP*, pp. 61–73, 115–126).

Festal/Festival Eucharist—A service on feast day or festival of the church; characterized by joyful music and celebration.

Fraction—Breaking of the bread in the service of Holy Eucharist.

Funeral—A service for a deceased person at which the liturgy of The Burial of the Dead is read. See *BCP*, pp. 469–489, 491–505.

Gifts—Bread, wine, and alms presented to the presider at the offertory of the Eucharist.

Gloria in Excelsis (Deo)—"Glory to God in the highest" in Latin; sung or said at the beginning of the Eucharist following the acclamation and/or collect for purity; most appropriate from Christmas Day through Epiphany, days of Easter Week, Sundays from Easter Day through Day of Pentecost, Ascension Day, festive occasions; not appropriate during Advent or Lent; *BCP*, pp. 52, 94, 324, 356.

Gloria Patri—"Glory to the Father" in Latin; praise to the Trinity; sung or said after Psalms and canticles in the Daily Offices; see *Doxology*. Full text: "Glory to the Father, and to the Son, and to the Holy Spirit: As it was in the beginning, is now, and will be for ever. Amen."

Grace—The unearned action of God toward us for our benefit.

Gradual—A liturgical anthem between the first and second lesson; usually a chant setting of the appointed psalm, sung by all, or by choir or cantor with refrain sung by congregation; term comes from the Latin *gradus,* meaning *step,* on which the cantor stood when singing the Gradual; dates from the mid-fourth century.

Gradual Psalm—Psalm sung by choir or congregation after the lesson; sometimes called the Responsorial Psalm.

Great Amen—The people's Amen at the end of each Eucharistic Prayer, the only Amen in the *BCP* that is capitalized; *BCP*, pp. 336, 343, 363, 369, 372, 375; EOW, pp. 59, 62, 65, 67, 68.

Great Litany—Intercessory prayers in versicle and response style; originally written to be sung in procession, now appropriate to sing or say, standing, kneeling or in procession; often done on First Sunday of Advent, in Lent, other times in the church year, before the Eucharist or after collects of Morning or Evening Prayer; first English-language rite created by Archbishop Cranmer. *BCP*, p. 148; EOW, p. 46.

Great Thanksgiving—Major prayer of the Eucharist begins with salutation/ *sursum corda* and ends with the Lord's Prayer.

Holy Communion—Name for the Holy Eucharist, Mass, Lord's Supper, Liturgy of the Table, or Divine Liturgy; used specifically for the second part of the Eucharist service, following the Liturgy of the Word, beginning with the offertory.

Holy Eucharist—See *Eucharist*.

Homily—Sermon.

Installation—A service at which a consecrated bishop is inaugurated as the diocesan bishop, or a priest as rector; a service at which a person is recognized as the official bearer of an academic position.

Kyrie Eleison—"Lord, have mercy" in Greek; may be sung at the beginning of the Eucharist as a song of praise after the acclamation; particularly appropriate in the more penitential seasons of Advent and Lent.

Lectionary—Appointed lessons and psalms for use at the Daily Offices and Holy Eucharist.

Lessons—Old Testament and New Testament readings, excluding Gospel and Psalm; in Daily Offices read one or two lessons and a Psalm; the service of Holy Eucharist service lists two lessons, a Psalm, and a Gospel.

Litany—A form of prayer with petitions and congregational responses.

Liturgy—"Work of the people" from two Greek words; the texts, ritual, ceremonial, public prayer and worship of the people gathered.

Liturgy of the Table—Second part of the eucharistic service, from the offertory to the end of the service.

Liturgy of the Word—The Word of God, the first part of the Eucharist, includes the lessons, Psalm, Gospel, Sermon, Nicene Creed, Prayers of the People, Confession, Absolution, and Peace.

Lord's Supper, the—See *Holy Eucharist.*

Mass—See *Holy Eucharist.*

Memorial Acclamation—Congregational part in the Eucharistic Prayers of Rite Two, said after the words of institution: Prayer A, *BCP,* p. 363 (*Christ has died. Christ is risen. Christ will come again.*); Prayer B, *BCP,* p. 368 (*We remember his death, We proclaim his resurrection, We await his coming in glory*); Prayer C, *BCP,* p. 371 (*We celebrate his death and resurrection, as we await the day of his coming.*), Prayer D, *BCP,* p. 375 (*We praise you, we bless you, we give thanks to you, and we pray to you, Lord our God*).

Morning Prayer—First service of the Daily Office in the *BCP*; Rite One, *BCP,* pp 37–60; Rite Two, *BCP,* pp. 75–102.

Nicene Creed—Statement of faith used in many Christian churches; written in the fourth century as a means of uniting the Christian church under the emperor Constantine.

Noonday Prayer—Short title for An Order of Service for Noonday. See *BCP,* pp. 103-107.

Oblations—Offerings to God; bread and wine offered for consecration at the Eucharist; may include alms (money gifts); may be an offering of ourselves, our lives and labors, in union with Christ, for the purposes of God. See *BCP,* p. 857.

Offertory—Collection of alms (money and other gifts); representatives of congregation present alms and oblations (bread and wine) to celebrant presider for reception and preparation and offering of the gifts at the beginning of Holy Communion, second part of eucharistic service.

Offertory Procession—Movement of representatives of the congregation to present bread, wine, money, and other gifts to deacon or presider. See *BCP,* p. 333 and p. 361.

Offertory Sentence—Scriptural passage that may be said or sung before the offertory begins; *BCP,* pp. 343–344, 376–377.

Ordinary—Texts of Daily Offices or Holy Eucharist which remain the same or with only slight changes regardless of the day or liturgical season.

Peace, The—Greeting of one another in Eucharist service, after confession and absolution (*BCP,* pp. 332, 360); also known as *passing the peace*; ancient sacramental greeting of the faithful, a sign of love and union in Christ. Priest says, "The Peace of the Lord be always with you." Congregation responds, "And also with you."

Postcommunion Prayer—Prayer of Thanksgiving for the Eucharist and for the grace and support for our ministries; follows the receiving of bread and wine at Holy Communion; *BCP,* pp. 339, 365–366.

Prayer of Humble Access—Prayer from 1548 that follows the breaking of the bread and precedes the distribution of the elements; not included in Rite Two, optional in Rite One; not titled as Prayer of Humble Access, but begins "We do not presume to come to this thy Table, O merciful Lord . . ." *BCP*, p. 337.

Prayers of the People—Intercessory prayers with congregational responses or silence (*BCP*, pp. 383–393) or prayer for the whole state of Christ's Church and the world, offered by deacon or other appointed person (*BCP*, pp. 328–330).

Preces—from the Latin, meaning "prayer"; short petitions, said or sung, in versicle and response form, between officiant and congregation in the Daily Offices.

Preface—First part of the Great Thanksgiving, from salutation/*sursum corda* through the *sanctus*.

Propers—Collect, lessons, proper preface; variable texts appointed for the day.

Proper Preface—Portion of the Great Thanksgiving that follows the *sursum corda* and precedes the *sanctus*; appointed for Sundays, liturgical seasons, and special occasions; required in Rite One (Eucharistic Prayers I and II) and Rite Two (Eucharistic Prayers A and B); Eucharistic Prayers C and D do not include a Proper Preface. Assigned Proper Prefaces are indicated at the end of each collect appointed for the day or occasion. See "Collect" for page numbers. Texts of Proper Prefaces are on pp. 344–349 (Rite One) and pp. 377–381 (Rite Two) of the *BCP*.

Psalm—One of 150 poems from the Book of Psalms. The Psalter is in *BCP*, pp. 585–808.

Requiem—Also, Requiem Mass, Mass for the Dead, or Solemn Requiem Mass; a service of Holy Eucharist offered on behalf of a deceased person. The music may include these or some of these sections and in this order: Introit, *Kyrie eleison*, Gradual, Tract, Sequence, Offertory, *Sanctus, Agnus Dei*, Communion, *Pie Jesu, Libera Me, In paradisum*.

Responsorial Psalm—A Psalm between the first and second lesson in the eucharist; sung by a cantor with a refrain by choir or congregation.

Rite One—The eucharistic liturgy in traditional language.

Rite Two—The eucharistic liturgy in contemporary language.

Rubric—Meaning "red" in Latin; directions for the conduct of worship found in *The Book of Common Prayer*; italicized in services and offices; lists of additional directions are at the beginning or end of the rites; in previous prayer books rubrics were printed in red so they would stand out from the black ink used in the rites.

Salutation—See *Acclamation.*

Sermon—An address to the congregation, offered by priest, deacon, or lay person, usually based on biblical text from proper of the day and delivered from the pulpit or in front of the congregation.

Song of Praise—Canticle or hymn following the acclamation at the beginning of the Liturgy of the Word. See *BCP*, pp. 324, 356.

Suffrages—Set of petitions set in the form of versicle and response, found in Morning and Evening Prayer after the Lord's Prayer. See *BCP*, pp. 55, 67–68, 97–98, 121–122.

Summary of the Law—The two commandments that summarize the Ten Commandments; found on p. 324 of *The Book of Common Prayer.* "Hear what our Lord Jesus Christ saith: Thou shalt love the Lord thy God with all thy heart, and with all thy soul, and with all thy mind. This is the first and great commandment. And the second is like unto it: Thou shalt love thy neighbor as thyself. On these two commandments hang all the Law and the Prophets."

Sursum Corda—"Lift up your hearts" in Latin; versicle and response of the preface in the Eucharistic Prayers; *BCP*, pp. 333, 361.

Tenebrae—Special service in Holy Week, usually on Wednesday night (*BOS*, pp. 74–90).

Tract—Sentence of Scripture sung or said in place of Alleluia verse between Epistle and Gospel, especially in Lent.

Trisagion—"Thrice Holy" in Greek; may be sung or said as a song of praise in Liturgy of Word of Holy Eucharist; "Holy God, Holy and Mighty, Holy Immortal One, Have mercy upon us." *BCP*, pp. 324, 356.

Versicle and Response—Brief lines of Scripture, often from psalms, sung or said as a call-and-response interaction between officiant and congregation.

Vigil—Evening service of prayer, preceding a major feast day; Great Vigil of Easter (*BCP*, pp. 285–295), Vigil of Pentecost (*BCP*, p. 227), prior to a funeral (*BCP*, pp. 465–466); Book of Occasional Services provides vigils for Christmas Eve (*BOS*, p. 35), for Baptism of Our Lord (*BOS*, p. 51), All Saints' Day (*BOS*, p. 106), and for Baptism (*BOS*, p. 131).

Wedding—Celebration and Blessing of the Sacrament of Marriage. See *BCP*, pp. 423–432.

Words of Institution—Narrative in the Eucharistic Prayer recalling the words and actions of Jesus during the Last Supper.

Sacraments and Sacramentals

Sacraments are outward and visible signs of inward and spiritual grace, words
and actions that acknowledge the presence of God in our lives.

Holy Baptism—Sacrament of full initiation by water, sign of the cross, and
Holy Spirit into membership in the church, Christ's body.

Holy Eucharist—Reenactment of the Last Supper shared by Jesus and his
disciples before the crucifixion; bread and wine are the outward and visible signs; all baptized people are welcome to receive communion.

Confirmation—Rite in which a bishop "confirms" the baptismal vows made
by or on behalf of an individual, and strength is received from the Holy
Spirit through prayer and the laying on of hands.

Holy Matrimony—Christian marriage between two people who make vows
before God and church, exchange rings, enter a life-long union, and receive the grace and blessing of God.

Ordination—Rite in which God gives authority and the grace of the Holy
Spirit to those being made bishops, priests, and deacons, through prayer
and the laying on of hands.

Reconciliation of a Penitent—Rite in which a penitent person may confess
his/her sins to God in the presence of a priest and receive the assurance
of pardon and the grace of absolution.

Unction of the Sick—Rite of anointing the sick, or for the sick, with oil and
the sign of the cross or laying on of hands, by which God's grace is given
for the healing of spirit, mind, and body.

Liturgical Traditions and Customs

Bowing—An act of reverence toward the altar, reserved sacraments, processional cross; a slight nod of the head and shoulders constitutes a simple
bow, bending at the waist is a solemn bow.

Ceremonial—Term for how liturgical rites are performed, including choice
of vestments, movement, and interactions throughout the service.

Fasts, Fasting—Specified days of discipline and self-denial (Ash Wednesday,
Good Friday, other weekdays of Lent and Holy Week, Fridays during the
year, except for Christmas and Easter Seasons, and Ember Days).

Genuflection—Act of reverence that involves bending the knee, sometimes
to the floor, then standing; people may genuflect when entering or leaving their seats, before the reserved sacrament in the tabernacle or aumbry;

clergy may also genuflect during the Prayer of Consecration and after the Great Amen.

Gospel Procession—Movement of the Gospel Book to where the Gospel will be proclaimed, either in the midst of the congregation, or to the lectern or pulpit, by the reader of the Gospel, deacon or priest; may be accompanied by processional cross, holder of book, candles/torches, incense.

High Church—In the early Episcopal Church, the high church stressed the historic episcopate, faithful use of the prayer book, sacraments of baptism and Eucharist, ministry, and sacraments as primary means of grace. High church also indicates a style of worship in which the presider sings or chants, rather than speaks, portions of the service not sung by the congregation; incense and/or sanctus bells may be used.

Intercessions—Prayers of petition on behalf of others and for the needs of the world.

Intinction—The manner of receiving communion by taking the bread or wafer and dipping it into the chalice of wine.

Kneeling—A posture indicating penitence or reverence, at times of personal and community prayers, Eucharistic Prayer, confession and absolution, blessing.

Liturgy—From Greek words meaning "people" and "work"; the public worship of God and the work of the Christian people.

Low Church—Historically, the low church stressed the importance of evangelistic preaching, disliked ritual, and demoted the importance of the sacraments. Today a low church might be one that is less formal in style, in which there is an absence of chanting by the presider, any singing beyond hymns and service music sung by the congregation and choir, incense, or sanctus bells.

Orans Position—A posture for praying, with hands extended outward and palms lifted upward; ancient tradition, used by priests and bishops; more common among laity since time of charismatic renewal.

Procession—A movement of people into or out of the church or to a specific location within the church (baptismal font, Paschal candle, site of dedication); may include crucifer, torches, acolytes, clergy, choir, non-vested members of the congregation participating in the worship service, thurifer, banners, and liturgical kites.

Recession—A procession out of church at the end of a service to go into the world to love and serve the Lord; the words "procession out" are preferred by many, believing we should never recess from God.

Reverence—A genuflection, simple or solemn bow before the altar or reserved sacrament, an act of adoration and honor.

Sign of the Cross—A hand movement, symbolizing the cross, first the vertical line, then the horizontal; made on the forehead by priest or bishop at baptism, confirmation, anointing in healing services; made in the air by priest or bishop at the absolution, consecration of bread and wine, blessing; made by individuals (forehead, diaphragm, left shoulder, right shoulder) at personal prayer, with holy water at entrance to worship service, at announcement of Gospel, at absolution and blessing, as desired; individual may make sign of cross first on forehead, then lips, then heart at announcement of Gospel.

"Smells and Bells"—Casual description of a church that is considered *high*, that uses incense and sanctus bells.

Vestments

Alb—Long (neck to ankle), white or natural-colored vestment with sleeves, worn by presider and other ministers at the Eucharist; often gathered at the waist by a cincture (rope), may be worn with stole, under chasubles, dalmatics, tunicles, and copes, over cassock, or by itself.

Amice—Square or rectangular piece of material (white or natural-color), worn under the alb as a hood.

Biretta—A square hat with raised corners and a pompom sometimes worn by priests (black hat) or bishops (purple hat).

Cassock—A long (neck to ankle), black vestment worn over street clothes by those serving in the worship service (chalice bearers, vergers, acolytes, clergy, choir members).

Chasuble—An oval-shaped garment with an opening for the presider's head; a long, wide and sleeveless vestment worn over all other vestments at a service of Holy Eucharist.

Chimere—Red or black sleeveless vestment worn by Episcopal bishops over a white rochet and purple or black cassock.

Cincture—A rope, usually white, worn with cassock or alb, knotted at one side and allowed to hang; the presider may knot the cincture in the middle, form side loops, and pass the ends of the stole through the openings.

Collar—White, detachable shirt collar, worn by ordained persons; the collar has no particular religious meaning, only identifies members of the clergy.

Cope—A long cape, usually made in liturgical colors and designs to match other vestments or hangings, worn in procession.

Cotta—Short white vestment worn over cassocks by choir members and acolytes.

Crook—The bishop's staff, resembling a shepherd's staff; long pole with a C-curve on top; see *crozier*.

Crozier (Staff)—The bishop's staff, resembling a shepherd's staff; long pole with a C-curve on top; see *crook*.

Dalmatic—Tunic decorated with two strips of material that run vertically from front to back over the shoulders, connected in the front and back with two horizontal strips of material; vestment of deacons, but may be worn by priests.

Deacon's Stole—A strip of material worn like a sash over the left shoulder, and tied on the right side.

Episcopal Ring—Ring worn by a bishop.

Eucharistic Vestments—Stole and chasuble, worn over alb, amice, and cincture, or over cassock and alb by presider; stole may be worn under or over chasuble, depending on custom.

Miter or Mitre—Hat worn by a bishop in procession and when pronouncing Episcopal blessings.

Orphery—An embroidered band on an ecclesiastical vestment or hanging.

Pectoral Cross—A cross with chain, worn by a bishop.

Rabat—A shirt-front with attached clerical collar, which can be worn over another shirt and fastened around the waist.

Rochet—A white, ankle-length garment with wide sleeves, gathered deeply at the shoulders and wrists, worn by a bishop over his/her purple cassock and under the chimere.

Stole—A long strip of material, often with religious symbols and in liturgical colors, worn by deacons, priests, and bishops at the Eucharist or other sacramental functions.

Surplice—An ample white vestment with round or square neck, full sleeves not gathered at the wrists, at least mid-calf in length, longer and fuller than a cotta, worn over the cassock by clergy officiating at a Daily Office or assisting clergy at the Eucharist.

Tippet—Black scarf, wider than a stole, often bearing the seal of the Episcopal Church or seminary crest, worn by a priest officiating at the Daily Offices; never worn when the priest is celebrating the Eucharist.

Tunicle—Almost the same as dalmatic, except the tunicle has one more horizontal stripe.

Liturgical Year

Advent—The first season of the liturgical year, includes the four Sundays before Christmas Day; liturgical colors are purple or blue (Sarum).

All Saints' Day—November 1, the day the church remembers the whole communion of saints; may be observed on the Sunday following November 1; liturgical color is white.

All Souls' Day—November 2, the day on which all the faithful departed are remembered; liturgical color is green.

Ascension Day—Thursday, forty days after Easter Day, ending the post-resurrection appearances of Jesus, marking Christ's ascension into heaven; liturgical color is white.

Ash Wednesday—Wednesday, forty-six days before Easter Day (forty days excluding Sundays); marks the beginning of Lent; ashes made from the previous Palm Sunday's palms are placed on worshipers' foreheads in the sign of the cross; liturgical color is purple.

Baptism of our Lord—Observed on the First Sunday after the Epiphany; liturgical color is white.

Candlemas—February 2, also known as the Presentation of Our Lord in the Temple; liturgical color is white.

Christ the King—Last Sunday after Pentecost, observes the authority of Christ over all; marks the end of the liturgical year before beginning another on the next Sunday, First Sunday of Advent; liturgical color is white.

Christmas—The Nativity of our Lord, celebrated on December 25; the Season of Christmas ends on January 6, the Feast of the Epiphany, thus marking the twelve days of Christmas; liturgical color is white.

Easter Day—Sunday of the Resurrection, the pinnacle and conclusion of Holy Week; liturgical color is white.

Easter Eve (Great Vigil of Easter)—Observed between sunset on Easter Eve and sunrise on Easter Day, consisting of lighting of Paschal flame, singing of the *Exsultet*, Old Testament lessons recounting God's saving deeds in history, baptism and renewal of baptismal vows, and the first Eucharist of Easter; liturgical color is white.

Easter Season—The Easter Season begins at sundown the evening before Easter Day and goes until the Day of Pentecost. The season, also known as Eastertide or the Great Fifty Days, includes six Sundays in addition to Easter Day; liturgical color is white.

Ember Days—Four separate sets of three days within the same week (Wednesday, Friday, Saturday), set aside for fasting and prayer; they occur before the Fourth Sunday of Advent, after the First Sunday in Lent, the weeks after Pentecost Day and Holy Cross Day (September 14); occur within the seasons and have no singular liturgical color.

Epiphany—January 6, Feast of the Manifestation of Our Lord Jesus Christ to the gentiles; liturgical color is white.

Feasts—Days of celebration: movable feasts are Easter and Pentecost, immovable feasts are Christmas, Epiphany, All Saint's Day, days honoring saints, and days of thanksgiving.

Fifty Days of Easter, The—From the Great Vigil of Easter through the Day of Pentecost, observing the appearances of the risen Christ to the disciples; includes Ascension Day; liturgical color is white.

Good Friday—Friday before Easter Day, on which the crucifixion of Jesus is observed with special devotion and without Eucharist; the liturgical color is red or black.

Holy Week—The week before Easter Day; liturgical color is red.

Lent—A period of forty weekdays and six Sundays from Ash Wednesday to Palm Sunday; a time of self-denial, preparations for Holy Week and Easter Day; liturgical colors are purple or the neutral color of unbleached muslin. Sundays are *in* Lent, not *of* Lent, as each Sunday includes the resurrection story of Easter.

Maundy Thursday—Thursday of Holy Week, commemorates the institution of the Lord's Supper and the washing of the disciples' feet; from the Latin *mandatum* meaning "new commandment" and referring to the great commandment "Love one another as I have loved you." The solemn stripping of the altar takes place at the end of the Maundy Thursday service; liturgical color is red.

Palm Sunday—Sunday before Easter, Sunday of the Passion, last Sunday in Lent and the beginning of Holy Week; a two-part liturgy marking the triumphal entry of Jesus into Jerusalem with the waving of palms and the passion of Jesus with the reading of the Gospel; liturgical color is red.

Patronal Feast—A day or occasion on which a congregation honors the one who was chosen as the patron saint, or namesake, of the parish.

Pentecost, Day of—The end of the Great Fifty Days of Easter and the celebration of the presence of the Holy Spirit bestowed upon the disciples; considered the birthday of the church; liturgical color is red.

Pentecost, Season of—Sundays and weekdays from the Day of Pentecost until the day before the First Sunday of Advent; liturgical color is green.

Rogation Days—Monday, Tuesday, and Wednesday after the Sixth Sunday of Easter, the three days before Ascension Day; originally designated to pray for a good harvest in a more agrarian society; now includes prayers for stewardship of creation, for commerce and industry; liturgical color is white.

Shrove Tuesday—Not an official observance in *The Book of Common Prayer*, day before Ash Wednesday, time for confession and absolution before the beginning of Lent; historically, a time when the faithful were forbidden by the church to eat eggs, milk, or butter so, with the addition of some flour, those stores of foods were eaten in the form of pancakes before the discipline of Lent began.

Transfiguration—An event recorded in Matthew, Mark, and Luke in which Jesus became radiant, was called *Son* by the voice of God, and spoke with Moses and Elijah; the Transfiguration is observed on August 6 and the Gospel story is also read on the Last Sunday after the Epiphany in all three years of the Revised Common Lectionary; liturgical color is white.

Triduum—Three days, beginning on the evening of Maundy Thursday, continuing through Good Friday, Holy Saturday, and Easter Vigil.

Music Terms

A cappella—From Italian, "in the manner of the church"; solo or group singing without accompaniment.

Ambrosian Chant—Plainchant repertory of the Ambrosian rite of the Roman Catholic Church, named after St. Ambrose; similar but distinct from Gregorian chant, named for Gregory the Great; Ambrosian chant and Gregorian chant are the only surviving plainchant traditions to still be approved by the Roman Church; see S 76, S 80, S 82, S 111, S 133, S 140, S 152, S 168, S 172 for examples.

Anglican Chant—A way to sing psalms and canticles, non-metrical prose translations of the original Greek, Aramaic, and Hebrew texts, by matching the rhythm of the words, as they would be carefully spoken, to a harmonized melody of ten or twenty chords (single or double chant).

Anthem—Choral music based on biblical and other sacred texts, sung by a choir, in English and usually accompanied.

Antiphon—Scriptural or traditional text sung or said before and after the Psalms in the Daily Offices (*BCP* 43–44, 80–81) and the Gradual Psalm of the eucharistic liturgy.

Antiphonal—Style of singing/reading with two or more groups alternating responsively.

Burden—A refrain or chorus sung at the beginning and then after each stanza of a song, especially of a fifteenth-century English carol; see 247 and 266 in *H82*.

Cadence—A progression of two or more notes or chords that concludes a musical phrase or portion of a chant.

Call and Response—Style of singing; cantor/leader sings a phrase, congregation repeats phrase.

Canon—Music form in which a melody is imitated in a different voice, either with exact rhythms and/or intervals or in a similar style.

Cantata—Musical setting of a text, often a sacred text, and may include solo arias, duets, chorale or chorus, interspersed with recitatives, and instrumental accompaniment.

Canticle—A hymn, usually a biblical text, not metrical, not from the Psalms; sung or said after the lessons at Morning or Evening Prayer; can be sung as a Song of Praise in Holy Eucharist service.

Cantoris—From the Latin, "of the cantor"; designates the side of a cathedral choir on which the precentor (cantor) sits, the north side of the cathedral or chapel; indicates choir section.

Cantus Firmus—From the Latin, "fixed song"; a melody, often from plainsong, providing the basis of a polyphonic composition.

Carol—A joyful song, usually celebrating the birth of Christ.

Cento—A literary work, such as a hymn text, which is comprised of phrases, verses, or text from other authors. See *H82* 215.

Chant—Rhythmic speaking or singing of texts.

Chorale—Metrical hymn tune with religious text, historically associated with the Lutheran Church in Germany.

Conductor—Person who leads a chorus or instrumental ensemble, using hand gestures and usually a baton.

Conductus—A sacred song for one or more voices, monophonic or polyphonic, from France in the 12th century. From the Latin *conducere*, "to escort," the conductus was most likely sung while the lessons were processed to the place of reading.

Counterpoint—Generally, counterpoint involves lines of music that are independent and sound different from the others, yet produces harmony and a pleasing sound when played together; such music created from the Baroque period may be described as contrapuntal, whereas before the Baroque period this music was called polyphonic.

Decani—From the Latin, "of the dean"; designates the side of a cathedral choir on which the dean sits, the south side of the cathedral or chapel; indicates choir section.

Evensong—Sung service of Evening Prayer; officiant leads/sings opening sentences and prayers, creed; choir sings responses, Psalm setting, two canticles after the two lessons, anthem and hymns.

Exsultet—Ancient song of rejoicing, sung by deacon or appointed person after the lighting of the Paschal candle and procession into the church for the Great Vigil of Easter.

Fauxbourdon—An arrangement of a hymn in four parts with the melody in the tenor voice; also, a harmony with melody and two other parts, a sixth and a perfect fourth below; see *H82* 378 for an example.

Flex—A note that indicates a short pause for breath in plainsong chant; see S 447 and S 448 for examples.

Full Anthem—An anthem with four or more parts, to be sung by the choir; no verses or solo passages like verse anthems.

Gloria—One word abbreviation for *Gloria in Excelsis* (*Deo*) or "Glory be to God on high" (*BCP*, p. 324) or "Glory to God in the highest" (*BCP*, p. 356), a hymn of praise sung near the beginning of a service of Holy Eucharist, most appropriately from Christmas Day through Epiphany, Sundays from Easter Day through the Day of Pentecost, Ascension Day, and other festive occasions.

Gregorian Chant—A form of monophonic, liturgical music, also known as plainchant, used in music of the mass and other celebrations of Western Christianity; named after Pope Gregory I, Bishop of Rome (590–604), who ordered the simplification and cataloging of such music.

Homophonic—A style of composition with one melody; all voices and accompaniment move together in the same rhythm.

Hymn—Sacred, metrical, poetic text set to music for the congregation to sing in praise of God.

Introduction—In hymns or anthems, a passage of music, organ or accompanied instrumental, that begins or precedes the singing of the anthem or hymn.

Introit—Hymn, psalm, or anthem sung or said at or before the entrance of participants at the beginning of a worship service.

Invitatory—Canticle (*Venite, Jubilate,* or *Christ our Passover* at Morning Prayer; *Phos Hilaron* at Evening Prayer) sung after the opening versicle and response and before the Psalter.

Isometric—Style of poetry with lines of the same length.

Jubilate—"O be joyful" in Latin, opening sentence of Psalm 100, canticle in Morning Prayer.

Kyrie Eleison—"Lord, have mercy" in Greek, may be sung or said at the beginning of the liturgy of Holy Eucharist; most appropriate in penitential seasons.

Lessons and Carols—A format for a service of worship, observing Advent or celebrating Christmas; an appointed number of lessons are read, each followed by anthems and/or hymns; a bidding prayer precedes the service, prayer and blessing conclude the service.

Magnificat—"Magnifies" in Latin; the Song of Mary as recorded in Luke 1:46–55; text traditionally used at Evening Prayer/Evensong, also used in Morning Prayer.

Mass—Celebration of the Holy Eucharist; originally the Roman Catholic name for the Eucharist, but also used by some Episcopalians; musical parts of the Mass are *Kyrie, Gloria, Credo, Sanctus* and *Benedictus, Agnus Dei.*

Melisma—One syllable of text sung over several or more notes; music sung in this style is named melismatic, the opposite of syllabic, where there is a single note for each syllable of text.

Metrum—Like the flex in a chant, the metrum marks a pause or breathing spot at the end of the first convenient stopping place or at the conclusion of a main clause. See S 447 and S 448 for examples.

Mode—A fixed arrangement of the diatonic tones (white keys on piano) in a pattern of semitones/half-steps (s) and whole tones/whole steps (T) over one octave:

I /Ionian—play one octave, C to C (T-T-s-T-T-T-s)—major key

II/Dorian—play one octave, D to D (T-s-T-T-T-s-T)—minor key

III/Phrygian—play one octave, E to E (s-T-T-T-s-T-T)

IV/Lydian—play one octave, F to F (T-T-T-s-T-T-s)

V/Mixolydian—play one octave, G to G (T-T-s-T-T-s-T)

VI/Aeolian—play one octave, A to A (T-s-T-T-s-T-T)—minor

VII/Locrian—play one octave, B to B (s-T-T-s-T-T-T)

Motet—Unaccompanied choral composition, usually in one movement, often polyphonic, based on Latin sacred text.

Mozarabic Chant—Also known as Hispanic, Old Hispanic, Old Spanish, or Visigothic chant; related to but distinct from Gregorian chant; few chants have survived; see S 123 and S 272 for examples.

Nunc Dimittis—"Now let us depart" in Latin; first words of the Song of Simeon as recorded in Luke 2:29–32; canticle used at Evening Prayer/ Evensong, Compline, Candelmas, and at Morning Prayer.

Octavo—A piece of sheet music containing vocal parts and accompaniment.

Oratorio—A large-scale musical composition for solo voices, chorus, and orchestra, designed for concert, portraying a sacred story with or without costumes or scenery or choreography or staging.

Ostinato—A repeated phrase.

Phos Hilaron—"O Gracious Light" in Greek; hymn/canticle sung in the Order of Worship for Evening, after the lighting of the vesper candle.

Phrase—A single line of music, played or sung; a musical sentence.

Plainsong Chant—A way to sing psalms and canticles; non-metrical prose translations of the original Greek, Aramaic, and Hebrew texts, using a single, unaccompanied melodic line.

Pointing—Method of marking a psalm or other text, fitting the words to the music.

Polyphonic—A style of composition in which each voice moves independently.

Postlude—Organ, piano, or instrumental music that concludes the worship service.

Preces—Responsive prayers based on short verses of Scripture, especially the Psalter, which may be sung or said; see S 33 and S 58 for examples.

Prelude—Organ, piano, instrumental, solo, or choral music that precedes the worship service.

Quilisma—A jagged marking found over a note between two notes which are a minor third apart; the manner of singing is to prolong slightly the note or group of notes that comes just before the note with the quilisma; see S 112, *sursum corda*, for an example.

Refrain—A phrase or verse repeated throughout a hymn, song, or poem; usually placed at the end of a stanza.

Requiem—Also, Requiem Mass, Mass for the Dead, or Solemn Requiem Mass; a service of Holy Eucharist offered on behalf of a deceased person. The music may include these or some of these sections and in this order: Introit, *Kyrie eleison*, Gradual, Tract, Sequence, Offertory, *Sanctus, Agnus Dei*, Communion, *Pie Jesu, Libera Me, In paradisum*.

Rote—A way to learn music by listening and repeating, without printed music.

Round—A canon in which each voice returns from the end of the music to the beginning, repeating the music ad libitum until a designated conclusion.

Sanctus—"Holy" in Latin, from Isaiah 6:1–3; sung at the end of the Preface of the Great Thanksgiving.

Schola Cantorum—From the Latin, a "school for singers"; originally dating from a Roman 4th c. papal singing school, but reorganized by Pope Gregory (d. 604) and formed to teach techniques of singing and plainsong chant over a nine year course of study. The term is sometimes used to indicate a school for church singers or a gathering of singers at a conference or convention, or a place where there is instruction in the singing of chant.

Sequence Hymn—Hymn sung between the Epistle and the Gospel.

Service Music—Music settings of texts used in liturgy, excluding hymns and anthems, including texts of the ordinary, canticles, psalms, chants for special services.

Simple Tone—Music for singing the Preface, using one note to a syllable; in use since Archbishop Cranmer recommended this style in the first English prayer book; characterized by the drop of a major third at the beginning of the concluding cadence.

Solemn Tone—Music for singing the Preface in a slightly more difficult and more ornamental way.

Song—Composition for solo singer, accompanied or unaccompanied, texts are usually poems or have a rhyming nature, may be sacred or secular; may be dance, ballad, folk, pop or art song styles; may be sung in two or three parts or larger group.

Song of Praise—Hymn or canticle sung after the acclamation at the beginning of the Eucharist.

Stanza—A line of poetry; can be synonymous with *verse*.

Te Deum—"You, God" in Latin; also known as *Te Deum Laudamus* ("You are God: we praise you"); canticle used at Morning Prayer, as song of praise in Eucharist, on special days of thanksgiving and praise.

Through-composed—A setting that has a different melody for each stanza.

Unison—Two or more singers or instrumentalists playing the same notes at the same time.

Venite—"O Come" in Latin, invitatory canticle in Morning Prayer, based on Psalm 95.

Verse—A brief biblical passage, sung by cantor or choir, before the Gospel.

Verse-anthem—Choral music in which the music alternates between a solo voice or small group and the full choir; organ and/or instruments provide accompaniment; popular during the early seventeenth century through the middle of the eighteenth century.

Voluntary—Music for a solo instrument or organ, often improvised, played before, during, or after the worship service; also used to refer to Prelude and Postlude.

Altar Vessels, Linens, Hangings, Supplies, and Liturgical Symbols

Advent Wreath—A circle, with four candle holders representing the Sundays of Advent, usually covered with evergreens, found in churches and homes. All four candles may be purple or blue; or three may be purple or blue and one rose or pink. The rose candle is lighted on the Third Sunday of Advent, *Gaudete (Rejoice)* Sunday. The rose candle does not represent Mary; her Sunday is the Fourth Sunday of Advent.

Alms Basin—A plate, bowl or basket used to collect the offering of the people.

Altar Book—A large book, also referred to as *Missal*, which is placed on the altar for use during services. The Altar Book contains texts from *The Book of Common Prayer* and music settings of collects, prefaces and other texts for the officiant or presider to sing, music for specific liturgies, responses, blessings and dismissals, and anthems (non-choral), as in the burial rite.

Altar Cloth—A piece of white cloth, usually linen, that covers the top of the altar and hangs down the sides or to the floor. It is also called the Fair Linen and may be embroidered with crosses or other symbols.

Antependium—From the Latin, "hanging before"; a liturgical hanging, usually made of fabric that matches the colors of the liturgical season, specifically for the front of the altar.

Aspergillum—A handle with pierced ball, brush, or branch of juniper or other plant used to sprinkle holy water on the congregation, altar, and vested participants.

Blessed Sacrament—Consecrated bread and wine, representing the body and blood of Christ.

Bread Box—A vessel for unconsecrated wafers, usually brought forward at the offertory.

Bucket—Container for water to be used in the asperges, or sprinkling of holy water.

Burse—An envelope-like pocket, covered with the same cloth/color for the current liturgical season or occasion as vestments and altar hangings, for the folded corporal; it is placed on top of the chalice, paten, and chalice veil.

Candles—Representing the light of Christ in a darkened world, two candles may be placed on the altar, at the four corners of the altar, as part of the reredos, in procession, in the Advent wreath, before icons and statues of saints, and also used at Candlemas, Epiphany, Easter Vigil liturgies, and evening services.

Censer—A metal container for burning charcoal and incense, with a pierced lid to release smoke, held by a chain to allow for swinging and rotation to disperse smoke; also called *thurible.*

Chalice—A stemmed cup used for communion wine.

Chalice Veil—A square piece of fabric, in the same liturgical color as vestments, to cover the paten and chalice.

Chrism—Consecrated oil, pure or scented olive oil, used at baptism and ministration to the sick.

Ciborium—A metal or ceramic vessel, shaped like a chalice with a top or lid ornamented with a cross or other symbol, used as a container for consecrated bread and stored in the aumbry or tabernacle.

Corporal—A large square of white cloth, usually linen, that is folded and stored in the burse when not in use, and unfolded and spread at the setting of the table. The paten and chalice are placed upon the corporal on the altar.

Corpus—Latin for "body"; carved body of Christ on a cross.

Crèche—An arrangement of the nativity scene that includes Jesus, Mary, and Joseph, the wise men, angels, shepherds, and animals.

Cross—Symbol of the crucifixion and sacrifice of Jesus Christ, symbol of Christianity. The most common cross, a Latin cross, consists of two lines at right angles to each other; used for processions, sewn on altar linens and vestments, found on altar vessels and reredos, attached or suspended inside church, placed on top of church roof or steeple, worn as jewelry; also the shape of Gothic architectural style for church buildings.

Crucifix—Cross with the carved figure of Jesus attached; may have crucified Jesus with crown of thorns or the risen Christ with eucharistic vestments and crown; see *Corpus.*

Cruets—Vessels used to carry water and wine to the altar, made of glass, silver, or ceramic and include handles and stoppers.

Dossal—Fabric hanging behind an altar that is attached to a wall, not free-standing.

Dust Cover—A white cloth placed over the altar cloth when the altar is not being used.

Elements—Bread and wine to be used for Holy Eucharist.

Ewer—A pitcher to contain and carry water for baptism; from the Anglo-French word for "water."

Fair Linen—See *Altar Cloth*.

Flagon—A large metal, ceramic, or glass pitcher for wine or water.

Frontal—A cloth, matching vestments of the liturgical season, that covers the front of the altar or all sides, often down to the floor. The altar cloth is placed over the frontal.

Funeral Pall—A large cloth with symbols and color appropriate for burial liturgy, placed on the casket before the liturgy begins; a smaller cloth is used for an urn containing ashes or cremains of the deceased.

Gospel Book—A book which contains the Gospel readings, carried in procession for the reading of the Gospel at a place of visual prominence during services of Holy Eucharist.

Holy Water—Water that has been blessed by a priest or bishop, and used at baptism, blessing of the people, house blessings, dedication of church objects, for personal devotions before or after worship services, and at the discretion of the priest.

Host—A large wafer made of unleavened bread, elevated by the celebrant and broken at the fraction, at the end of the Eucharistic Prayer and before the distribution of elements.

Incense—A wood or resin burned in a thurible or censer, producing smoke and a fragrant aroma. Frankincense, a symbol of divine priesthood, was a gift of the wise men. A symbol of prayer and reverence, incense adds solemnity to the liturgical service in procession, at the reading of the Gospel, and in preparation for the Eucharist.

Lavabo—The ceremonial washing of the celebrant's hands at the offertory before the Eucharist, after using chrism, and after the imposition of ashes on Ash Wednesday.

Lavabo Towel—A cloth used to dry hands after the lavabo.

Lenten Array—The use of unbleached muslin or sackcloth in place of purple for paraments and vestments during Lent and Holy Week.

Lenten Cross—A cross of wood in place of a ceremonial cross, or a cross draped in purple or black for the Season of Lent.

Missal—See *Altar Book.*

Missal Stand—A metal or wood support, or in some cases a pillow, to hold the large Altar Book.

Pall—1) A large cloth draped over a casket during a funeral; see *Funeral Pall;* 2) a white, cloth-covered board positioned over a chalice, on top of which are placed the burse and veil.

Paraments—The liturgical hangings on the altar (frontal, altar cloth) and near the altar, including those on the pulpit and lectern.

Paschal Candle—A large white candle, often decorated with a cross, symbols of alpha and omega, and the year; lighted at the beginning of the Easter Vigil and present for all services during the Great Fifty Days of Easter; carried in procession or placed by caskets for funerals; kept near the baptismal font and lighted for baptisms.

Paten—A shallow or flat dish of ceramic, silver, or gold, that contains the priest's host or unleavened wafers for communion; a basket, bowl, or tray may be used for real bread.

Processional Cross—A wood or metal cross, occasionally a crucifix; attached to a long pole, held high for all to see, carried by a crucifer in procession.

Purificator—A cloth, often linen, used to wipe the chalice during the administration of wine during communion and for cleaning the chalice at the end of the distribution.

Pyx—Small silver box or container used to store consecrated bread for visitation to the sick.

Reserved Sacrament—Consecrated bread and wine, kept in the tabernacle or aumbry, reserved for visitations to the sick or a future service.

Sanctus Bell(s)—A single bell or set of bells rung during the Eucharistic Prayer, usually at the saying or singing of the *Sanctus* and at the elevation of bread and wine.

Stoup—A vessel for holy water, usually placed near a church entrance, for worshipers entering or leaving the church to dip their fingers into the water and make the sign of the cross on themselves, a reminder of their Baptismal Covenant.

Super-frontal—A cloth that is placed over the top of an altar and hangs down a few inches over the frontal.

Tabernacle—A container for the reserved sacrament.

Thurible—See *Censer.*

Torch—A candle on a pole, placed in a stand, carried by an acolyte in procession.

Architecture and Church Furnishings

Altar—A table on which bread and wine are placed for the celebration of the Eucharist. The word is derived from the Latin *altare*, indicating a place where sacrifice is offered. A "high altar" may be found against the eastern wall; other altars are placed in the crossing or in a position of visibility closer to the people or in side chapels.

Altar of Repose—An altar or area of the church set aside for bread and wine consecrated on Maundy Thursday to be used on Good Friday.

Altar Rail—A railing made of wood, metal, marble, or other material that sets apart the sanctuary from the rest of the worship space, where people stand or kneel to receive communion.

Ambo—A raised platform, also known as lectern or pulpit, from which the lessons are read or the sermon preached.

Aumbry—A receptacle for the reserved sacrament, either an indentation in the wall, a shelf set apart from the altar, or a cabinet fastened to a wall, often marked by the presence of a sanctuary lamp or light; also spelled *ambry*.

Baptismal Font—A container for the water of baptism.

Bishop's Chair—A designated seat, also called the bishop's throne or cathedra, reserved for the bishop in cathedrals and churches.

Cathedra—See *Bishop's Chair*; the Latin word *cathedra* means "chair."

Cathedral—The official church of the bishop and which contains the bishop's chair.

Chancel—The area of the church between the nave and the sanctuary, east of the crossing, often called the choir; in some places, the chancel is the area between the front pew and the altar.

Chancel Screen—A screen of wood or metal, also called a rood screen, that divides the nave and chancel.

Chapel—A small place of worship within or attached to a larger structure; place of worship associated with a college or university or seminary; may be large or small, private or institutional.

Cloister—A covered walkway around a courtyard or between buildings, often part of a convent or monastery.

Columbarium—A space reserved on church grounds or in a church wall or cemetery containing niches for the interment of ashes of the dead.

Crossing—The intersection of aisles in the front of a church; in a cruciform (cross-shaped) church the crossing joins the choir and sanctuary (east) with the nave (west) and the transepts (north and south.)

Credence Table—A small table or shelf near the altar used to hold vessels needed for Eucharist.

Dossal—A fabric reredos, hanging above and behind the altar.

Episcopal Church Flag—A flag bearing the red cross of St. George, patron saint of England, on a white field, with blue field in the upper left corner containing nine crosslets in the x-shape of the cross of St. Andrew. The colors are the same as the national flags of both the U.S. and England. The crosslets represent the nine dioceses when the Protestant Episcopal Church was founded in Philadelphia in 1789. The cross of St. Andrew honors the consecration of Samuel Seabury, first bishop of the Episcopal Church, by the Anglican Church of Scotland.

High Altar—The main altar for celebrating the Holy Eucharist in a church or cathedral; centered against the east wall in older churches; often on a raised platform and placed near the people as a sign of unity and community gathered for the Eucharist.

Lectern—A stand for holding the Bible or other readings in a raised, visible position in the front of the church; also known as *ambo*.

Narthex—The space between the main entrance to the church building and the door to the nave.

Nave—The large portion of a church, from the narthex to the chancel, where the congregation sits; from the Latin *navis* meaning "ship," a symbol of Christian journey; often the ceiling vaulting or beams resemble the overturned keel of a ship.

Parish Hall—A place for coffee hour, church gatherings, and meetings that is separate from the worship space but in the same building; a Parish House would be a structure separate from the church building for similar purposes.

Pew—Long bench with back support for congregational seating.

Piscina—A sink, usually in the sacristy, that drains directly into the ground, not into a sewer system; used for disposing consecrated wine not consumed at communion, cleaning the chalice and paten, and pouring out holy water from the baptismal font.

Prayer Desk—A kneeling bench with a shelf for a book or support, occasionally with a cushion for knees, used for private devotions or leading prayers in public worship.

Presider's Chair—Seat used by the presider of the liturgy. See *Sedilia*.

Prie-dieu—See *Prayer Desk*; French for "pray God."

Pulpit—A raised platform, often with wood or metal railing and enclosure, from which the sermon is preached; located in the front of the nave or in a highly visible location.

Rectory—The residence of the rector, provided by the church.

Reredos—Decoration above or behind the altar, may include wood or stone carvings of Christ, Mary, apostles, saints and angels, tapestries, icons, banners, stained glass, scriptural texts.

Rood Screen—From Old English, *rood* means "cross"; used as early as the twelfth century to separate the chancel or choir from the nave or to separate the clergy in the chancel from the lay people in the nave; often a crucifix and statues of the Virgin Mary and St. John were placed on top of the rood screen.

Sacristy—A room located near the worship space for the storage of vessels, supplies, candles, and linens for use at the Eucharist and in other liturgies, and for their preparation and cleaning.

Sanctuary—Refers to the area around the altar in the Episcopal tradition; synonymous with the whole interior of the church in other denominations.

Sanctuary Light or Lamp—A candle, oil lamp, or electric light that continues to burn or be seen when the reserved sacrament is present.

Sedilia—Seat used by the presider during the Liturgy of the Word, also called *Presider's Chair*.

Table—See *Altar*.

Transept—In a cross-shaped (cruciform) building, the horizontal part of the cross, the north and south arms, at right angles to the nave and chancel.

Sources Used for the Compilation of Terms and Definitions.

The Book of Common Prayer. New York: The Church Hymnal Corporation, 1979.

The Episcopal Handbook. New York: Church Publishing, 2008, pp. 211–225.

Armentrout, Don S. and Robert Boak Slocum, editors. *An Episcopal Dictionary of the Church: A User Friendly Reference for Episcopalians.* New York: Church Publishing, 2000.

Guilbert, Charles Mortimer. *Words of Our Worship: A Liturgical Dictionary.* Church Publishing, 2000.

Hatchett, Marion J. *Commentary on the American Prayer Book.* The Seabury Press, 1980.

Pfatteicher, Philip H. *A dic-tion-ary of Liturgical Terms.* Philadelphia: Trinity Press International, 1991.

Randel, Don Michael, ed. *The Harvard Dictionary of Music.* Belknap Press of the Harvard University Press, Cambridge, Massachusetts, 2003.

Wall, John N., Jr. *A New Dictionary for Episcopalians.* San Francisco: Harper & Row, Publishers., 1985.

Westerhoff, The Rev. Dr. John H. *A People Called Episcopalians: A Brief Introduction to Our Peculiar Way of Life.* Harrisburg, PA: Morehouse Publishing, revised 1998.

Bibliography

Alternate, Emergent, Blended Worship, Language and Cultural Inclusion

Baker, Jonny, Doug Gay, and Jenny Brown. *Alternative Worship: Resources from and for the Emerging Church.* Grand Rapids, MI: Baker Publishing Group, 2004.

Duncan, Geoffrey. *Courage to Love: Liturgies for the Lesbian, Gay, Bisexual, and Transgender Community.* Cleveland: The Pilgrim Press, 2002.

Everett, Isaac. *The Emergent Psalter.* New York: Church Publishing, 2009.

Gibbs, Eddie and Ryan K. Bolger. *Emerging Churches.* Baker Academic, 2005.

Giles, Richard. *Times and Seasons: Creating Transformative Worship throughout the Year.* New York: Church Publishing, 2008.

MacDonald, Mark L., ed., for the Standing Commission on Liturgy and Music: *The Chant of Life: Inculturation and the People of the Land,* Liturgical Studies Four. New York: Church Publishing, 2003.

Meyers, Ruth A. and Phoebe Pettingell. *Gleanings: Essays on Expansive Language with Prayers for Various Occasions.* New York: Church Publishing, 2001.

Tirabasse, Maren C. and Kathy Wonson Eddy. *Gifts of Many Cultures: Worship Resources for the Global Community.* Cleveland: United Church Press, 1995.

The Book of Common Prayer

The Book of Common Prayer. New York: The Church Hymnal Corporation, 1979.

The Revised Common Lectionary—Years A, B, C, and Holy Days—According to the Use of The Episcopal Church. New York: Church Publishing, 2007.

Black, Vicki K. *Welcome to the Book of Common Prayer.* Harrisburg, PA: Morehouse Publishing, 2005.

Hatchett, Marion J. *Commentary on the American Prayer Book.* New York: The Seabury Press, 1980.

Marshall, Paul V. and Lesley Northrup, editors. *Leaps and Boundaries: The Prayer Book in the 21st Century.* Harrisburg, PA: Morehouse Publishing, 1997.

Mitchell, Leonel L. *Praying Shapes Believing: A Theological Commentary on The Book of Common Prayer.* Harrisburg, PA: Morehouse Publishing, 1985.

Stuhlman, Byron D. *Prayer Book Rubrics Expanded.* New York: Church Hymnal Corporation, 1987.

Children and Youth: Music Ministry

Bertalot, John. *5 Wheels to Successful Sight-Singing: A Practical Approach to Teach Children (and Adults) to Read Music.* Minneapolis: Augsburg Fortress, 1993.

Cooksey, John M. *Working with the Adolescent Voice.* St. Louis: Concordia Publishing House, 1992.

Dawn, Marva J. *Is It A Lost Cause? Having the Heart of God for the Church's Children.* Grand Rapids, MI: William B. Eerdmans Publishing Company, 1997.

McRae, Shirley W. *Directing the Children's Choir: A Comprehensive Resource.* New York: Schirmer Books, 1991.

Rotermund, Donald, ed. *Children Sing His Praise: A Handbook for Children's Choir Directors.* St. Louis: Concordia Publishing House, 1985.

Roth, Robert N. and Nancy Roth, eds. *We Sing of God: A Hymnal for Children. Teacher's Guide.* New York: Church Hymnal Corporation, 1989.

Stultz, Marie. *Innocent Sounds—Building Choral Tone and Artistry in Your Children's Choir—A Personal Journey.* St. Louis: MorningStar Music Publishers, 1999.

Choral Training

Bertalot, John. *Teaching Adults to Sight-Sing.* Buxhall, U.K.: Kevin Mayhew Publications, 2004.

Ehmann, Wilhelm and Frauke Haasemann. *Voice Building for Choirs.* Chapel Hill, NC: Hinshaw Music, Inc., 1982.

Haasemann, Frauke and James M. Jordan. *Group Vocal Technique: The Vocalise Cards.* Chapel Hill NC: Hinshaw Music, Inc., 1992.

Henry, Earl. *Sight Singing.* Upper Saddle River, N.J.: Prentice Hall, 1997.

Perona-Wright, Leah, ed. *Voice for Life.* Salisbury, U.K.: Royal School of Church Music, 2004.

Church History

Prichard, Robert W. *A History of the Episcopal Church—Revised Edition*. Harrisburg: Morehouse Publishing, 1999.

Webber, Christopher L. *Welcome to the Episcopal Church*. Harrisburg, PA: Morehouse Publishing, 1999.

Church Music

Doran, Carol and William H. Petersen. *A History of Music in the Episcopal Church*. The Assocation of Anglican Musicians, 2001.

Eskew, Harry and Hugh T. McElrath. *Sing with Understanding: An Introduction to Christian Hymnology*. Nashville, TN: Church Street Press, 1995.

Haskel, Marilyn L., ed. *What Would Jesus Sing? Experimentation and Tradition in Church Music*. New York: Church Publishing, 2007.

Parker, Alice. *Melodious Accord: Good Singing in Church*. Chicago, IL: Liturgy Training Publications, 1991.

Westermeyer, Paul. *Te Deum: The Church and Music*. Minneapolis: Augsburg Fortress, 1998.

Wilson-Dickson, Andrew. *The Story of Christian Music—From Gregorian Chant to Black Gospel, an illustrated guide to all the major traditions of music in worship*. Minneapolis: Fortress Press, 1996.

The Episcopal Church

The Episcopal Handbook. New York: Church Publishing, 2008.

Armentrout, Don S. and Robert Boak Slocum, eds. *An Episcopal Dictionary of the Church: A User-friendly Reference for Episcopalians*. New York: Church Publishing, 2000.

_____. *Discovering Common Mission: Lutherans and Episcopalians Together*. New York: Church Publishing, 2003.

Guilbert, Charles Mortimer. *Words of Our Worship: A Liturgical Dictionary*. New York: Church Publishing, 2000.

Markham, Ian S. *Liturgical Life Principles: How Episcopal Worship Can Lead to Healthy and Authentic Living*. Harrisburg, PA: Morehouse Publishing, 2009.

Westerhoff, The Rev. Dr. John H. *A People Called Episcopalians: A Brief Introduction to Our Peculiar Way of Life*. Harrisburg, PA: Morehouse Publishing, 1994.

Hymnals, Hymnody, Hymns & Spiritual Songs

El Himnario. New York: Church Publishing, 1998.

The Hymnal 1982, Accompaniment Editions; Volume 1 (Service Music) and Volume 2 (Hymns). New York: The Church Hymnal Corporation, 1985.

Hymns of Glory Songs of Praise. New York: Church Publishing, 2009. Official hymnal of The Church of Scotland; contains traditional hymns, new songs, and global music.

Lift Every Voice and Sing II: An African American Hymnal. New York: Church Publishing, 1993.

Music by Heart—Paperless Songs for Evening Worship. New York: Church Publishing, 2008.

Music for Liturgy: A Book for All God's Friends. Saint Gregory of Nyssa Episcopal Church, San Francisco, CA, 1999.

My Heart Sings Out. New York: Church Publishing, 2004.

Taizé: Songs for Prayers. Chicago: GIA Publications, 1998.

Voices Found. New York: Church Publishing, 2003.

Wonder, Love, and Praise. A Supplement to The Hymnal 1982. New York: Church Publishing, 1997.

Eskew, Harry and Hugh T. McElrath. *Sing with Understanding: An Introduction to Christian Hymnology.* Nashville, Tennessee: Church Street Press, 1995.

Glover, Raymond F. *The Hymnal 1982 Companion, Vols. 1–4.* New York: Church Hymnal Corporation, 1990.

Haskel, Marilyn L. and Lisa Neufeld Thomas. *Voices Found: Leader's Guide.* New York: Church Publishing, 2004.

Hooker, John L. *Wonder, Love, and Praise, A Supplement to The Hymnal 1982: Leader's Guide.* New York: Church Publishing, 1997.

Routley, Erik, ed. and expanded by Paul A. Richardson. *A Panorama of Christian Hymnody.* Chicago, IL: GIA Publications, Inc. 2005.

_____. *Christian Hymns Observed: When in Our Music God is Glorified.* Princeton, NJ: Prestige Publications, Inc., 1982.

Vidal-White, Fiona. *My Heart Sings Out, Teacher's Guide.* New York: Church Publishing, 2005.

Williams, John E., ed. *Simplified Accompaniments: 97 Hymns from The Hymnal 1982.* New York: The Church Hymnal Corporations, 1994.

Liturgy and Worship

A New Zealand Prayer Book. Auckland: William Collins Publishers Ltd., 1989.

Holy Women, Holy Men: Celebrating the Saints. New York: Church Publishing, 2010.

Lesser Feasts and Fasts-2003. New York: Church Publishing, 2003.

Dawn, Marva J. *Reaching Out without Dumbing Down: A Theology of Worship for the Turn-of-the-Century Culture*. Grand Rapids, MI: William. B. Eerdmans Publishing Co., 1995.

_____. *A Royal "Waste" of Time: The Splendor of Worshiping God and Being Church for the World*. Grand Rapids, MI: William B. Eerdmans Publishing Co., 1999.

Doran, Carol and Thomas H. Troeger. *Trouble at the Table: Gathering the Tribes for Worship*. Nashville, TN: Abingdon Press, 1992.

Galley, Howard E. *The Ceremonies of the Eucharist: A Guide to Celebration*. Boston, MA: Cowley Publications, 1989

Haskel, Marilyn L., ed. and Clayton L. Morris, ed. *As We Gather to Pray: An Episcopal Guide to Worship*. New York: The Church Hymnal Corporation, 1996.

Keating, Thomas. *The Mystery of Christ: The Liturgy as Spiritual Experience*. Amity NY: Amity House, 1987.

Mitchell, Leonel L. *Pastoral and Occasional Liturgies: A Ceremonial Guide*. Boston, MA: Cowley Publications, 1998.

_____. *Lent, Holy Week, Easter and the Great Fifty Days*. Boston, MA: Cowley Publications, 1996.

Morris, Clayton L. *Holy Hospitality: Worship and the Baptismal Covenant*. New York: Church Publishing, 2005.

Portaro, Sam. *Brightest and Best: A Companion to the Lesser Feasts and Fasts*. Boston, MA: Cowley Publications, 1998.

Price, Charles P. and Louis Weil. *Liturgy for Living*, revised edition. Harrisburg, PA: Morehouse Publishing, 2000.

Saliers, Don E. *Worship Come to Its Senses*. Nashville, TN: Abingdon Press, 1996.

Smith, George Wayne. *Admirable Simplicity: Principles for Worship Planning in the Anglican Tradition*. New York: Church Hymnal Corporation, 1996.

Webber, Christopher L. *Welcome to Sunday: An Introduction to Worship in the Episcopal Church*. Harrisburg, PA: Morehouse Publishing, 2003

_____. *A User's Guide to the Holy Eucharist Rites I & II*. Harrisburg: Morehouse Publishing, 1997.

Weil, Louis. *A Theology of Worship*. Cambridge, MA: Cowley Publications, 2002.

Music and Liturgy Planning—Episcopal Resources

Psalm settings and resources are listed in a separate section below.

The Book of Occasional Services-2003. New York: Church Publishing, 2004.

Enriching Our Worship: Morning and Evening Prayer, The Great Litany, The Holy Eucharist. New York: Church Publishing, 1998.

Enriching Our Music 1: Canticles and Settings for the Eucharist. New York: Church Publishing, 2003

Enriching Our Music 2: More Canticles and Settings for the Eucharist. New York: Church Publishing, 2004.

Musical Settings for Noonday and Compline. New York: Church Publishing, 2000.

The Revised Common Lectionary: Years A, B, C, and Holy Days according to the use of the Episcopal Church. New York: Church Publishing, 2007.

Black, Vicki K. *Welcome to the Church Year: An Introduction to the Seasons of the Episcopal Church*. Harrisburg, PA: Morehouse Publishing, 2004.

Bock, Susan K. *Liturgy for the Whole Church*. New York: Church Publishing, 2008.

Collins, Dori Erwin and Scott C. Weidler. *Sound Decisions: Evaluating Contemporary Music for Lutheran Worship*. Minneapolis: Augsburg Fortress, 1997.

Daw, Carl P., Jr. and Thomas Pavlechko. *Liturgical Music for the Revised Common Lectionary, Year A*. New York: Church Publishing, 2007.

_____. *Liturgical Music for the Revised Common Lectionary, Year B*. New York: Church Publishing, 2008.

_____. *Liturgical Music for the Revised Common Lectionary, Year C*. New York: Church Publishing, 2009

Elwood, Frederick C. and John L. Hooker, eds. *In the Shadows of Holy Week—The Office of Tenebrae*. New York: Church Publishing, 2000.

Giles, Richard. *Times and Seasons: Creating Transformative Worship throughout the Year*. New York: Church Publishing, 2008.

Glover, Raymond F., ed. *The Hymnal 1982 Companion*. New York: The Church Hymnal Corporation, 1994.

Hatchett, Marion J. *A Liturgical Index to The Hymnal 1982*. New York: The Church Hymnal Corporation, 1986.

_____. *A Guide to the Practice of Church Music*. New York: Church Publishing, 1989.

_____. *A Scriptural Index to The Hymnal 1982*. New York: The Church Hymnal Corporation, 1988.

Kucharski, Joseph A., ed. *The Episcopal Musician's Handbook: Lectionary Year C, 2012–2013*. Milwaukee, WI: The Living Church Foundation, Inc. 2012. (Published annually)

Mason, Monte, ed. and Larry Reynolds, composer. *Great Paschal Vespers*. Instant download. New York: Church Publishing, 2009.

MaultsBy, Carl. *Afro-Centric Liturgical Music: Settings for Morning and Evening Prayer and the Holy Eucharist*. New York: Church Publishing, 2008.

Music and Liturgical Planning—Lutheran Resources

The Evangelical Lutheran Church has many resources that parallel and augment those of the Episcopal Church. Although some other Augsburg Fortress publications are included in various categories in this bibliography, those listed next are particularly relevant to music and liturgy planning. Check the Augsburg Fortress website for additional information on these books.

Our liturgies are very similar, our hymnals and supplements are all superb; both the Episcopal Church and the ELCA use the RCL, and we are Full Communion partners. I have regularly used ELCA materials in my church work and highly recommend them for your consideration.

Minneapolis, MN: Augsburg Fortress www.augsburgfortress.org

Evangelical Lutheran Worship: Service Music and Hymns (ELCA hymnal, 2007, which comes in full accompaniment, 2-volume edition, and compact accompaniment editions)

Evangelical Lutheran Worship: Service Music and Hymns. Simplified Keyboard Accompaniment Edition, 2007.

Evangelical Lutheran Worship: Psalter for Worship, Year A, 2007.

Evangelical Lutheran Worship: Psalter for Worship, Year B, 2008.

Evangelical Lutheran Worship: Psalter for Worship, Year C, 2006.

Choral Literature for Sundays and Seasons (anthem suggestions for specific liturgies, including numerous styles, levels of difficulty, composers, and publishers), 2004.

Guitar Accompaniment Edition: Service Music and Hymns (2 volumes), 2007.

Hymnal Companion to Evangelical Lutheran Worship (reference information on hymns and commentary on hymn texts, authors, composers, and tunes), 2010.

Indexes to Evangelical Lutheran Worship (prayer of the day, gospel acclamations, listings of appropriate hymns and songs, index to RCL, topic and scriptural indexes). 2007.

Musicians Guide to Evangelical Lutheran Worship (introduction to how music serves worship, suggestions for each piece of service music, hymn and song), 2007.

Psalm Settings for the Church Year: Revised Common Lectionary, 2008.*Sundays and Seasons: Year B-2012* (worship planning resources for worship leaders, musicians, visual artists, educators, altar guilds, and pastoral liturgists; published annually).

This Far By Faith—Accompaniments to the Liturgies: An African American Resource for Worship, 1999.

With One Voice (Accompaniment Edition and Pew Edition; supplement to *Lutheran Book of Worship* (*LBW,* 1978), previous hymnal, 1995.

Worship and Praise (Full Music Edition and Songbook Edition with melodies and chords; songs of the faith, mostly composed in the past twenty years), 1999.

Music Leaders: Skills and Resources

Lord, Open our Lips: Musical Help for Leaders of the Liturgy. New York: Church Publishing, 1999.

Bertalot, John. *Immediately Practical Tips for Choral Directors.* Minneapolis: Augsburg Fortress, 1994.

Cronin, Deborah K. *O For A Dozen Tongues to Sing: Music Ministry with Small Choirs.* Nashville: Abingdon Press, 1996.

Devinney, Richard. *The Wednesday Workout: Practical Techniques for Rehearsing the Choir.* Nashville: Abingdon Press, 1993.

Donathan, David F. *How Does Your Choir Grow? Recruitment, maintenance, organization, growth, publicity, development, fun and fellowship.* Nashville: Abingdon Press, 1995.

Farlee, Robert Bucklee and Eric Vollen. *Leading the Church's Song.* Minneapolis: Augsburg Fortress, 1998.

Laird, Robert C. *Tell Out My Soul: Guitar Lead Sheets for Favorite Hymns, Vol. 1.* Instant Download. New York: Church Publishing, 2006.

Keiser, Marilyn J. *Teaching Music in the Small Church.* New York: The Church Pension Fund, 1983.

Owens, Bill and Herb Miller, ed. *The Magnetic Music Ministry: Ten Productive Goals.* Nashville: Abingdon Press, 1996.

Pfautsch, Lloyd. *Choral Therapy: Techniques and Exercises for the Church Choir.* Nashville: Abingdon Press, 1994.

Roberts, William Bradley. *Music and Vital Congregations: A Practical Guide for Clergy.* New York: Church Publishing, 2009.

Sirota, Victoria. *Preaching to the Choir: Claiming the Role of Sacred Musician.* New York: Church Publishing, 2006

Thompson, Martha Lynn. *Handbell Helper: A Guide for Beginning Directors and Choirs.* Nashville: Abingdon Press, 1996.

Tyree, Debra. *The Reluctant Soloist: A Director's Guide to Developing Church Vocalists.* Nashville: Abingdon Press, 1994.

Wallace, Robin Knowles. *Things They Never Tell You Before You Say "Yes": The Nonmusical Tasks of the Church Musician.* Nashville: Abingdon Press, 1994.

Westermeyer, Paul. *The Church Musician.* Minneapolis: Augsburg Fortress, 1997.

Willetts, Sandra. *Upbeat Downbeat: Basic Conducting Patterns and Techniques.* Nashville: Abingdon Press, 1993.

Organ and Keyboard Resources

Cherwien, David M. *Let the People Sing!* Saint Louis, MO: Concordia Publishing House, 1997. A keyboardist's creative and practical guide to engaging God's people in meaningful song.

Fesperman, John. *Organ Planning: Asking the Right Questions,* Hymnal Studies Four. New York: Church Publishing, 2000.

Fishell, Janette. *But What Do I Do With My Feet? The Pianist's Guide to the Organ.* Nashville: Abingdon Press, 1996.

Leppert-Largent, Anna. *Sacred Piano Literature: A Comprehensive Survey for the Church Musician.* New York: Church Publishing, 2003.

Lovelace, Austin C. *The Organist & Hymn Playing,* revised. Carol Stream, ILL: Agape, 1981.

MaultsBy, Carl. *Playing Gospel Piano: The Basics with Examples from Lift Every Voice and Sing II.* New York: Church Publishing, 2003.

Schmidt, Dennis. *An Organist's Guide to Resources for The Hymnal 1982*. New York: The Church Hymnal Corporation, 1987.

_____. *An Organist's Guide to Resources for The Hymnal 1982, Volume II*. New York: The Church Hymnal Corporation, 1991.

Williams, John E., Editor for the Standing Commission on Church Music. *Simplified Accompaniments*, 97 Hymns from *The Hymnal 1982*. New York: The Church Hymnal Corporation, 1994.

Pastoral Resources

Each edition of the Enriching Our Worship Series contains lists of hymns appropriate for the various liturgies.

Enriching Our Worship 2: Ministry with the Sick or Dying, Burial of a Child. New York: Church Publishing, 2000.

Enriching Our Worship 3: Burial Rites for Adults, together with a Rite for the Burial of a Child. New York: Church Publishing, 2007.

Enriching Our Worship 4: The Renewal of Ministry and the Welcoming of a New Rector or Other Pastor. New York: Church Publishing, 2007.

Enriching Our Worship 5: Liturgies and Prayers Related to Childbearing, Childbirth, and Loss. New York: Church Publishing, 2009.

Prayers and Meditations

Baker-Trinity. *Soli Deo Gloria: Choir Devotions for Year B*. Minneapolis, MN: Augsburg Fortress, 2011.

Chamberlain, Martha E. and Mary B. Adams. *Hymn Devotions for All Seasons: Fifty-two Favorite Hymns*. Nashville, TN: Abingdon Press, 1989.

DeHoog, Genevieve and Herman. *Devotions for Choirs*. Nashville, TN: Abingdon Press, 1997.

Guenther, Margaret. *The Practice of Prayer*. Boston, MA: Cowley Publications, 1998.

Hunt, Jeanne. *More Choir Prayers*. Washington, D.C.: The Pastoral Press, 1990.

Johnson, Kenneth. *Pilgrim Prayers for Church Choirs*. Cleveland, OH: The Pilgrim Press, 2002.

Mueller, Craig M. *Soli Deo Gloria: Choir Devotions for Year A*. Minneapolis, MN: Augsburg Fortress, 2010.

Roger, Brother, of Taizé. *Life from Within*. London, England: Geoffrey Chapman Mowbray, 1990.

Roth, Nancy. *A Closer Walk: Meditating on Hymns for Year A*. New York: Church Publishing, 1998.

_____. *Awake, My Soul! Meditating on Hymns for Year B*. New York: Church Publishing, 1999.

_____. *New Every Morning: Meditating on Hymns for Year C*. New York: Church Publishing, 2000.

_____. *Praise My Soul: Meditating on Hymns*. New York: Church Publishing, 2000.

Rowthorn, Jeffery W. *The Wideness of God's Mercy: Litanies To Enlarge Our Prayers*. Harrisburg PA: Morehouse Publishing, 1995.

Smylie, James H., Mary Nelson Keithahn, ed. *Between Warm-Up and Worship: Prayers for Choirs on the Run*. Nashville, TN: Abingdon Press, 1998.

Wold, Wayne L. *Soli Deo Gloria: Choir Devotions for Year C*. Minneapolis, MN: Augsburg Fortress, 2009.

Psalm Settings and Resources

Gradual Psalms: Holy Days and Various Occasions. New York: The Church Hymnal Corporation, 1981.

Gradual Psalms for the Occasional Services. New York: Church Publishing, 2000.

Daw, Carl P., Jr. and Kevin R. Hackett. *A Hymn Tune Psalter: Book One—Gradual Psalms: Advent through the Day of Pentecost*. New York: Church Publishing, 1998. (*BCP* Lectionary)

_____. *A Hymn Tune Psalter: Book Two—Gradual Psalms: The Season after Pentecost*. New York: Church Publishing, 1998. (*BCP* Lectionary)

_____. *A Hymn Tune Psalter, Book One: Advent through the Day of Pentecost*, RCL Edition. New York: Church Publishing, 2007.

_____. *A Hymn Tune Psalter, Book Two: Gradual Psalms: The Season after Pentecost*, RCL Edition. New York: Church Publishing, 2008.

Daw, Carl P., Jr. *To Sing God's Praise: 18 Metrical Canticles*. Carol Stream, IL: Hope Publishing Company, 1992.

Everett, Isaac. *The Emergent Psalter*. New York: Church Publishing, 2009.

Ford, Bruce E. *Gradual Psalms with Alleluia Verses and Tracts, Years A, B, C*. New York: Church Publishing, 2007.

Hawthorne, Robert A. *The Portland Psalter Book One: Liturgical Years A,B,C*. New York: Church Publishing, 2002. (*BCP* and RCL lectionaries.)

_____. *The Portland Psalter Book Two: Responsorial Psalms for Congregation, Cantor & Choir.* New York: Church Publishing, 2003, *BCP* and RCL lectionaries.

Litton, James, editor. *The Plainsong Psalter.* New York: The Church Hymnal Corporation, 1988.

Pavlechko, Thomas, arr. *St. Martin's Psalter: The Revised Common Lectionary, Years A, B, and C, Based on Hymn Tunes and Other Familiar Melodies.* Tryon, NC: St. James Music Press, 2004.

Pulkingham, Betty and Kevin Hackett. *The Celebration Psalter, The Lectionary, Years A, B, and C.* Pacific, MO: Cathedral Music Press, 1992 and 1991.

Roberts, William Bradley. *Simplified Anglican Chants / Anglican Chants.* St. James Music Press, 2011.

Shafer, Keith, ed. *Psalms Made Singable: The Psalms of David set to Anglican and Plainchants* with text and music aligned. Church Music Services, 2011.

Webber, Christopher L. *A New Metrical Psalter: Revised Common Lectionary Edition.* New York: Church Publishing, 2008.

Wyton, Alec, editor. *The Anglican Chant Psalter.* New York: The Church Hymnal Corporation, 1987.

Spirituality

Guenther, Margaret. *The Practice of Prayer.* The New Church's Teaching Series, Volume 4. Boston, MA: Cowley Publications, 1998.

_____. *Toward Holy Ground: Spiritual Directions for the Second Half of Life.* Boston, MA: Cowley Publications, 1985.

Hanh, Thich Nhat. *The Miracle of Mindfulness: An Introduction to the Practice of Meditation.* Translated by Mobi Ho. Boston, MA: Beacon Press, 1976.

Nouwen, Henri J. M. *Life of the Beloved: Spiritual Living in a Secular World.* New York: The Crossroad Publishing Company, 1999.

Saliers, Don and Emily Saliers. *A Song to Sing, A Life to Live: Reflections on Music as Spiritual Practice.* San Francisco, CA: Jossey-Bass, A Wiley Imprint, 2005.

Sprague, Minka Shura. *Praying from the Free-Throw Line—for Now.* New York: Church Publishing, 1999.

Index